O. Olsson

OLOF OLSSON

The Man, His Work, and His Thought

BY

ERNST WILLIAM OLSON, L.H.D.

AUGUSTANA BOOK CONCERN
ROCK ISLAND, ILLINOIS

[PRINTED IN U·S·A·]

AUGUSTANA BOOK CONCERN
Printers and Binders
Rock Island, Illinois
1941

CONTENTS

INTRODUCTION by JULIUS LINCOLN, D.D.

OTHER WORKS BY THE SAME WRITER

History of the Swedes of Illinois, 1908
En bokhandelshistoria, 1909
The Swedish Element in Illinois, 1917
Svenskarna i Amerika (Collaborator), 1925–26
Augustana Book Concern, Monograph, 1934
Swedes in America (Collaborator), 1938

INTRODUCTION

This biography of Olof Olsson, seasoned for forty postmortal years in a constant process of appraisal by a contemporary and following generation, traces the development and achievements of a devout, versatile man and resourceful leader against a historical background of pioneering along idealistic and geographical frontiers.

The compelling story begins with childhood in a humble home in Värmland, Sweden, from which the light of evangelic piety shone out into spiritual darkness that enveloped a naturally beautiful region. The unerring beams of that lamp, tended and trimmed by the hands of an understanding mother, led her gifted son upon paths of wide-spanned preparation to outstanding accomplishments, of which the titles of chapters in this faithful sketch are reliable indicators. In the gradual unfolding of exceptional talents and the enlargement of range under the tuition of neighborhood, rural schoolmasters, or at famous institutions of learning in Stockholm, Leipsic, and Uppsala, the direction pointed out by this mother, who was his first teacher, was held unswervingly by Olof Olsson with an intensification of true glow in his great heart.

In the summer of 1893, when official duties in connection with the commencement exercises at Augustana College and Theological Seminary and the celebration of the 300th anniversary of the Decree of Uppsala, demanded the personal attention of President Olsson, his mother passed away peacefully at Lindsborg, Kansas, in her eighty-seventh year. At the interment, thoughtful old friends, who knew of this son's deep gratitude to his mother, caused a wooden tube to be placed in the grave, extending from the lid of the casket to the top of the mound, so that Dr. Olsson, in person, might later dedicate the precious remains to the ground, in accordance with the familiar church ritual. A small company of fellow pioneers in the Smoky Valley and their sons then stood by as Dr. Olsson performed the last rites, reading the Ninetieth Psalm, and closing with: "Dust thou art . . ." At the conclusion of the committal no one stirred. That circle of intimates sensed that words not printed in the book would also be spoken. Who could have written for that son what he wanted to say at his mother's grave? In a voice vibrant with strong emotions came the tribute: "Mother, my mother! For loving guidance and burning prayers, I thank thee. Farewell."

That little cemetery lies on the slope of a high bluff that commands the fair valley and the winding river that flows through it. From the summit the homes, plantations, and corrals of pioneers, and the monuments they and their children have built can be seen and identified. It has become the hill of reveries and memories for four generations of Northland folks. Chroniclers relate that Spanish conquistadors under Coronado pushed onward in 1541 from the Pacific to take and hold the fabulously rich, mythical town of Quivira, another theme for reverie on the hill that bears the name of the Castilian adventurer. No city of gold, silver, or gems was found at the end of that wearisome march. Fragments of Spanish chain-mail armor in the museum of a real city, reared by another race three centuries later where Quivira was supposed to have been, are the only mementos of that earlier expedition to central Kansas.

In the year 1869, a vanguard of two hundred and fifty men and women, having carefully weighed the values of what they were about to leave with corresponding idealized standards, set out simultaneously from Värmland, Sweden, with the courage and warmth of laic evangels, to match endurance with faith in fashioning fresh patterns for their civic and spiritual lives. For the launching of that large enterprise the virgin prairies of Kansas had been hopefully and prayerfully chosen. To guide them in their bold new-world venture, these emigrants had sought and secured the ready consent of twenty-eight-year-old Pastor Olof Olsson, who arrived on the Kansas scene after a separation from them of only two months.

That summer afternoon in 1893, exactly twenty-four years had elapsed since the reclaiming and reshaping of the valley had been begun by the Swedish frontiersmen. The few advance countrymen and other hardy settlers already on the ground, located in widely scattered dugouts and cabins, welcomed their fellow pioneers to share with them the thrill of being among the first to break the fertile sod in a land of challenging opportunities. Herds of buffalo and bands of Indians ranged the region— a new territory that awaited the magic touch of men with stout hearts and unwearying arms. They came, upstanding men in the grip of a shining ideal, who strode their prairie acres undaunted even by the lack of an implement in their willing hands. Compensating the longing for the old homeland with its wholesome climate,

deep forests, brooks and lakes, its tender associations
and memories, even tempo and quaint customs, the hot,
mostly treeless plains yet offered a land in which to start
anew, a land where initiative and diligence would reap
their reward. Not a familiar object was in sight over that
vast expanse, except the eternal stars in the sky at night,
when tear-dimmed eyes were often turned to the North
Star, for under it lay the old Fatherland. But, they were
sturdy, these men and women, well equipped physically,
mentally, and spiritually for the hard and long struggle
ahead. The mainspring of their action was reverence and
responsiveness to the wise counsel of their leader.

In close historical sequence the panorama of twenty-
four years unrolls its farflung and proximate scenes to
the spectators on the look-out heights of the Valley. The
start is in rural and small-town parishes in Värmland,
Sweden, where a mysterious restlessness seizes some
people, who in turn disturb the general complacency.
Attempted restraint merely accelerates the growth of the
movement until it bursts the bounds to search for full
freedom elsewhere. The decision is unwaveringly made
by the young pastor, his family and kinsfolk, in faith
and hope, to embark for the United States and there to
found a new order upon the old, tried fundamentals.
What locality could be more suitable to that holy experiment than the open prairies, bordered only by the horizon? As was to be expected, the first public assembly of
these newcomers to the Smoky Valley is a service of
thanksgiving to God and a prayer for His mercy and
blessing, held in a lowly, scantily furnished home, even
before the dwellings of all arrivals had been completed.

There could be no delay in translating their vision into tangible form. Gratification of personal needs must not interfere with the building of a house of God. On the nineteenth day of August, 1869, Pastor Olof Olsson and twelve men organized a Christian fellowship, naming it Bethany, an open, hospitable house for the Lord and His friends. Down yonder on the slope a little stone church is erected, 36 x 24, and in it choral music is heard for the first time in Lindsborg, Pastor Olsson being accompanist and conductor. Directly in line with that church from our point of observation is a house, also of stone, erected for the pastor and his family by devoted parishioners. In the rooms of that plain prairie parsonage, Pastor Olof Olsson's pen begins to wield a mighty influence that goes far beyond the limits of his parish and draws attention to a scholarship and other qualities of leadership that mark him for elevation to posts of eminence in the expanding Augustana Synod. That editor's sanctum also becomes the office of the first Superintendent of Public Instruction in that Kansas county and of the member of the State Legislature from the district. The little church is gone, but down on the Valley's level floor gleams the tall spire of a large temple in the sunlight and a busy city that has grown up around it. To the left is a group of imposing buildings among the trees, halls of learning, peopled with happy boys and maidens, and a temple of music where rings Handel's oratorio, "The Messiah," to the enjoyment and marvel of throngs of visitors from near and afar.

All this in twenty-four years! The prairie, uninhabited and untilled from "the beginning," has become a cultural center and a garden.

Viewing that panorama on a Sunday afternoon in the summer of 1893 from Coronado Heights, a realization came to the group that standing in its midst by the grave of his mother was the man who had laid the groundwork and given direction and inspiration to his brilliant and indomitable pupil and successor in Lindsborg, Carl Aaron Swensson, to enlarge the vision and to see it successfully consummated. It is recorded that Pastor Olsson, the founder, had been instrumental in securing the glebe for Bethany church that produced the original education fund and upon which Bethany College has been erected.

The introduction of Handel's oratorio, "The Messiah," into Swedish Lutheran circles in the United States is straightly traceable to a memorable day in London, England, in April, 1879, when Pastor Olsson listened to its rendition in Exeter Hall and later so rhapsodically described the experience that a start was made at Augustana College, Rock Island, Illinois, to produce it. An epochal event in musical development in the Augustana Synod was the journey from Rock Island in 1882 of the Augustana College orchestra to Lindsborg, Kansas, to accompany the young Bethany College Chorus in giving that oratorio. The fame of Bethany College throughout the nation and abroad rests largely upon the annual presentation of Handel's "The Messiah" in Holy Week.

This volume will also reveal that in arousing the church to a consciousness of its high calling in the field of charity, Dr. Olof Olsson's challenge: "The Augustana Synod can not hope to live and grow without deeds of mercy," gave impetus to a magnificent eleemosynary program.

A full and remarkable Augustana career, finished altogether too soon at the age of fifty-nine years, had its beginning at the extreme periphery of the then Synod. That Swedish settlement in Kansas was the most distant outpost of the church toward the setting sun, far removed from the center. For ten years it had no railway connections, except by long and slow horse and wagon routes over the prairies to main-line railroads. Visitations of relentless droughts and sudden plagues dashed the farmers' hopes of reward for a year of toil in the sweat of their brows. Total destruction of a season's crops while the building of the second church was in progress dismayed pastor and congregation. Money was needed, but none was to be had in the stricken community. Not without many misgivings did Pastor Olsson consent to call on a few sister churches to the east for aid. The result, however, exceeded all expectations, and the Lindsborg church was speedily completed. That pleading voice, even then irresistible, on behalf of a distressed flock, was thus being pitched to ring later through the entire Synod with amazing results for Augustana College and Theological Seminary, for which institution Dr. Olof Olsson became a living, unfailing endowment in a critical period. Unknowingly, the plainsman preacher was being drawn by a popular confidence in his extraordinary qualifications toward a unique place in the affections of a loyal constituency and to positions of larger responsibility and distinction.

Woven into the tapestry of the story of Olof Olsson's splendid achievements are also threads of pathos to give it a finish of softness. The parting from the cherished spot in Kansas and from fellow pioneers, many of whom

remained his life-long friends, seemed like leaving behind
something infinitely and inexplicably precious, that could
not be recovered elsewhere. Healed were the gashes of
conflict in the days of inevitable disillusionments and
estrangements, and valiant opposing combatants again
smiled, talked, and walked together. Horny-handed men
were ready to grasp the banner of a large idealism and
begin the march to a noble destiny. The settlement had
become a Valley of Peace under the blue haze of the
Smoky Hills, and to it Olof Olsson went frequently in
after years for brief rests.

We linger over a page in this book that contains a
description of Olof Olsson's visit to his beloved Kansas
community with a band of musicians from Augustana
College, after a year's leave of absence to hold a chair as
professor in the Augustana Theological Seminary. On
an early October evening, 1877, Olof Olsson led this group
and some local friends to the top of the historic bluff.
Onrushing memories prompted him to tell the story of
the colony and to pour out his heart in fervent thanksgiving to God for His guidance. That was Olof Olsson's
"farewell to a prospect he greatly admired and to a scene
he could not leave without regret." The Augustana Silver
Cornet Band played a number of selections. Among
those young musicians was Carl Aaron Swensson, who
was soon to take up and continue at Lindsborg the work
of Olof Olsson, who now returned to Rock Island and
Augustana College to remain there for the rest of his
days.

Thus Olof Olsson left the proving ground, where he
passed every test, to enter the larger sphere of action.
Preacher, Teacher, Executive, Theologian, Philosopher,

Humanitarian, Linguist, Legislator, Musician—all things
unto all men—his memory is kept in reverence and love
by all who came under the influence of his versatile and
consecrated personality, among them by one who now is
sincerely grateful for Olof Olsson's fatherly solicitude
which began at the baptism of an infant and persevered
through life.

JULIUS LINCOLN

I

THE EARLY YEARS

In the parish of Karlskoga, province of Värmland, Sweden, lies a modest farmstead by the name of Björtorp, which about the middle of last century was the home of Anders Olsson and his wife Britta. The house, small and commonplace as it was, gave the appearance of poverty, yet these folk were not needy; by thrift and frugality they made a living such as that of the average small farmer of their day. This did not mean much at a time when, as economists tell us, Sweden was still one of the poor countries of Europe and living conditions of the greater part of its rural population were so disastrously low that they can not be measured by present standards.

The simple life lived by Anders Olsson and his family had its compensations. There was an air of neatness and comfort, peace and contentment about their little home. Moral strictness, fear of God, kindness to neighbors, and a rather too eager desire to share their scant means with the very poor—these were some of the virtues that had gone into the make-up of these two. Throughout the community they were held in great esteem. This was true more particularly of "Mother Britta," whose efficiency as a housemother, her capable and sympathetic way with people, but chiefly the way she lived her Christian faith, had earned her that title of endearment and

15

respect. Her husband was much of an opposite type.
His reticence led to aloofness, and he grew severe and
legalistic in the practice of righteousness, leaving him
little contact with the people about him. It was not
until much later in life that Christianity to him became
a vital thing and a faith to live by.

When the son Olof was born to these good people in
1841, on the last day of March, such was the outer
environment and such were the social conditions and
spiritual influences that were to shape this boy's life in
his earliest years. Whatever some have said to the contrary, it does matter what one's father's occupation was
and what use one's mother made of her duty as the child's
first teacher. In the case of Olof Olsson, the molding of
his life and character is so clearly traceable to his mother
that a fuller characterization of her is essential to a true
portrayal of her son. It is drawn from a life sketch of
Olof Olsson, written by Johannes Nyvall, whose parents
stood close to the Olsson family in Karlskoga.

In the forties a spiritual revival took place in the
parish, through the efforts of a zealous pastor named
Berggren, who assumed that charge about 1846. Although gratified at the arrival of a "spiritual" clergyman, the "worldly" kind being only too prevalent in
those days, Mother Britta at first looked askance at the
movement he set on foot, but she was soon reassured by
the results, and from that time her home was open to
the new converts, and it became known as headquarters
for private devotional gatherings in the community, the
kind of meetings which under the name of "conventicles"
for decades in the Church of Sweden were proscribed by
law. She rejoiced at the activity stirred up among the

Lithograph by Birger Sandzén

THE OLOF OLSSON HOMESTEAD NEAR LINDSBORG

laymen of the church. The movement was indeed pietis-
tical, but churchly withal, and its adherents, soon found
in groups throughout the province, were in no sense dissenters. They retained their reverence for the established
church, and they would travel long distances to hear men
known as true spiritual teachers and to seek their advice
in private. Mother Britta was of that type of pietism,
as ardent as any new convert, but strictly loyal to the
church. She insisted that its pastors should be twice-born
men. After Pastor Berggren moved from Karlskoga, she
would often make long pilgrimages to churches known
to have truly devout ministers. On these journeys she
was usually accompanied by another zealous Christian
woman, the wife of a miner, Maria Jonsson, of Vall, in
the same parish. She became the founder and patroness
of an orphanage at Vall, and her son, under the name of
Carl Johan Nyvall, became widely known as a lay preacher and educator. He figures prominently in the life of
Olof Olsson.

Whatever may be laid against this pietist movement,
which later, in Värmland and elsewhere in Sweden, went
to regrettable extremes, counteracting the beneficial results earlier achieved, this much is to be said for it: At
the outset it was a wholesome and fully loyal lay movement within the church, and had its ministers understood
it rightly, sponsored it, and guided it in a true, Christian
spirit, great blessings from that wave of spirituality and
religious awakening, instead of sects and schisms, might
have accrued to the Church of Sweden. The opposition
and, in rare instances, persecution which met these
pietists, known by the general term "läsare" (readers,
devotionalists), tended only to estrange them from the

church and hasten the forming of groups of religious dissenters. So concludes Johannes Nyvall, a pastor of the Augustana Synod and a son of Carl Johan Nyvall, one of the founders of the Mission Covenant of Sweden, the largest dissenting denomination.

From the very first, the boy Olof and his brother Carl were brought up in the fear of God—and of their father, for he was as harsh as their mother was kind. If Luther's precept for rearing children was followed by these parents, it was he who wielded the switch and she who offered the apple. Be that as it might, natural instinct drew the boys very close to their mother, and their rearing from infancy up to school age fell almost entirely upon her. To the end of his twelfth year, Olof had no other teacher than his mother. The Bible was almost her only book, but that she knew better than many a theologian. Leading a life of prayer, she passed to her sons this key to spiritual understanding. Noting early Olof's quick perception and ready absorption of all that she had to teach him, she gave herself more and more to the task of instruction. An apt pupil makes an ambitious teacher. She cherished the thought that this boy of hers might be fitted for high service, and, like Hannah of old, she offered him to the Lord for service in His temple as a minister of the church. Olof never forgot his mother's teachings and admonitions. The prayers learned at her knees not only never faded from his memory, but they shaped his life. From her he learned that intensive searching of the Scriptures which later in life made him a profound Biblical scholar. His kind heart and sympathetic disposition was a maternal inheritance, as was also his cheerful outlook on life, later clouded at times by obdurate opposition and stupendous obstacles. Like her, he wished to see all happy about him, and it saddened him equally not to be able to right some great wrong or to give aid to those in need.

The price the family had to pay for its existence was hard and constant work. At a tender age, Olof and his brother Carl had to begin to help out in work of one kind or another, and the strength of the boys was not always equal to the tasks set for them. Their strength would often be completely exhausted when at the end of the long day they sat down to a frugal meal and then, after the never-failing evening devotions, fell suddenly asleep. For labor and prayer were the order of the day, followed perhaps more scrupulously here than in many a home with "Ora et labora" as a motto on the wall. In this way Olof was taught the sanctity of work, a lesson which he never forgot. At least it implanted in him the habit of strenuous application and the love of work which grew with the years. To it may no doubt be traced that profound respect for labor and sympathy with the working class which not only showed through in his personal life but often found expression in his sermons and writings.

Although not physically strong, Olof did his fair share of work. At an early age he loved to read and showed an aptitude for study which did not escape his mother's notice. The boy could join with zest in the games of playmates, but these he would often forego for the pleasure of reading some book his mother had borrowed. At other times he would roam all alone through the woods and over the hills. The natural beauty of the region must have strongly impressed this boy who, grown to

manhood, could go into ecstasy over a beautiful land-
scape and whose writings abound in poetic descriptions
of nature and inspired apostrophes to God for the glories
of His creation.

Olof's favorite pastime was to climb the linden that
grew in the dooryard and, concealed from view, sit reading, dreaming, or engaged in building air castles. With
his brother's help he had built among the branches of
the old tree a rude arbor which, as likely as not, may
have been his first castle in the air. As in this crow's
nest he listened to the song of birds and held communion
with nature in his boyish way, there is no telling what
impressions stamped themselves upon his mind, yet we
have it from first sources that he would sometimes surprise his parents with snatches of song or bits of fancy
which he had got from they knew not where. The lad
was gifted, there was no doubt about it, and the dis-
covery eventually prompted them to relieve him of the
drudgery of daily chores and send him to school.

At the age of twelve, Olof had studied only the first
of the "three R's," and had become a fluent and avid
reader. Besides the primer, the textbooks used were
Luther's Catechism, the Swedish Psalmbook, and the
Bible. The first he had learnt by heart, as all Swedish
school children were supposed to do, and in the others he
was very well versed, having not only read them through,
but also memorized most of the favorite hymns and a
great number of chapters from the Bible in their entirety.
The knowledge thus stored up in his mind proved a valuable and convenient fund for him to draw from in his
career as a pastor and theologian. His appetite for learning was whetted by this process, and, combined with his

mother's guidance in the Christian faith, it proved a decisive factor in the shaping of his life. Part of his duties on the little farm up to this time had been to tend the sheep. Mounted on some rock or stump, the lad would sometimes be seen or heard preaching fervently to his flock in the approved manner of the parish parson. While not a sure mark of destiny, this form of play is noted in the early life of several eminent divines in the Church of Sweden, and in the case of Olof Olsson it certainly proved a true forecast of his future career.

II

THE STUDENT YEARS

When a new parish schoolmaster, a devout man as compared to his predecessor, was engaged, the parents decided to let Olof, now in his thirteenth year, have the benefit of his instruction in the ordinary subjects of study, but through private tutorship, as the boy evidently could not be spared during school hours. Finding Olof an apt and diligent pupil, the schoolmaster did his best to gratify the boy's desire for knowledge. Soon, however, he discovered gifts in him, such as a good voice and love of music, the development of which did not lie within his field. So he advised sending him to Anders Fredrik Sedström, a schoolmaster, precentor, and organist at Fredsberg, Västergötland, whom he highly recommended. At thirteen, Olof was still a rather frail boy, and by that time his parents had little hope that he would ever grow strong and be of much use on the farm or as a worker in the neighboring mining region. Hence, without much persuasion, they took the advice offered and decided to send the boy away for a more thorough schooling, whatever that might lead to. Most likely a presumptive position as organist was in the father's mind, while the mother must have cherished the fonder hope that her son might devote his life to still greater service to the church in the holy ministry.

At this point, events took a decisive turn for the first

time in the boy's life. His character had been primarily
molded by parental influence in the Christian home at
Björtorp. At Fredsberg, in the home of Sedström, the
process of systematic education practically began for him.
This teacher had much to give, and it appears that his
pupil acquired a great deal from him in the short time
spent under his guardianship and skillful tutelage.

Sedström was a man of parts. His was a many-sided
education, and his biographer speaks of him as "a man
of remarkable capacity and great originality." From the
Academy of Music at Stockholm he was graduated as
both organist and precentor, and from the teacher's seminary in the same city as schoolmaster. He served in all
three capacities at Fredsberg from about 1852 almost to
his death in 1904, a period of more than half a century.
During that time he grew to be part and parcel of the
community so that hardly anybody would think of the
one without the other. As a champion of temperance he
joined the movement led by Per Wieselgren and in his
community vigorously fought the secret distilleries that
flourished under the law permitting household distilling
until the law was revoked as a result of the temperance
campaign.

At the time Olof was sent from Värmland to be his
charge, Sedström had served at Fredsberg only a year or
two. What with his church duties, his school of about
one hundred and twenty-five pupils, a farm of about
thirty acres to oversee, and a family of four children, it
might seem that the man had his hands full without
taking in a strange child to teach and board. But he
needed to do precisely that to eke out his income, salaries
in those days being what they were—a paltry 150 crowns

a year for a schoolmaster and for an organist no doubt still less.

Olof spent only one year at Fredsberg, but it was a period of intense study during which the boy's receptive mind was literally crammed with elementary knowledge. All the regular subjects except reading and Christianity were new to him and, as such, of absorbing interest. The curriculum of the Swedish folk school at that time did not stop with reading, writing, and arithmetic, but comprised grammar, history, botany, zoology, geometry, and perhaps other studies. In Sedström's school, at least, all these subjects were taught, and as he was a hard taskmaster and a strict disciplinarian, yet an efficient and interesting instructor, there was not much in his teaching that escaped the alert and receptive boy from Värmland.

After school hours came daily music lessons. The teacher and his pupil spent long hours with the intricacies of harmony, the art of singing, and the technic of playing the organ. Time was not an essence of the contract between them. With half-hour lessons, as is now the practice, it would not have been possible for this lad of fourteen to lay a good theoretical foundation for his musical education and at the same time learn to sing and to play the church organ fairly well all in one short year. As it was, his playmates did not see a great deal of Olof after school. "Värmlands-Olle" they nicknamed him, but not from disrespect; he stood too well in his classes for that. One might rather infer that it was a sort of title of honor spontaneously conferred by the school, for it is referred to in the published biography of Sedström, by Gustaf Hultgren, who in a letter written almost eighty years later says: "Of 'Värmlands-Olle' I have been told a great deal, for he and I had the same teacher, although at different times." It seems that later generations of pupils had not forgotten the boy from Värmland, and it is known that Sedström himself took great pride in his former ward and pupil and held him in life-long esteem.

The tutor did not overwork his pupil, irksome as the lesson assignments seem to have been. He knew how to combine hard work with wholesome recreation. A man of powerful physique and robust health, he took care to teach his pupils healthful habits and ways to keep fit and strong. In him a sound mind dwelt in a sound body. "One has no right to be in bad humor," was one of his maxims. "Stop eating while food tastes the best," was another. By moderation in food and drink he preserved his physical health and mental vigor to the end of his life. As for drink, it should be explained that while he fought the use of distilled liquors and ardent spirits of all kinds, fermented beverages were not barred from his table. He would likewise enjoy an occasional pipe of tobacco or a cigar. In summer he went down to the near-by river almost daily for a plunge and a brisk swim. Often he took a flock of boys with him, and these he taught to swim by a method of his own. He simply threw them in and offered assistance only when needed. The common-sense ways and habits of this teacher must be noted inasmuch as his influence is easily traceable in the life of his pupil.

In Sedström the boy found a spiritual father, adviser, and guide, and however much of secular knowledge Olof acquired from him, it was far exceeded by the religious influence wielded by him over this young soul, still malleable though already cast in the mold of strict and rigid pietism. Out of the man's admiration for the boy's attainments and his mature insight into spiritual things, rare in one so young, and the latter's whole-hearted confidence in his instructor, there soon grew a mutual attachment closer and more intimate than the ordinary relationship between teacher and student. It is hardly to be assumed that Sedström could have deepened the faith implanted in the heart of Olof from childhood by his pious mother, but rather that the schooled and disciplined mind of this young and devout schoolmaster exerted a steadying, sobering, and broadening effect on the youth's Christian life and outlook. It is a matter of record that he was heartily encouraged in his early ambition to become a minister of the gospel, while we have no other gauge of Sedström's influence on his religious views than the lifelong friendship of the two. They exchanged many letters across the sea, and their affectionate meeting in Fredsberg church decades afterwards is worth recording in its proper place.

It had been the parents' design, as Sedström understood it, that Olof was to prepare for a career as organist and schoolmaster. Before long, however, he had manifested traits and inclinations which led the sincere and modest teacher to conclude that his pupil was fitted for a calling higher than his own, so when he sent him back home it was with this farewell message: "Tell your parents, my dear Olle, that you are cut out for a higher calling than that of schoolmaster and organist. You must study for the ministry."

It was with deep regret that after one year Olof was obliged to leave the teacher who had opened up so many

fields of knowledge to him and return to Björtorp to take
up anew his share of labor on the home farm. These
duties, while scarcely more strenuous than his studies,
were much less to his liking, and his heart was not in
that kind of work. Intensely, hopelessly, he longed to
continue his studies. Year after year passed by without
holding out any prospect to him. But this drab stretch
of time's woof was shot through here and there with
stripes of brighter color, and the monotony of toil had
its compensations.

Of this period in Olsson's life, Johannes Nyvall says:
"In Karlskoga as in other parts of the Värmland province, the pietist movement had spread in ever-widening
circles, and that type of Christianity had become firmly
rooted in many parishes. Together with his mother, Olof
faithfully attended the devotional gatherings, known as
conventicles, held in various homes, most often in Vall,
the home of the aforesaid Nyvall family. This had become the center of the movement after the eldest son,
Carl Johan Nyvall, fervently supported by his devout
mother (popularly known as "Mor i Vall"), gave all his
time and powers to evangelistic preaching and gave freely
of his means to the support of the movement. At this
time Olof Olsson and this young man were bound together
in a bond of friendship which, although put under severe
strain by subsequent controversies and schisms in the
church, was never broken.

"The benevolent activities of these pietists, especially
in behalf of children and the youth through the establishment of homes for children, such as the orphanage
at Vall, and of private schools for young people, known
as mission schools, as also through the devotional gather-

ings, all this made indelible impressions on Olof's mind. Though but a youth, he took note that in this revival many who had been sleeping for decades, rocked in the cradle of rationalism and false orthodoxy, had their consciences awakened. He saw how persons living lives of sin, steeped in vice, heedless of their fate, were truly born again. He saw, too, how these devout people, despite suppression and persecution by both ecclesiastic and political powers, clung to their faith and loved their very adversaries. He was a witness to the fact that their persecutors eventually revealed themselves as enemies of all forms of religion and would suppress even freedom of conscience. But to see Christian men and women hounded for the sake of their conscience and their faith stirred him to the depth of his soul. These things were enough to fix his attitude in future years both to pietism and toward the enemies of devotionalism. From this time on, Olof Olsson was a sincere and ardent pietist. This attitude of honest, unfeigned, strictly churchly and Lutheran pietism he maintained throughout his student years and subsequent period of pastoral service in Sweden, and from that position he did not shift during his career in America; on the contrary, he remained unalterably true to its principles throughout his fruitful and sanctified life."

To Olof's work on the farm during these years might be applied the passage in 1 Corinthians 7—old Swedish version—for indeed, he "used this earth as if not using it." True, he did his best to be useful on the farm, his health none the worse for a year's hard study, but the lack of opportunity to continue his schooling constantly burdened his mind. His parents could not spare the means—that seemed to have settled the matter.

About that time, Peter Fjellstedt's missionary call
rang through the Church of Sweden. It reached the
ears of young Olof Olsson, and his heart warmed at the
thought of serving God in some foreign mission field. He
solemnly resolved, God willing, to dedicate his life to the
cause of foreign missions as soon as a way opened.
Friends in Karlskoga, learning of his resolve and knowing him as a gifted and sincere youth, encouraged him
and did what they could to help make his promise good.
Just then Doctor Fjellstedt opportunely made a visit to
Karlskoga on one of his many missionary journeys, and
they met this eminent divine to plead the young man's
cause. At this interview it was arranged, to Olof's great
joy, that he should enter the mission institute founded by
Fjellstedt in Stockholm and prepare to go out as a missionary to the heathen. This was in the year 1858, and
Olof was registered at the institute that fall, elated at
the thought that his dearest wish would now come true.

In the mission school with its warm evangelical atmosphere the vivacious country boy from Värmland felt very
much at home, and the rapid progress he made in his
studies was somewhat of a surprise to his teachers. By
his natural gifts and his uncommon capacity for work,
combined with an exemplary Christian life, he drew the
attention of the directing board, who, disregarding his
inexperience and immaturity in spiritual things, sent him,
with four other young men, to a mission institute in
Leipsic the very next year.

At this noted German mission school he was to finish
his preparation for a missionary career, but the plan did
not work out well. The spirit and environment of the
German institute apparently were not congenial to the

young Swedish student. They served to unsettle his determination to enter the foreign mission service. Too late the board in Stockholm discovered their mistake, and Doctor Fjellstedt felt profound regret that one of his most promising students seemed lost to the cause of heathen missions. Olsson's change of mind, which was only temporary, is thus explained:

To the young Swedish student, a child of the conventicles whose spiritual experience had been wholly derived from the devotionalism of Värmland, the year spent amid the stale orthodoxism and high-churchliness of Germany was nothing short of martyrdom. For the first time in his life Olof Olsson here came in contact with this form of Lutheranism and felt its oppressive weight. Inexperienced as he was, and still without any very clear doctrinal conception of true and living Christianity, he could not bring himself to believe that a life of grace could exist under the form of such orthodox frigidity and high-hatted, long-faced, circumspect ecclesiasticism. Empty formalism, spiritual paresis—that was all he saw in it. He got a distaste for everything taught at the institution and even began to doubt that it was a Christian school. All this depressed him, made him morose, and steeped him in melancholy speculation. His power and will to study was well-nigh lost, and all spiritual interchange between him and his teachers seemed to be cut off. They began to doubt his fitness for the missionary's calling, and eventually, to his great relief, Olsson was released from the institute. He returned to Sweden after a year's stay in Leipsic. Sad, disillusioned, sick in body and sick at heart, the brilliant student came back home. To this account of Olsson's stay at Leipsic, based on Olsson's own letters, may be added his words to a brother pastor many years afterward: "That was a hard and dark year for my inner man. We Swedish students, free and joyful Christians that we were, used to gather on Sunday afternoons to sing and pray in our mother tongue. Those Germans did not understand either our Swedish temperament or our buoyant type of spirituality, but took us to be fanatics, or the like. We were partly misunderstood, partly understood not at all."

After another short period at the Fjellstedt school, Olsson returned to his home. He did not stay long with his parents, but sought his friends at Vall. There they put him to use keeping records and doing odd jobs in the recently established orphanage and private school. The sixty children in the school were more than could be managed by the teacher, an inexperienced young man, who was further handicapped by lameness, so it became a part of Olof's duties to assist him in his work. This he did by working out arithmetical tables and furnishing copy for the penmanship class. Work among the children caused a wholesome change in the young man and soon drove away all melancholy thoughts from his mind. The group of friends who had sent him away to school had not yet despaired of his future, but did what they could to cheer him up. At this point another factor entered in to revive the spirit of the disappointed young student and restore his interest in life. While at the Vall children's home, he met a charming young woman who soon won his heart and who had it in safe keeping not only until she became his wife but until death parted them.

The pessimist was gone. A most hopeful young man dismissed the past and faced the future. Shaking off all gloomy thoughts of his wrecked plan, he resolved, after prayerful consultation with his parents and such others as were still interested, to take up studies anew, this time with the regular ministry in the Church of Sweden as his goal. He would go to Uppsala and pursue the required courses, and somehow the means were found to put the plan through. With a slender purse, made up in part by his parents, but for the most part by friends of the family, he left for the university town in the fall of the year (1860). His previous preparation stood him in such good stead that with intense work he was able to finish college by the following January, after only one semester, and with excellent grades. His diploma was dated January 22, 1861. With this passport he entered the university department of theology and plunged at once into divinity studies. Here he was in his natural element. His two years at different mission institutes were not thrown away after all. That background gave him a great advantage over the average theological student.

After his graduation, Olsson had severe attacks of headache, making him unfit for any kind of employment that summer. The malady would not let him continue his studies that fall, so he took a position as private tutor, reading up on his courses in the meantime. In spite of this handicap, he finished the heavy courses required by the theological faculty ahead of his class after only a short stay at the university. Final examinations completed, he was solemnly ordained to the holy ministry December 15, 1863, by Archbishop Henrik Reuterdahl, in the ancient cathedral of Uppsala.

III

THE YOUNG PASTOR

The ordination of Olof Olsson marks the beginning of
the third distinct period of his life, namely, his six years
as pastor in the church of his native land. Shortly after
New Year's, 1864, he was assigned to the parish of
Brunskog, of the Karlstad diocese, as assistant pastor.
The young clergyman, not yet twenty-three years of age,
put into his new work the same enthusiasm that had
inspired him as a student at Stockholm and Uppsala,
barring of course the Leipsic period. He set out to win
the people of the lower level in the community, leaving
the class of habitual church-goers and those established
in faith to the care of the parson himself. Knowing the
value of the laymen's movement of the past few years in
these parts, he did not hesitate to make full use of it in
his pastoral work. He knew personally some of the lay
preachers and workers in the devotionalist groups and
had never had any reason to doubt their sincerity or the
purity of their motives. So he became one of the few
pastors who sought to conserve this spiritual force and
to keep these devout people active within the pale of the
established church, while the clergy in general, who stood
pat on formalism, by their intolerance and petty annoy-
ances under cover of the old Conventicle Edict promoted
nonconformity while they thought they were discouraging it.

Without neglecting his parish duties, Olsson made occasional tours to preach to groups of pietists in various parts of the province. His boyhood friend, Carl Johan Nyvall, twelve years his senior and now developed into an ardent lay preacher, furnished the conveyance on many a long home mission trip and usually had a preaching part in the meetings. The two would speak daily in any convenient place opened to them, a private home, an empty barn, a grove, a parish house or school, or some church where a friendly parson presided. Often these devotional gatherings grew into great mass meetings. In times of spiritual awakening, such as this, people would come miles on foot—and the Swedish mile is a long one—to hear a preacher who spoke, they felt, moved by the Spirit of God.

A regularly ordained pastor could not, however, take part in this movement, promoted chiefly by lay preachers, without incurring suspicion from official quarters and from the greater part of the clergy. While Olsson's participation met with the enthusiasm of the devotionalists and the approval of a group of true shepherds of their flocks, he faced the opposition of all the rest as well as the derision of the rank and file of the people. For it must be understood that the name *läsare*, as applied to devout readers of religious books, was a popular term of opprobrium, and *läsarepräst*, as applied to pious and faithful ministers, a shade more derogatory, a learned man being supposed to know better.

As a matter of fact, Olsson's position was at odds with the official attitude of the church in this matter. A bit of Swedish church history inserted here will serve to explain a controversy which had agitated portions of the

Church of Sweden for more than a century, and incidentally to justify his action.

Philip Jacob Spener, sometimes called the Father of Pietism, sought to deepen spiritual life in the Lutheran church of Germany by means of private gatherings for prayer and study of the Word which might be led by laymen. As pietism spread northward to the other Lutheran countries, these meetings, known as conventicles, began to be held by its adherents here and there in Sweden. It had been far from Spener's mind to cause separation from the church or disrespect for its clergy, its practices, and the regular order of worship. Yet after his death the movement degenerated into nonconformism. Suspecting the pietists of heresy and schism, the ecclesiastical authorities in Sweden looked with disfavor upon all devotional gatherings not conducted by the clergy. On January 12, 1726, previous regulations were embodied in a "Royal edict, forbidding the impermissible meetings in private houses which are arranged as a special and distinct form of divine worship, and specifying the punishment of those found guilty of such services." The holding of any religious meetings by laymen, except household devotions conducted by the head of the family, was punishable by fine and imprisonment. This was the so-called Conventicle Edict, which for more than four generations shackled the spiritual life of the church. It grew especially odious during the spiritual awakening about the middle of the nineteenth century with its demand for freer evangelistic activity. From many parts of the country came demands for the revocation of the edict. The regrettable decree was finally revoked by an act of the riksdag dated October 26, 1858. The new act still forbade conventicles during the hours for regular worship, but ten years later this restriction, too, was abolished, the last vestige of the edict being a needless ordinance forbidding the holding of conventicles so close to the church as to disturb the regular services. It appears that this edict, like the English Conventicle Act of 1664, directed at the Presbyterians, always was in bad odor. Far from discouraging nonconformity to established church practices, it had the opposite effect, by virtually restricting liberty of conscience. Judged by the bitter denunciation of the edict by P. P. Waldenström, as late as the end of the century, forty years after it was revoked, it must have been the entering wedge starting the rift that eventually severed the Mission Friends from the state church, their denomination, the Mission Covenant, being the largest body of dissenters in Sweden.

Thus the right to worship God according to one's own conscience in or outside the church was vindicated at last. As this occurred five years before Olsson was ordained, he was clearly within his legal rights in pursuing his evangelistic work with the aid of laymen, the opposition being a hangover from the past and now having no support in church law. Within the Brunskog parish the warm-hearted and eloquent young assistant pastor was held in high esteem, and by his ministration, it is said, many souls were won for the kingdom of God. There were regrets on both sides when, after a short period of service there, Olsson was assigned by the diocesan chapter at Karlstad to serve as vice pastor in the congregation of Elgå, in Arvika parish. Very shortly after his transfer, he applied for the vacant position of pastor at Persberg, near Filipstad. Among several applicants the choice fell on him, and shortly after his election he removed to his new field of work.

In 1864, only a short time before coming to Persberg, Olsson had been united in holy wedlock with Anna Lisa Jonsson of Agen, in Karlskoga, the miner's daughter who had won his heart before he took up divinity studies at Uppsala. So here the young couple established what was practically their first home. Persberg was not the most desirable charge a young pastor might choose. It was a very active mining and factory community. A large part of the population consisted of young workingmen attracted by the fair wages paid. There were the usual drawbacks of an industrial town—many led a wild and coarse life, indulging in drinking, gambling, and other dissipations. Over this naturally picturesque region there hung a pall of spiritual darkness. Here, if anywhere, was a field to test the capacity of any clergyman, especially one who, like Olsson, was gifted, zealous, inspired by his divine calling, and burning with a desire to lift the lower classes, spiritually and physically, to a higher plane of living. And it was here, rather than in Brunskog, that Olsson's pastoral work bore its best fruit. Not only did he wage a brave fight against vice and ungodliness among the rougher element, but he fearlessly attacked wickedness in high places as well. The "better classes," so called, he found little better than the common run of miners and mill workers. In addition to his constant struggle with these social evils, he had to contend with his superiors in the churchly offices who did not approve of what they called his "pietistic methods" and his incessant preaching of repentance. With the evil forces massed against him on the one hand and discouragement

and obstacles on the other, he won the day in many a
battle. The gospel made headway in the whole iron
region as never before, chiefly through his efforts. When
he could spare the time from preaching and from caring
for the souls in his home congregation, he would make
trips to other fields, near or far, to whatever place whence
the call came.

Due to the friction with the church authorities, whose
attitude had changed little although the ban on conventicles was raised, Olsson, while serving at Persberg, acquired a distaste for the state church system which never
left him. These first years in the ministry revealed to
him the revolting fact that many of the religious leaders
led a coarse, worldly life and were inimical to every form
of genuine Christianity. He discovered that in large
areas ecclesiastical law, with its demand for church discipline, was a dead letter. The artificial union of the
church with the state seemed to the tender conscience of
the young pastor to hamper the work and stifle the spirit
of the church. He did not conceal his aversion to that
arrangement, but spoke his mind freely. At that time he
wrote: "Oh, how my soul burns with zeal for the propa-
gation of the truth and the advancement of God's work!
Would that I might work right powerfully for the accomplishment of good, but within the state church it seems
to become less and less possible to do anything at all."

Besides being assistant pastor at Persberg, Olsson was
director or superintendent of the local school and, as
such, had a considerable share in the teaching. One who
had him as his teacher jotted down his recollections of
Olsson some fifty years later from a retentive memory.
These give us a picture of the young pastor as he appeared

to a schoolboy of about ten years of age, named Nils J. Forsberg, who like his teacher became a pastor of the Augustana Synod.

"We had been told," he wrote, "that we would soon have a new superintendent who would also teach; that he was a learned man and very 'spiritual.' His learning naturally inspired fear, but how, we reasoned, could a spiritual man permit himself to pull our hair, use the rattan on us, or be severe in his reprimands. As compared to the common run, he would probably be welcome as a teacher after all. One day, as we were practicing writing, he came, looked at the penmanship of some of the older boys, smiled, and looked quite good-natured. Then he came over to me and guided my hand as I was struggling with the curves and ovals. In writing I was a beginner, although I had read the Psalmbook and the New Testament through once or twice and recited the Large Catechism eight times by heart. No wonder, then, that the nine-year-old knew his sinful heart well enough to fear the 'spiritual' young clergyman. But all at once this fear left me, and I was filled with childlike confidence. . . . We schoolboys presently found ourselves recognized as real scholars. Some of us were skilled penmen; Härdig was a historian, Planman a mathematician and geographer, etc.

"Now the school got a blackboard and a new organ. The first thing he wrote on the board was the musical scale in figures, for now we were to learn singing. All new and hard to understand, yet how interesting! But singing in parts was the best of all. And when the pastor sat down and played the organ, we were thrilled. He put life into everything. How fast and still how well he could write! A boy who had his name on his copybook written in a good round hand by the new teacher was so proud that we all remembered that name forever after. Absolute obedience was required. Yet there were only five cases of discipline during the years he taught, three boys getting a taste of the rod and two girls being spanked. We never, before or after, saw a teacher exercise discipline with such calm and without a sign of anger. His face registered profound sadness, but on these occasions not one harsh word was uttered. The morning when the young pastor, called to another charge, stood ready to leave, he visited the school to bid us all good-bye. When he uttered these farewell words, 'Remember to read the Word of God and keep His precepts in your heart, then it will be well with you,' the moment was solemn and seemed to mark a turning-point in our lives. That the Scriptures should mean so much to us, this we could not then grasp, but many of us later realized the truth of his words."

After having thus portrayed Olsson as a pedagogue who had a firm hand with his pupils, yet a kind heart for them, the erstwhile schoolboy of Persberg drew a picture of the young clergyman which, to judge from the incidental details and intimate characterization, seems equally true to life.

"As a pastor, he had to undergo many a trial like those of his Master. The theology of Parker and Strauss had spread a new kind of Sadduceeism even in Sweden, and rationalistic books by Lilja—such as, "Man; His Origin, Life, and Destiny" (1858); "Christian Doctrine and Priest Doctrine" (1862); "Bible History Based on Science" (1865)—were being read in a number of homes in Persberg at that time, scattering seeds of disbelief in the truth of the Bible and raising opposition and ill will against the clergy. Such teaching and influence the young pastor had to counteract, but so successfully did he cope with them that a number of persons in the parish credited their conversion to his ministration and guidance.

"It was no uncommon sight of a Sunday afternoon to see the pastor and his radiant young wife, laden with packages, on their way to the huts of the poor, who at these visits were given both bodily and spiritual food. An old cotter, who had never known anything but hard treatment and who was the dread of the small boys of the whole neighborhood, was so touched by the benevolence shown him and his 'old woman' that he melted into tears whenever he told of the visits of the preacher and his 'angelic lady.' He became a new man, with the transformation reflected in his very appearance.

"One fine spring day," the narrative runs on, "we saw the pastor looking quite dapper in a nice, new, well-fitting gray summer suit. The next morning a ragged journeyman came along, and when he stopped to show some of us boys what he had in his bag—there was that same gray suit, just given him by the 'preacher,' he explained.

"On his way home on foot through mud and melting snow some five miles after having preached in the Filipstad church on Easter morning, Olsson met another pedestrian, a poor fellow with shoes so worn that his toes were sticking out. 'My friend,' said the pastor, 'have you no better footwear for this kind of going?' 'Sure I'd use 'em if I had 'em,' said the weary wayfarer. Moved with pity, the pastor pulled off his new buskins, procured for just such preaching tours as this, told the stranger to put them on, and wished him Godspeed. When Olsson reached his home, his best Sunday boots were a sight to see." This episode is verified by a second pupil of Olsson's, who adds: "The buskins were exchanged for strong drink at the nearest tavern, where the disillusioned benefactor redeemed his property when told about this a few days later."

The person last quoted tells of another episode in testimony of Olsson's benevolent activities among the poor of the parish: "A poor widow was living alone not far from our home. When the pastor learnt that she was taken sick, he at once visited her, bringing with him some food he thought she might be in need of. Finding the woman lying on a hard bed, the first thing he did was to go to a farmhouse near by and purchase a bundle of straw which he carried back with him. After a more comfortable bed had thus been made, he cooked coffee and served some of the food with it. Meanwhile a storm came up, followed by an incessant rain, and the pastor, it was said, slept that night on the kitchen floor with a wicker broom for a pillow."

Olsson was always kind and tender-hearted, often generous to a fault, as some of these incidents show. It has been said of him that while he was pastor in the Filipstad mining region, the poor in the various parishes he served got more of his none too liberal salary than he kept for himself. Those who did not love the pastor feared him as a holy man to whom their thoughts and lives were like an open book.

The reputation of "Värmlands-Olle" as a preacher of unction and power had gone out over the surrounding region from the time he began to serve the Karlskoga parish at the age of twenty-four. But the first clear picture we have of Olof Olsson in the pulpit is that imprinted on the mind of his observant pupil, Nils Forsberg, two years later when the lad of twelve heard him preach the sermon at high mass in the Filipstad church on Christmas Day, 1866. His account is here somewhat abridged: "Many people had come in to town from the surrounding country, attracted by a notice in *Filipstads Tidning* announcing that Pastor O. Olsson of Persberg was to preach. The weather was clear and bitterly cold that Christmas Eve, and at early dawn the sky was more green than blue. The big stone church was not heated—hardly a church in the realm was, in those times. It was tolerably cheerful at the early morning services (*julotta*) when the hundreds of burning candles gave an illusion of warmth, but during the following services we were far from comfortable, sitting for two hours watching our breath and shivering with cold. All the people had remained for the second service, making themselves comfortable as best they could in various quarters during the long interval.

"At last the church bell rang again. The church was soon crowded with people eager to hear the Persberg preacher. The liturgy was read by the local minister. Then, while the pulpit hymn is being finished, a young man mounts the stairs, enters the pulpit, and bows his head in silent prayer. Now he raises his eyes, glances over the audience, and begins his sermon. From the very first word, he speaks clearly and fluently, without any labored start or apparent effort. There was no manuscript, no written notes that one could see. Rather unusual! Still the words come easily and the sentences flow on, clear and lucid, understood without strain or effort. It was as if a new message were being brought—a message which concerned us in particular. Olsson was not in the habit of writing his sermons, but when he did write one, it was almost memorized at the same time, so retentive was his memory. Only recently we have learnt from a published collection of his sermons that this particular sermon had been written out, but apparently the manuscript was reposing in his pocket if it had not been left at home. He knew full well that it would have been inadvisable for any young preacher to step poorly prepared into the pulpit, when A. F. Björlin, the scholarly and critical parson of the church, himself a noted preacher, would be sitting in the pew just below.

"We find, however, in reading the sermon now, no trace of any effort at parade. In those early days Olsson spoke more rapidly and with greater fervor than in his later years, but his presentation was always such that the man in the last pew had no difficulty in following him."

The disfavor with which the local church authorities looked upon Olsson's evangelistic methods at length wore him down, and in his discouragement he applied for transfer to another charge. The position of associate pastor in Sunnemo, in the rural deanery of Älvdal, was vacant, and to this he was assigned by the Karlstad chapter, the place being within the same diocese in which he had been serving. Here he labored with the same unremitting zeal as before, but apparently relieved of the former restraint. In his new field he found quite a group of like-minded men and women who welcomed him cordially and gladly accepted his spiritual leadership. But from that other burden on his heart, sympathy for the poor, he was to find no relief. The rural districts had their share of poverty as well as the industrial areas, and Olsson's tender feeling for those in want and misery moved him to acts of helpfulness and charity that put a heavy strain on his limited resources. He never wearied in well-doing, and apparently it did not occur to him to count the cost. Of his living he distributed so large a part among the needy of the parish that he soon found himself in economic straits.

IV

PLANNING EMIGRATION

In the middle decades of the nineteenth century the flow of emigration from Sweden to the United States was going on in ever-increasing volume. The so-called "America fever" was taking its toll in every part of central and southern Sweden, and Värmland was not immune. Few were the regions that had not added their quota to the exodus. In most localities, letters from America, with or without remittances for the purchase of tickets for the earliest sailings, but almost always containing glowing accounts of the opportunities the new country held out to all comers, were circulating among the folks at home, feeding the outflowing stream. When the Civil War was over and the heyday of reconstruction was on in the reunited States, many more were minded to help build up the land of freedom and incidentally to build their own fortune, and thus Swedish emigration got a new impetus in the late sixties, each west-bound ship carrying more passengers than the one before.

For a number of reasons Olsson was watching this movement and studying its implications. Since the time when he planned to go out as a foreign missionary, the idea of leaving Sweden was familiar to him. Now other factors had entered in. His devotion to the church of Christ could not blind him to the drawbacks of the state church system. His contacts with it in two or three

different charges had opened his eyes to glaring incon-
sistencies between confession and practice, not to mention sordid tendencies in the administration of church
affairs. Where, he asked himself, might a purer fellowship of believers be found or established? The answer
was gradually evolved as the thought of emigrating was
ripening in his mind.

Through trustworthy persons already located in the
United States he was informing himself about the new
country, its economic and social conditions, the advantages it had to offer newcomers with limited means or
none at all, particularly the generous terms on which the
government was offering land almost free to immigrants
who were willing to settle in the great wide West and
till its fertile soil. In the meantime he had secured
copies of the constitution of the Augustana Synod, the
new Lutheran free church in America formed chiefly by
Swedish immigrants, and minutes of its annual meetings,
and he was studying its structure and mode of administration. The great American West appealed mightily to
Olsson, but the question of affiliating with the Synod was
left open until a later day. Many of Olsson's friends had
sought his advice and conferred with him about all these
matters in advance, and when he definitely decided to
emigrate, a large number of his friends soon agreed to
join him. Plans were matured by leaders in the group
to leave Sweden in a body and upon arriving in America
to locate all in one place and form an independent communion of their own, with him as their leader and pastor.

Influences had been at work for some time before
Olsson arrived at his decision. One of the men who had
sought to induce him to take this step was Eric Norelius,

a young pastor of the Augustana Synod who on a visit to Sweden made his acquaintance at a religious conference in Stockholm. Of this meeting Norelius many years later gave this account: "Since I may possibly have had a part in influencing Olsson's decision to come to America and to this particular locality [Lindsborg], I wish to say a word about our first meeting and the acquaintance then formed. This occurred in June, 1868, during a convention of Fosterlands-stiftelsen [The Fatherland Foundation], when a social gathering was held at the Phoenix hotel for fellowship and fraternal exchange of opinions. To me the convention was of great interest as I there met and learnt to know quite a number of the men of whom I had been reading in the church papers. There was the caustic Professor Elmblad; there was the profound Johan Bring, the court preacher; there the devout parish rector, Jos. Colliander; there the genial and fatherly Doctor Forsell, who had not forgotten the Helsingland dialect of his ancestors; there that practical man and court preacher, G. E. Beskow, and many others, most of whom are now dead. Yet none of these engrossed my attention as did a slender young pastor from Värmland, in whose wideopen, jovial eyes there was a background of melancholy, the mark of all profound souls. He was very simply dressed, his clerical coat of very scanty cut, as if the owner had been obliged to save on broadcloth.

"The reason why I became so attached to the young cleric from Värmland was probably a laudable self-interest, rather than anything else. I had been authorized to look around for pastors suitable for America during my stay in Sweden, and it occurred to me that here was legitimate prey for the Augustana Synod. Through folks from Karlskoga living in America I had heard of 'Pastor Olsson of Persberg,' and when I saw him standing at a window, I walked right up to him as if guided by instinct, and without waiting for an introduction I said in my abrupt American fashion, 'I suppose this is Pastor Olsson of Värmland, that is, if you were born in Karlskoga' . . . Yes, I had found my man. There followed a very interesting conversation in the course of which I sought to lay upon his heart the burden of our need of pastors, and I pleaded with him to come over and help us."

Norelius, who seems to have elicited a tentative promise from Olsson, induced one of the Minnesota Conference churches to extend a call to him or at least a letter of invitation. This appears from a letter to T. N. Hasselquist, written by Olsson after his decision to come to America, but before he had determined where to locate. Part of this letter gives personal facts not elsewhere recorded:

"I thank you heartily for your letter received a good while ago. My delay in replying is due to the fact that I have been attacked from all sides with requests not to go to America. That these insistent requests have made me hesitant you may well understand. Nevertheless, I have now decided, God willing, to come to you. A few days ago my petition to be released from service in this diocese was forwarded to the chapter [at Karlstad]. Should the Lord put no unforeseen hindrance in my way, I will be with you late in June next year. Of late my powers have been reduced, due to several years of overwork, hence I need to save my strength until I have recuperated. For that reason you must not expect too much of me at first. I should prefer a small congregation

to begin with; beyond that, I will gladly do what I can.
I have had a communication from N[ew] Stockholm, and
have promised to come, but have not said how long I
will stay. You will not, I hope, look upon my promise
to N. Stockholm as an indignity to your Board. Naturally I do not know how strictly you stand on centralization in church government . . ."

Shortly afterward, Olsson informed Hasselquist that
his petition for release had been declined by the Karlstad
chapter, but would doubtless be granted by His Majesty
without the necessity of his resigning from the ministry.
He said further: "I have just had a letter from Ahlberg
asking me to help a few young men from there [the Ahlberg school] who intend to work among the Negroes. If
such a mission is begun in Kansas, I will gladly take part
in it and do what I can by the grace of God. An agricultural company has been formed near Salina by Christian
men known to me. I intend to take a share in this company in order to have a sure footing for my family. . . .
When I wrote, I had not received Ahlberg's letter, nor
did I know much about the Kansas company, but that
I must keep my promise to New Stockholm is clear. I
must go there for a time, at least, if their call is sure.
They wrote me that a formal call would be issued. That
has not reached me. If it does not come, the invitation
is purely personal, and my promise has been given only
to an individual. However that may be, I would ask
permission to go to Kansas sooner or later, trusting that
you do not look with disfavor on my plans."

By February 1869 Olsson had made his choice, select-
ing the Kansas settlement as against that of New Stockholm for valid reasons stated to Hasselquist. There

follow Olsson's very pronounced views on the emigration from Sweden and the serious conditions that forced people out of the country. He said: "Emigration is going to increase. It is a necessity for people who must find a way to live. It is a necessity for Sweden, for the country is over-populated in many regions. Besides, the economy of the country is in a sad state. The greater part of the farm owners are being ruined by mortgage loans and unlimited free trade. Lawmaking has lost its way, and unless God graciously puts things to rights, the end will be bankruptcy. I see God's mercy in this, that with you He has land enough for the many who need it. Here we are overrun by beggars. In Småland there is famine to a frightful degree. Unemployment prevails all over the country. And yet the riksdag is about to vote a gift of 196,000 crowns to the newly engaged princess. Meanwhile a private subscription is afoot to provide her a most luxurious home. If you can do anything for the sufferers in Småland, in the Lord's name do so. Royalty have, indeed, given something to the starving; a loan to provide relief is also proposed in the riksdag, but among so many that will not go far. The Lord has visited His wrath upon our beloved land. Many of its lawmakers seem to have been stricken with blindness. Pray for our country!"

Although some of Olsson's statements sound extravagant in our day, a comparison with authorities will bear him out, showing that he correctly gauged the economic causes for emigration. At the middle of last century Sweden was one of the poor countries in Europe. Toward 1860, skilled mechanics in Stockholm received an hourly pay of 10 to 15 öre, that is, 3 to 4 cents. The wages of

farm workers were even lower than that. In the United
States industrial wages at that time were about four
times as high and farm wages in proportion. Emigrants
writing back home gave the general impression that
a dollar was more easily earned here than a krona in
Sweden. Conditions being what they were, the Swedes
who left their country about the middle of the nineteenth
century knew precisely what they most wanted—to make
a living; and Olsson and others who brought groups of
them to this country were their real benefactors.

Even after Olsson moved to Sunnemo, he and his
friend Nyvall made occasional preaching tours together.
The evangelization work in which they and others were
engaged had the support of the independent Lutheran
organization known as the Evangelical Fatherland Foundation (Fosterlands-stiftelsen). Pastor Ahlberg and other
well-known pietists visited Värmland and spoke at the
mission meetings of the Ansgarius societies. Peter Fjellstedt, the noted Biblical scholar and commentator, is
known to have looked kindly upon the movement, and a
number of clergymen favored it without directly affiliating with it. Typical of their attitude was the answer
given by Rector Hammargren of Karlskoga when asked
how he stood in relation to the free religious work in the
community and whether it were not detrimental to the
church. His words were these: "As for me, I have seen
no bad effects in our parish, nor heard of any such in
neighboring parishes. On the contrary, formerly when
out on the roads, especially at night, I would often hear
rocks come whizzing past my head, but now that is a
thing of the past. I am convinced that this change among

the young people is due to this evangelizing movement. It may go on without any interference on my part."

The seeds from which germinated a free church movement had already been sown, and at the very time when Olsson was preparing to emigrate, plans were being discussed which several years later took definite form in the Mission Covenant. We are told that Nyvall, Lundborg, and other adherents of the movement were studying the organization of the Free Church of Scotland, founded as recently as 1843, as a suitable model for a free church in Sweden. Olsson was an interested participant in these discussions, for David Nyvall tells us: "With no other of his associates could my father talk so unreservedly about free-church matters, and feel certain of being fully understood, as with Olsson of Noretorp until, to my father's deep regret, he betook himself to America . . . How intimately my father was bound to Olsson at the time by the idea of a free church is shown by this note in his diary under date of September 15, 1868: 'How about Olsson's going to America? Lord, help us soon to a free church in our own country and grant also a change in temporal conditions. Otherwise America will become a refuge for the poor children of God.' He added: 'Therefore, shouldst Thou, O Lord, call me and aid me to visit the friends in America for half a year, I should gladly go.' Father's visit to America, contemplated or at least hoped for at that time, was put off until several years later; but Olsson left for America not long after. On February 1, 1869, my father sought Olsson at Noretorp, but did not find him at home . . . He had not yet given up the hope of binding Olsson to the homeland, a hope expressed by him in this proposal, made March 25, 1868:

'Let us unite in asking Olsson to become our traveling representative.' He also had his eye on his friend Olsson as teacher in a prospective school at Kristinehamn. But the latter was firmly resolved to leave Sweden.

"On May 2 my father met Olsson at Sunnemo, where the latter preached, and the two friends had an opportunity to talk over religious matters . . . On May 3 he made this notation: 'Bade Olsson farewell. Lord, Thou knowest how I felt. May we meet in heaven, if not before.' Then followed his repeated wish that a call from America might come to him as well."

Later events in Olsson's career as a champion of the traditional Lutheran doctrine of the Atonement, as against the interpretation by P. P. Waldenström soon adopted generally by the Mission Friends, lend peculiar interest to the events thus minutely recorded by Nyvall.

V

FOUNDING THE LINDSBORG SETTLEMENT

In the spring of 1868, on April 17, there was organized in Chicago a land company to promote the settlement of Swedish immigrants in larger communities rather than small, widely scattered groups. It was named the First Swedish Lutheran Agricultural Company of America. McPherson County, Kansas, was its choice as the location of the first settlement. The first paragraph of its constitution characterized the enterprise in a few words: "Every person who joins this corporation shall have the Christian spirit and shall adhere to the evangelical Lutheran doctrine, be zealous and industrious, and do all in his power to promote the progress and development of the company."

Olsson and his friends had the prospectus of this company before them while planning to emigrate. Many of them even became members of the company before leaving Sweden. The idea of recruiting companies of emigrants for the purpose of colonizing them was quite common at the time, but this particular plan differed from most others in this, that the organization of a Lutheran communion was fundamental. The religious interest was uppermost in the mind of this group, in whose plans entered even the founding of a "pure" congregation; hence that feature had for them a peculiar appeal. One of their group, C. R. Carlson, a close friend

of Olsson, departed for America in August 1868, as a sort
of unofficial observer and investigator. After contacting
officials of the company at Chicago, he came out to their
new settlement in November. After talking over the
matter with the first few members of the company already located there, he brought it about that an informal
call was issued shortly before Christmas asking the young
Sunnemo pastor to become their spiritual leader. It was
on the basis of this invitation that Olsson definitely
resolved to leave Värmland and take up pastoral work
in the Smoky Hills region of Kansas.

Individually and in very small groups, Swedes had
settled in central Kansas from 1855 on. With a party of
sixteen Gustaf Johnson located on land in the neighborhood of the present city of Lindsborg in 1866. Some of
the settlers had no religious interests; others had been
members of the Swedish pioneer churches in Illinois or
elsewhere. Religious work among them was not begun
until 1868. That spring S. G. Larson made a preaching
tour of the region, and A. W. Dahlsten, who followed
him in the fall of the same year, later organized and
served Swedish congregations at the neighboring points
Fremont and Salemsborg. When C. R. Carlson arrived,
he gathered for regular devotional services the few settlers
belonging to the Chicago company, while Dahlsten
worked chiefly among the members of a similar company
operating from Galesburg, Illinois.

The president of the agricultural association was John
Ferm, a devout man from Storfors, Värmland. The chief
purpose was to obtain land and secure homes for settlers.
With the provision that all should be true Lutheran
Christians did not go any precise stipulation by the com-

pany as to forming a congregation at once, that being left to the settlers themselves. The strict Lutheran spirit that pervaded the enterprise was the result of the personal piety of its promoters, who preferred like-minded people in their settlement.

When the plans began to take shape, Ferm wrote to friends in Sweden who were his brethren in the faith. Thus correspondence was opened with John Johnson, then of Backa, Värmland, and C. R. Carlson, a schoolmaster in Filipstad. These two began to influence others in favor of the emigration and settlement plan, and they were instrumental in gaining the attention of Olsson and his prospective party of emigrants, who eventually cast their lot with the company, which, after having considered various localities, decided in favor of the Smoky Hill Valley.

The land company negotiated with the Kansas Pacific (Union Pacific) Railway Company for the purchase of 16,000 acres of land and finally procured 13,160 acres at a total price of about $30,000. The tract acquired consisted of alternate sections of railroad land, every other section being homestead land secured from the Government. This made a solid tract, six by nine miles, located in the south part of Saline and the north part of McPherson counties. The deal was closed with the railway company on September 1, 1868.

It was several weeks later that emissaries from the Chicago company located the first section-line markers and began to stake out its holdings. There had been no real settlement on the land so far. Only a few scattered pioneers were located on the tract before midyear 1869, when the large party of emigrants direct from Sweden

arrived. Thus, it was to the people Pastor Olsson led
out of Värmland that the company's land was for the
most part parceled out. With their coming the community virtually sprang into being, and due credit given to
those who first planned the enterprise does not obscure
the fact that Olof Olsson with his party became the actual
founder of Lindsborg. The records of the company show
that not much more than a hundred farms were sold to
individuals while it is known that most of the eighty
families who came over with Olsson located in that
community.

The records of the agricultural company and the contracts issued to purchasers of land and town lots add
touches to the picture of conditions in the early years
of this settlement, which was not a "colony" in the
specific sense, but a community of independent settlers.
These gleanings from the records of the corporation are
part and parcel of the history of the settlement:

In January 1869, it was proposed to build a church,
but the matter was tabled until a committee should make
inquiries and bring in a plan. In February 1870, thirteen
months later, the following entry is made: "§12. The
church Ferm speaks of as having been built on the company's land is supported by the company to this extent,
that we wish them [the builders?] and those who belong
to it that they may have success and may bring blessings
with them and that every member of the company is
urged to contribute as much as he is able." The church
was built by the settlers on their own initiative, and a
statement that the Chicago and the Galesburg land companies each had a church erected for the settlers is clearly
in error as touching the former corporation.

The name Lindsborg was adopted February 20, 1869. It was suggested by the prominence of S. A. Lindell, S. P. Lindgren, J. O. Lindh, A. P. Linde, and D. Lindahl among the promoters and directors of the company. On April 30, 1869, the foreman was ordered to do two days of breaking with a team on ground allotted to Pastor Olsson in advance of his arrival. In June the directing board ordered the purchase of "47 guns, 4 revolvers, and 6 pistols, together with ammunition, to be paid for at once by the treasurer and sent to Salina for the protection of our workmen against the Indians."

There was talk of a new railroad in these parts, as evidenced by this entry in the minutes for February 11, 1870: "The proposed railroad which would cross our land those in Lindsborg are urged to work for all they can and to try if possible to have it pass through Section 7." There is nothing to show that the board in Chicago took any direct action to further a project that would mean so much to the new settlement beyond recommending it to the local people. Among these there was one man who saw, perhaps more clearly than the others, the tentative value of the proposed railway to the community, and that man was the new pastor. His correspondence with the president of the Kansas Pacific is noted elsewhere in this volume.

As early as 1870 the records take note of a plan to lay out a town site and seek to make Lindsborg the county seat. Both projects were endorsed May 30 by the board, which assumed the cost of surveying and plotting the town site. In June it was decided to distribute one hundred lots free, every third lot in the town

site to be given to any person who built a house on it
or planted forty trees along the street.

The settlement was just a year old and the town of
Lindsborg had just been laid out when it was proposed
to start a newspaper there. An entry in the minutes
dated September 27 reads: "§4. After a long discussion
for and against the value of a newspaper, it was unanimously decided to ... set apart the company's house and
lot [in Lindsborg] as the property of a political newspaper,
with the proviso that it shall be a weekly paper to promote the progress of the town by telling the truth
inexorably and faithfully and not resort to lying and
jocularity, as do most of the small papers hereabout."
This particular newspaper project was not carried out.
It remained for Pastor Olsson to start the first publication issued from Lindsborg—a religious periodical of
which there is more to be said later.

The sale of the surplus lands, which was to take place
after five years, as stipulated in the by-laws of the corporation, was undertaken in 1871, after only three years.
On the remaining land, auctioned off to members February 21, a total sum exceeding $75,000 was realized.
The price for the whole tract was $29,625 or $2.25 per
acre. According to the original pact, the surplus funds
were to be distributed among the members after five
years, or in 1873. The land had been fully paid for by
November 2, 1872, yet the distribution was put off. The
company was chartered in 1870 as the "First Swedish
Agricultural Company of McPherson County," its business to be transacted at Lindsborg and Chicago and its
directors being divided between the two places. Action
taken by the directors in Lindsborg did not always suit

those in Chicago, and vice versa. There was friction at times, and interests conflicted, but no open rupture resulted. The deferring of the dividends by decision passed in 1871 at Chicago seems to have caused dissatisfaction among the settlers, and that feeling apparently prevailed among them for several years. The matter came to a head in 1877, as borne out by the record for March 28. This entry is typical:

"Owing to the fact that the members in Lindsborg have resolved that a dividend be declared, contrary to a decision by the general meeting in Chicago, April 14, 1871, and whereas they threaten suit if their resolution is not carried out, and whereas here also there is threat of going to law unless the dividend is distributed as previously decided, and whereas this company was organized on a Christian basis, be it resolved according to Paul's 1 Eph. ch. 6 [sic] to appoint a court of five members to be selected as follows: two to be elected by each party, these to select two others who shall draw lots to decide which is to serve as judge. The winner shall serve and the other withdraw. All are to be selected from among the members of the company."

A proposal from Lindsborg looking toward the dissolution of the corporation was found impractical and illegal, and a more suitable plan was asked for. A compromise was then reached, whereby the resources were to be equitably divided among the original members "according to the proposition from Kansas." A committee was chosen to wind up the affairs, and on June 16, 1877, the agricultural company was dissolved.

The Värmland emigrants left their homes early in May 1869, heading for the port of Gothenburg. There were really two groups, both looking to Olsson as their leader. He and a group from Sunnemo, who started first, were followed by another group from Persberg and the surrounding mining region. When these reached Gothenburg, they found that Olsson and his party had sailed the day before, so they embarked on another ship. Eighty families are said to have made up the two groups, the emigrants numbering about two hundred and fifty in all.

Without serious incidents the two parties reached Chicago and, shortly afterward, McPherson County, somewhat ahead of Olsson, who was detained in Illinois. There he met with Swedish pastors and attended the annual convention of the Augustana Synod, which was in session at Moline June 17–23. His presence was recognized on the 22nd, when he was received as an advisory member. Later he was invited to preach a sermon before the synod. In the session of the day before, there was reported a request from the Minnesota Conference, "That the Synod would ask Pastor O. Olsson, newly arrived from Sweden, to accept a call from Stockholm and Säbylund." The petition is evidence of the great need of Swedish pastors for the new churches springing up. At the time it was drawn up, the Conference did not know that Olsson was already committed to the charge of the prospective congregation at Lindsborg.

At midsummer, Olsson joined his people in the Lindsborg settlement. He took up his work at once, preaching here and there in the few homes that could accommodate a gathering. Francis Johnson, one of the first Swedish settlers in Kansas, has noted down interesting reminiscences, and we will let him tell us of Olsson's arrival and the events immediately following.

"The first time I saw Olsson was on my way to Salina. I met him sitting on top of a load of lumber, reading a newspaper. He wore a slouch hat, bought in Salina for a dollar. 'This is the new pastor just come from Sweden,' said the driver by way of introduction. 'What kind of a preacher is that, coming in such fashion,' I thought to myself.

"The first thing to do was to rig up something for the new pastor to live in. Coming from a comfortable home as curate of Sunnemo, here he had to live in a twelve-by-fourteen hut. It had to serve for living room, dining room, bedroom, and kitchen. But Olsson seemed quite satisfied. 'I am glad to be rid of the bonds of the state church,' he would explain. 'Never did I get worse abuse from anyone than I got from the archbishop of Sweden for preaching the Word of God on week days here and there in the villages. . . . Here we will form a congregation of believers only. It will be a paradise on earth, where we will be free to worship God in peace and contentment.'

"Now it was time to organize a church, and one Sunday it was announced that all who desired to take part in the founding of a Swedish Lutheran congregation were asked to meet at the company house on the 19th of August. We were many at that meeting, but only twelve signed up for membership, and the first constitution was adopted. The rest of us, who did not like it, did not join the church until 1872, when the constitution drawn up for the churches by the Synod was adopted.

"The building of the parsonage was begun in the fall of 1869. We all took part, even those who were not members. There was plenty of rocks in the hills and lots

of sand in the creek, but where get money to buy lime?
We raised cash enough for a shingled roof and lime for
outside mortar, while the inside was plastered with sand
and clay. Those used to handling rock did the masonry
work. Magnus Carlson bossed the job. Olsson was there
all the time. We began and closed the day's work with
meditation on the Word of God and with prayer.

"Olsson at once moved into the house, which was
built on his own land. It was poorly constructed, of
course, and within a year large cracks opened in the walls,
so that snakes and other vermin crawled through. One
morning a big snake lay coiled up on the pastor's study
table.

"We built the first church on section 7. This, too,
was built of stone, and having no money we did our own
work. Poor were we, and poor was our pastor. After
some time he was short of clothes. He used to borrow
suits from Jon, his brother-in-law, but the trousers would
be two inches too short. In those days it was not so much
a matter of thine and mine: we had to help one another
in every way. When I came to the parsonage one day,
Mrs. Olsson said, 'I ought to ask you to stay for coffee,
of course, but we have had no coffee for three days.' Poor
as we were, we never suffered want outright, for we had
all become landed gentry, each one with a farm of his
own.

"The church was finished. It was thatched with grass.
There was no floor and no ceiling. In January 1870, we
moved in. Divine services were held there regularly, and
a Sunday school was started at once, Olsson teaching a
Bible class of adults. I was one of the members of the

class, and the impressions received there have stayed with me all my life."

Many of the newcomers came from the mines and smelters and knew little about cultivating the soil. They farmed with but little success the first years. Either drought reduced their crops or grasshoppers took their toll of what little was raised. In 1871 Olsson sought to induce the railway company to take back half of the land sold to the settlers. This the company would not do, but deferred their payments so that no one would be forced to give up his farm. Very soon, however, most of them learnt how to till the new soil, and the more industrious and enterprising among the settlers prospered in due time.

Olsson came to America with a family consisting of no less than six persons. Besides himself, with wife and a young child, there were his parents and his brother Carl. One of the earliest settlers, who owned a 10 x 12 frame dwelling, opened his home to them, and there they all lived for the first few weeks until the first rude "parsonage" could be built for them. The pastor, like the other newcomers, had a farm allotted to him, and there, in Section 7, a little house was built in the early fall, with rock brought from the Smoky Hills. It was a makeshift of rock and sod, and within a year or two the mortar began to crumble, and the hut was not considered safe to live in, so it was torn down when in 1872 another and better house had been completed.

This first dwelling provided scant protection against the weather and none against snakes and other vermin. In the winter the dipper would freeze fast in the water bucket overnight. One summer day, while the pastor was engaged in the preparation of the next Sunday's sermon, he heard a frightened outcry from his little daughter: "Papa, a snake!" Looking around, he found a rattler stealthily making his way through the crevices in the wall. He had to fetch a stick and put out of the way this unpleasant reminder of another wily old serpent before the sermon preparation could go on. Not even in the little sanctuary was the preacher safe from uncomfortable intrusion. In the course of divine services one Sunday, it is said, a skunk suddenly came out from his hiding place under the pulpit, causing an anxious interval for the pastor and no little disturbance among his hearers.

The second prairie home of the Olsson family still stands as a landmark in those parts, and it has been found worthy of perpetuation in lithography by Birger Sandzén, local artist of Lindsborg and celebrated painter of the Rockies and the scenic Southwest.

The hardships shared by Olsson with the early settlers at Lindsborg and the conditions under which they lived have been described, not only by the pioneers themselves, but by Ernst Skarstedt, Alfred Bergin, and others, who have lived in Lindsborg at later periods.

Many of the newcomers lived in dugouts, the inside sometimes lined with logs brought from the nearest creek or river. The walls extending above the ground were of sod or rock; the roof was either flat or pitched, and consisted of poles or logs placed close together and covered with turf or a thatch of coarse grass. At one end was the door, at the other a small window. "Life in such a hovel could be made fairly tolerable, but that called for unlimited patience and presupposed a contented disposition," remarks Skarstedt with the inference that these virtues were not always present. The hazards of these pioneers were many and their discomforts varied. One family had the roof of their dugout punctured by the hoofs of a stampeding buffalo herd. During violent rainstorms the earthen floors of the huts would often be flooded and turned into soft mud. Olsson himself told of an instance when a garden snake unexpectedly dropped from the ceiling directly into the soup tureen while a family sat at the dinner table.

Such mishaps, however, were mere trifles as compared to the greater reverses during the first few years, such as recurring epidemics of malaria, periodic drought, and occasional visits by swarms of grasshoppers.

VI

THE PIONEER CHURCH

When Olsson left Värmland, destined for Kansas, the adventure was greater than anything he could have foreseen. True, the missionary zeal kindled in his heart years before was still alive, and it doubtless prompted his going. An ordinary missionary, starting for a foreign field, is definitely called and is sent out after an official commissioning by a church body or some missionary society, but Olsson had no commission, and his call was tardy in coming. The understanding was that he would be the spiritual adviser of those who joined the party of emigrants, but on coming to Kansas they found no congregation for him to serve, no church for him to preach in. The missionary had to build his own mission.

Devotional services were held in various homes for a few weeks after the arrival first of the Olsson party, later of Olsson himself, but they were not slow in organizing for regular church work. At an out-door meeting held in the evening of August 19, outside of the company house, a church congregation was organized by Pastor Olsson, twelve of the men present joining then and there. The small number and the absence of women is explained in part by the rigorous requirements for membership set up in advance. It had been agreed by the organizers that they would not knowingly admit any but devout believers into this congregation. In order to put this puritan principle into practice, these pietists from Värmland and all other applicants had to submit to a strict test, only professed converts being accepted. The pastor's own wife is said to have submitted to an inquiry as to the soundness of her Christian life. With so thorough a discipline, it goes without saying that all others were required to give proof of their faith. The constitution drawn up for adoption at the organization meeting and there signed may well be held to have expressed the views of the newcomers, particularly Olsson and C. R. Carlson, a leading layman, as to religious communions. Of its nine short paragraphs, the following are rendered from the Swedish original:

"§2. This congregation recognizes the evangelical Lutheran confession as its rule of faith, yet it desires to stand in friendly and brotherly relation to Christians of other Protestant persuasion.

"§3. Being convinced by the Word of God and holding that participation in Holy Communion does not serve to reclaim the unconverted, but tends rather to his destruction, the congregation will admit to participation in this sacrament no one but those who have been gently but thoroughly tested by the pastor and the deacons, according to the Word of God, as to their true conversion.

"§6. Children within the congregation and those without shall be instructed in Christianity at the proper time by the pastor, and those desiring to partake of the Holy Communion with the congregation shall be admitted to membership in the manner prescribed by this constitution for other persons.

"§7. As deacons and trustees shall be elected men known in the congregation as living Christians, in so far as men guided by the Word of God are able to judge.

"§8.   Each deacon shall seek to ascertain by conversation the spiritual condition of the person who applies for membership in the congregation and shall report to the church council, which shall then decide according to Paragraph 3 what action shall be taken with regard to the applicant."

Bethany was the name adopted for the church. The earliest divine services were held in the home of Mr. Carlson, where the first communion was administered by Pastor Olsson.   The company house was occasionally used for worship, but the erection of a small church, as elsewhere described, was undertaken not many weeks after the congregation was formed. The church was built in the center of Section 7, doubtless because the company house was located there and the site adjoined the pastor's farm.   The little edifice was not finished until the last days of the year; hence Christmas matin services were deferred until New Year's Day (1870), when the congregation worshiped in the new church for the first time. The congregation very soon outgrew this first church, but it had to serve for more than two years.

The constitution adopted by Olsson and his parishioners had no heterodox elements, and it was considered "peculiar" in a questionable sense by other Lutheran pastors although in spirit it was much like that governing their own congregations, even though differently worded.   The suspicion attached to it was voiced by the president of the Augustana Synod, Jonas Swensson himself, who wrote to A. W. Dahlsten, Olsson's neighbor pastor, under date of April 23, 1870:

"You mentioned that Pastor O. Olsson and his congregation intend to ask for admittance to the Augustana

Synod next summer. It would then be necessary to find out what kind of constitution the congregation has adopted, so that we do not let into the Synod a congregation which ignores the confessions of the Lutheran church, just as the old General Synod admitted a synod which had not even on paper adopted the Augsburg Confession. Be so kind as to inform yourself definitely on their constitution. I suppose it is not printed; if so, you might secure a copy. But living so near by, you might go there and read it through, taking notes on matters in which it differs and making a copy of its doctrinal article in particular. Do not neglect this. It is of great importance that you get this matter clear should they ask to be admitted; but do not take anything on mere hearsay; see that you get a look at the constitution and read it for yourself."

The inquiry seems to have allayed all fears, for a few months later Olsson and his church were welcomed into the Augustana communion, the synodical constitution as well as the uniform constitution for its congregations being readily accepted by them as rules of faith and practice. Olsson's attitude to lay evangelism had been challenged by officials of the state church in Sweden, and with others he had been vindicated on that point by legislative enactment. Labeled a free-church man at home, as Olsson was, his stand, oddly enough, was questioned, upon his coming to the United States, by a Lutheran free church founded here by men who over there had sided with the new-evangelical movement and had held with him against the state church on many points. The reason for the indirect investigation does not appear from any records. The Bethany church con-

stitution was no secret document, and a transcript might
have been had for the asking, including its orthodox
confessional article. In any event, uniformity and good
order required a change to the congregational constitution prescribed by the Synod, and the ease with which
the transition was made proved groundless any suspicions that might have existed. The step taken made the
church founded by Olsson one of the first of the many
churches since then established in Kansas through the
missionary activities of the Augustana Synod.

Joining the Synod was the only sensible thing for the
pioneer church to do, yet there were those in the congregation who complained of the action taken. The murmur
grew ever louder, nourished by the agitation of the mal-
contents. The pastor sought to show them that they
could not long endure as an independent, isolated congregation, and he maintained that a group of Swedish
Lutherans like themselves was the church body most
natural for them to join. There were many who would
not yield, and from then on the pastor's peace of mind
was frequently disturbed. He had discovered very early
that in the flock of exclusively faithful Christians they
had aimed to gather certain of the sheep were prone to
stray to other pastures. Some of the loudest confessors
of the holy life proved to be the most unruly, and their
shepherd sadly admitted that many who had gone in for
purity and perfection in the church were themselves
something less than perfect. When he saw that no human
searching of hearts and reins had sufficed to establish a
communion of *only* saints, he resigned himself to the task
of preaching to sinners as well.

Within a year the dissension had grown so strong that

an itinerant preacher named Blom was called in by the minority to preach to them one Sunday. The message was such that Pastor Olsson was compelled to register a warning against error in teaching.

The leaven of Waldenstromianism was being added to the lump here as in other congregations, and the ferment kept working. By 1872 Olsson deemed a second public warning needful. On Trinity Sunday he read to his congregation the sermon in which Peter Paul Waldenström of Sweden propounded his own view of the meaning of Christ's atonement—a departure from the Lutheran doctrine. The reading finished, Olsson put the question to his hearers whether anyone had noted doctrinal error in Waldenström's discourse. No one being prepared to point out any dangerous teaching, the pastor stated emphatically, "Well, if you assent to this, then it is time I hand in my resignation." At this point, it is reported, Mr. Ferm, one of the elder members, raised his voice in vigorous protest, saying, "What Waldenström here teaches is a doctrine from blackest hell."

Whether or not the words were so overemphatic in the mouth of the speaker or merely so in the report of the incident, they were typical of the heat and rancor with which the ensuing controversy among the Swedish Lutherans here and elsewhere over the doctrine of Atonement was carried on throughout that decade and after. The schism in the Bethany congregation certainly gave its pastor no peace during his four remaining years at Lindsborg. To get Waldenström's point of view at first hand, Olsson wrote him a letter of inquiry which was duly answered. These letters, both very long and doubtless covering every point of the famous theological controversy, are not found among the papers left by Olsson. He became the staunchest defender of the orthodox doctrine held by the greater number of Lutheran church members as against the dissenting views of Waldenström and his adherents. These letters would have had value as fundamental documents, showing the precise position of the two champions at the outset.

The internal strife in the Bethany congregation was not of the pastor's making. Olsson was not by nature contentious, but he saw it as his clear duty to guard his flock against erroneous teaching, and he stood his ground on the established doctrine of the Lutheran church without yielding an inch. He would have greatly preferred to act the part of peacemaker, but it was not to be.

A sketch of Olsson as a pioneer pastor of the Kansas prairies by Dr. Ernst F. Pihlblad, himself a Kansan, contains this word picture of the battlefield and the conflict there waged:

"The dove of peace was too soon to be driven from their settlement whose membership had sought to keep themselves 'unspotted from the world,' and who supposedly were of one heart and one mind in Christ. The Waldenstromian heresy in the matter of the Atonement had found its way across the sea from Sweden to remote Lindsborg. It became a very personal question with every man and woman and led to interminable debate, not only as they gathered for service on Sunday, but it carried into every home. Men brought their Bibles with them to the work on the farm, they were in evidence on the counters of the community store to be at hand for the belligerents on both sides to prove their point. Families were torn asunder, and bitter enmities sprang up among those who had been childhood friends.

"In this theological melée Pastor Olsson bravely stood his ground, contending without compromise for the truth of the Bible as taught by the church. The contention finally grew to such heat that when parishioners came to visit their shepherd in a period of illness, there were those who prayed aloud that the Lord might permit him to die. There were even whisperings about ambush to do him harm on his lonely journeys as he traveled in the night to minister to his people.

"The matter reached a crisis on Good Friday, 1874. Sixteen members were separated from the fellowship of the church. The experience through which this consecrated, zealous man of God had lived broke his health and saddened his days. On the other hand, his unflinching stand in championing the truth, linked with a tact born of the ardent love for souls, saved Bethany Church, now the largest and one of the most influential in this region, from complete collapse. During the years, it has proved a center of inestimable blessing. In its bosom was born Bethany College. In the struggles of the institution in its formative years it was tenderly nurtured and generously supported by the limited means of this devoted people.

"Time heals all wounds, even those which ache the most. In after years, when this storm of the spirit had spent itself, friend and foe alike recognized the Christian fairness of the great leader. Both yield respect for the convictions and affection for the personality of this Pastor of the Prairie."

A summary of the church records gives this picture

of the breach between the two leaders, which precipitated the so-called crisis. C. R. Carlson, prominent from the founding of the settlement, together with his wife asked for dismissal from the church on the grounds that (1) they had been warned and censured for receiving in their home preachers outside the Lutheran denomination whom they nevertheless held to be true Christian teachers, (2) Carlson had been severely reprimanded by the congregation on the charge of misinterpreting its holy faith and doctrine, (3) he had been unwilling to pledge loyalty to the Augustana Synod. In a written statement to the church council Carlson, however, promised to remain a member and do his duty as such on condition that he would be permitted to entertain in his home, without disapproval, Christian preachers of other denominations, and to support missions of his own choice; and he agreed to invite the pastor and the board of deacons to be present and pass on the orthodoxy of any and all such preachers visiting his home. The case having been duly discussed, the board on April 10 took this action: "The Church Council can not on its own behalf, neither on behalf of the congregation, grant the request of Mr. Carlson. Those persons who have so requested are therefore dismissed from membership, but should Mr. Carlson or any of the others desire to join the congregation later without setting up specific conditions, they will be welcome so to do." Far from being a peremptory dismissal, this was granting the petition of the dissenters, who could hardly have expected any other action. The withdrawal of Carlson and his wife together with fourteen others was publicly announced two days later. That was the wedge that threatened to split the church.

A second event of like nature but without group secession took place about a year afterward. It served to draw the line more clearly between the two contending factions. At a council meeting May 19, 1875, heresy charges were preferred against two church members, A. John Nilson and John Ferm. Now Olsson presented as a basis for discussion the following statement:

"Waldenström's interpretation of the doctrine of Atonement is unbiblical and un-Lutheran—

"1. Because P. W. segregates the attributes of God, making love alone a characteristic of His heart and being, with the exclusion of righteousness and divine wrath;

"2. Because P. W. denies the suffering of Christ as a punishment for our sins;

"3. Because P. W. denies propitiation in the Lutheran sense;

"4. Because P. W. denies that Christ was a Mediator between God and man;

"5. Because P. W. denies that God is merciful to us for Christ's sake;

"6. Because P. W.'s book on the Atonement and his sermons in general run counter to and subvert true Lutheran doctrine."

The ensuing discussion ran to great length, as indicated by a report covering eighteen closely written pages, and long excerpts were read from Lutheran books to prove or disprove the six theses. Nilson maintained that Waldenström's writings were being either wilfully misinterpreted or their meaning distorted through ignorance or thoughtfulness. The verdict was: "Resolved that John Ferm and A. J. Nilson, who, after having been warned privately and admonished by the church council, still persisted in their statements, be, and they are hereby, excommunicated on the ground that they hold, and defend, and seek to disseminate a doctrine foreign to the congregation, namely, the teaching of Peter Waldenström on the Atonement, and thus have deserted, misconstrued, and openly opposed the holy faith and doctrine of our church."

On the turn events took after the excommunication of the sixteen members on April 12, 1874, Dr. Alfred Bergin, who succeeded to the pastorate of Bethany in 1904, has this comment: "Among those dismissed were some who had been Olsson's most intimate friends. The prediction was triumphantly made that the Bethany congregation would go to pieces in a very short time. It is said, however, that its regret at the loss was measurably lessened by the accession of more than sixteen new members about the same time. But Pastor Olsson was keenly pained by the fact that Lutheran faith and love of the brethren had proved so weak in some of those to whom he had been most warmly attached. It was doubtless Olsson's uncompromising position and the firmness of his action that staved off the threatened breakup of his congregation. The heat of conflict may have made him somewhat hard, but now both sides justify his action, those who left the church, as well as those who remained, conceding that their love for him and their respect for his opinion has never ceased." But at the height of this controversy, with incessant debating, speaking, and writing on the subject of the Atonement, Olsson's strength was sapped, his health suffered, and his spirit was depressed at the estrangement of some of his best friends and the failure of a noble but futile experiment—the founding of a pure and perfect church.

In certain quarters Olsson's zeal for the doctrines of his church has been characterized as rank and unreasoning partisanship. A search of his own writings and of what has been written about him, as also the reading of some of his letters, yields scant support to such a view. There is evidence quite to the contrary. Far from recklessly sacrificing his old friends, Olsson was aggrieved at every such loss and sought by all means—except compromise in matters of Christian doctrine—to forestall any threatened breach of friendship. He was forbearing in love even to the brethren who were not of one mind with him on all points, and, according to the admonition of Paul, he diligently sought to keep the unity of the Spirit in the bond of peace. When the turbulence in his church was at its height, Olsson received a letter which is proof in point. From Nora, Sweden, C. J. Nyvall wrote under date of June 20, 1873, addressing him affectionately as "My Beloved Brother Olle." Much of the letter is pertinent to the times. The writer dealt with the religious ferment then working both here and in Sweden and at the same time stated his own attitude. About the annual meeting of the Fatherland Foundation (Fosterlandsstiftelsen) Nyvall wrote: "I will only say this, that there arose general dissatisfaction with Stift[elsen] among the friends from the country districts because Waldenström, who was in attendance, was not asked to preach. But through the insistence of friends he was given leave by Beskow to preach Sunday morning in the Blasieholm church to such an attendance that crowds stood around the doors and many were turned away. Stift., with its many orthodox clergymen, must of course maintain its churchly position, and it acted thus because of that sermon of Wald-m on the Twentieth Sunday after Trinity. A man whose activities appear so clearly to all eyes as a work for the kingdom of God is passed by while half-dead ministers are trotted out—that may well cause disgust among the friends of missions."

The writer then goes on to explain his personal attitude: "My own position as to that sermon I find it hard to state; as you know, I am no profound thinker; I cannot see that there is such an enormous difference, and it is not easy for me to contradict Waldenström's explanation of the subject in his theses for the ministerial examination last March which earned him the highest mark. In Werml[and], God be praised, there has as yet been no real controversy on this matter; we preachers have made no issue out of it. Nilsson in Kristineh[amn] is against Waldenström, and when we two are together, I am quite unable to parry his arguments with my own; still I can not say that he has brought me to the point of certainty. Such an attitude as this might seem peculiar, yet I am certain that through Jesus all the sins of the world have been paid for, and that He redeemed us from the curse of the law when He became a curse for us, and that God in His everlasting love gave us this sacrifice, and that he who hears and believes this is saved; this I preach according as grace is given me; then the learned may wrangle to their heart's content as to whether God was changed by the fall of man; restoration has been made, God be praised. As for the pattern for our sermons, I can not but say that the presentation of the Word by Waldenström as well as by Rosenius in *Pietisten* is in as

perfect accord with the Word as anything I get to hear
or read, also that the preachers in Werml[and] bear a
more evangelical stamp than formerly, thank God."

Of his contemplated visit to the United States and
his expected contacts with the Augustana Synod Nyvall
has this to say: "The matter of my trip is still rather
uncertain, at least this year. . . . Wherever I come, I am
besieged by friends who implore me not to go. . . . I can
well understand that those belonging to the smaller
synods have lesser standing; you mean that I might therefore be hampered in my activity; but as a traveling
preacher I could not possibly preach about matters in
dispute, and maybe the Augustana people are such as
will have nothing to do with other than those who do
all they can to gain members for their congregations. If
so, I would not fit. But as I, for my part, am a Lutheran
and can so remain with a good conscience, I had thought
best to secure a call or commission from August[ana] or,
as you suggest, from your Conference. I have also thought
it might be still better to accept a call from the Alliance,
which, I presume, has a branch in America that sends
out preachers. As far as I know, one is not required to
sink one's convictions, only to refrain from partisan propaganda. I have always had a dislike for the latter and
have become more and more set against such, so it would
be impossible for me to begin preaching and working in
a congregation of one confession to win it over to another . . . Should the good Lord desire to bring me over
there, it would give me indescribable joy to see and talk
with you again."

So intimate a correspondence as this letter indicates
could not then have been carried on with this apologist

for, yet not a convinced adherent of, Waldenström had Olsson been the ruthless antagonist some have made him out. The letter bears rather clear testimony to a conciliatory attitude on his part. Apparently he was not averse to a visit by his old friend to his own and other churches of the Synod, despite the latter's leaning to the opposition, prompted no doubt by the hope that his presence might serve as oil on the troubled waters here and there, even if the general storm would not abate. There was as yet no rupture in the personal friendship between these two men, though their diverging views altered their relations after Nyvall later made his decision and took his stand with Waldenström on most points. When Nyvall two years later, after having abandoned the long harbored desire to emigrate, compromised on a short visit to America, a letter from Olsson bade him heartily welcome, although it was C. R. Carlson and others who had withdrawn from Olsson's church that were sponsoring his visit and defraying his expenses, as Nyvall tells us in his *Reseminnen*, a book recounting his first visit to the United States.

The secession from the Bethany church due to the doctrinal schism was not as great as had been feared. A published list of those who relinquished their membership for that and other causes in the years 1873–76 comprises only forty-three communicants. These soon formed their own little congregations, one at Rose Hill and the other in the town of Lindsborg, each erecting a small meeting house.

In the group that withdrew from the Bethany church in 1874 was J. A. Pihl, later a pastor of the Mission Covenant. As a partisan, he might have judged his pastor less fairly at the time, but years afterward his reasoned and unbiased opinion of Olsson was expressed in terms of praise and just recognition of his worth. Writing of those first years, he gives this testimony: "Pastor Olsson was here then. He was faithful to his calling and equal to his task, working with diligence and devotion. At first there was peace and quiet. We had full confidence in one another. That was a precious time. I have been told that some were brought to life and peace even in the little church on Section 7.

"Pastor Olsson was a man of peace; he loved both liberty and peace. His purpose was to found an independent congregation, but he found it necessary for a local church to belong to some synod, and so he and his congregation joined the Augustana Synod. That displeased some, and when later the controversy over the doctrine of the Atonement arose, a mighty storm broke out. Many of Pastor Olsson's friends then left his church and joined the Mission Friends. From that time there was complete separation between the Lutherans and the Mission Friends. For many that was a time of testing, and unwise zeal cost them many tears and great anguish. O God, save thy children from schism and partisanship! To get down to serious work and the desired order was no easy thing, for many were ignorant and very unreasonable. They pushed their demand for freedom to the extreme, their action bringing down ridicule upon themselves and breeding levity in the church. Such unseemly procedure was encouraged even by certain visiting brother ministers."

As a pastor, Olsson did not confine his work to the local church, even though its care and nurture in the circumstances proved to be a man-size job. His missionary activity extended far and wide over the Kansas plains. According to his records, he was often called to distant points to christen children of Swedish settlers, and many were his preaching visits to the little Swedish settlements springing up roundabout Lindsborg. Neither did he fail to visit the camps of the men working on railway construction and the building of Fort Riley and other frontier outposts, a number of the men of his church being scattered around among these workmen in their effort to eke out the scant livelihood yielded by their farms the first years. As early as 1872, he organized the settlers at New Gottland into a little church which he had to serve on occasion. For three years, 1873–76, the Free Mount congregation in the neighboring settlement of Fremont, on the Smoky Hill River, a few miles to the west, was served by Olsson jointly with his home church.

During the years he served at Lindsborg, Olsson combined the office of pastor with that of cantor and organist, serving as precentor alone for the first few months until the first reed organ was procured. From the very first, he saw to it that the activities essential to the life of a Christian church were promoted. An adult Bible class formed and taught by the pastor was the nucleus of a Sunday school, a class of children being soon added. The need of the settlers to learn English without delay caused him to begin teaching them the language even in the Sunday classes. A parish school for the teaching of Christianity and Swedish seems to have antedated the first public school in the settlement, opened in 1871. One branch of religious education especially stressed by Olsson was the instruction preceding confirmation and admission to full church membership. The first class was confirmed in October, 1870. After that the confirmation school extended over two or even three years, and the instruction was methodical and thorough, written exercises and themes being required in addition to oral answers.

Olsson's sense of the importance of song in Christian worship prompted him to start drilling the congregation in singing as soon as it was organized. From the best singers he formed a choir directed by himself and rehearsing mostly in his home, with a tuning fork the only instrument. Its first public appearance was at the early morning service in the first little church on New Year's Day 1870. It was arduous labor training singers most of whom first had to be taught to read notes. Yet this choir soon appeared at various church festivals in Fremont, Salina, and probably elsewhere. After 1873, the young people of the Free Mount church joined the choir, adding greatly to its strength and bringing its membership up to almost forty. About that time they began rehearsing the compositions of Gunnar Wennerberg on the text of the "Psalms of David," adding several of these to their repertory, such as Psalms 24 and 150. The new church built at Lindsborg in 1874 was about to be dedicated, and for that occasion the choir prepared a musical program of no little merit. The interest in sacred song inspired by Olsson in those early days is said to have been the seed from which sprang the choir formed at Lindsborg to sing "The Messiah" of Handel, a choir which developed into a great oratorio chorus of national reputation. Later he gave the direct impetus which brought that organization into being.

The Bethany church grew to considerable size under

Olsson's charge. From the very beginning it possessed greater vitality than most pioneer organizations of its kind. There was large attendance at divine services and prayer meetings; the newcomers were known as great readers of religious books, and most of them worshiped God in the home, each housefather being a priest in his own household. Carl J. Stromquist, a leading member of the Galesburg land company that founded the Fremont settlement, has characterized the good folk of these two churches, the principal ones served by Olsson as pastor. He says in part:

"There was a certain difference in disposition and character between the two groups. The Lindsborg people, most of them from Wärmland, were very lively, temperamental, and talkative; very devout they were and discussed religious questions in season and out of season, it seemed to us. To each other they were very free and blunt in their mode of expression. I chanced to listen to one of their religious debates one day and was shocked to hear one say to another, 'There, now, that's a lie.' I expected a brawl to follow, but seemingly it was not said in anger, for the opponent good-humoredly accepted the remark as harmless. In fact, true brotherly love appeared to prevail among them all until the schism over the Atonement divided them.

"The Free Mount settlers were mostly natives of Småland, those from Dalarna being next in numbers, with a sprinkling of folk from Östergötland and Skåne. All of them were less glib of tongue and did not talk religion as freely as the Lindsborgians. Possibly they were less devout, I dare not say, but I do know that in the Free Mount congregation there were not only individuals but many families all of whose members were God-fearing, so far as men can judge."

The numerical strength of the Bethany church was reported officially as follows:

	1872	1873	1874	1875	1876	1877
Communicants	162	181	193	241	292	315
New members	26	21	18	79	58	33
Dismissed members	...	...	16	9	18	17
Total membership	259	300	327	430	500	544

It will be seen that the normal growth year by year increased greatly after 1874, making up many times over for the secession caused by the doctrinal schism.

The Free Mount congregation, which was only lightly touched by the storm that swept over Lindsborg, prospered in a like degree under Pastor Olsson's charge, as the corresponding figures show:

	1874	1875	1876	1877
Communicants	219	246	265	285
New Members	16	17	14	17
Total membership	321	374	412	450

When, in the fall of 1876, Olsson relinquished his charge of the two churches, these corresponded to a parish of one thousand members, the figures being for the beginning of each year. Viewed in the large, however, Olsson's work as a missionary had encompassed a vastly larger field, he having visited many of the smaller Swedish missions in the state and preached in churches whose pulpits stood vacant much of the time owing to lack of pastors. At one time Olsson as a member of a committee on missions reported to the Synod no less than a score of such vacancies in the Kansas Conference. This condition is readily understood from the fact that during this

period new settlements and new churches were springing
up by the score and as many as thirty-eight congregations were admitted into the Augustana Synod in one
year (1875). It might be said without gross exaggeration,
therefore, that while Olsson was stationed at Lindsborg,
all Kansas was his parish.

The little church first built by the pioneers had not
been planned to serve its purpose for long. It had grown
too small after a few years, and in 1874 the congregation
set about erecting a larger and more commodious sanctuary. Like the first, it was built by the members themselves, all but a couple of foremen giving their labor free
of charge. The story of the building of this house of
worship, written late that year, we have from the hand
of the pastor himself. It is typical of similar pioneer
enterprises mostly coupled with hardship and hampered
by lack of means; in its essential parts it reads as follows:

"Our congregation had for a long time had to be
contented with the extremely shabby church building we
hastily put up when we first came here; hence, for the
sake of our health, if not with a view to comfort and to
satisfy our sense of beauty, we felt constrained to undertake the erection of a new church. The decision was made
last winter. We had hoped from the outset to be able to
complete the undertaking without the necessity of appealing to our sister churches for help. So we began work in
the spring, with willing hands, and hopeful hearts, and
with prayers to the faithful Shepherd, Bishop, and Head
of His church. In this way we laid the foundation and
were able to get some work done on the walls before
summer came with its busy harvest season.

"We all looked forward to that time with tense expectation, for it was to bring the money needed for lumber and other building material, which we could not produce with our own hands. It should be stated that we decided to build the church of stone because that material would in our circumstances undeniably give us both the cheapest and the most durable structure. God had prepared the hearts of men among us who were willing and able to do the principal construction work so that the labor would be had without cost in money. Draft animals we also had for use free of charge for hauling building material. A sum of money had also been subscribed among ourselves in the spring, sufficient, it was then thought, for the purchase of all the lumber needed. Thus, we thought, we had carefully and not lightly counted the cost, and we were prepared to meet it. So matters stood when harvest time approached. Then the Lord permitted a long and destructive drought to befall our part of the country. After having for weeks in our weak way besought the Lord for rain and looked with longing eyes for every fleck of cloud that appeared in the sky, suddenly one Sunday evening we saw the heavens darkened by what looked like snow flurries. What could it be? To our consternation we soon learnt that it was the vanguard of an army of locusts, a host sent by the Almighty for our punishment. I need not describe the desolation caused by this plague. There we stood, with our church building little more than begun. What were we to do? . . .

"No one wonders that in our sad strait the thought grew strong in us that the Lord perhaps had chosen another, and for us a more humiliating, way to help us complete the building of our church. All were as willing and eager as before to do the masonry and all the other

work, but they all asked: If we finish building the walls,
where will we get the money for roof, windows and doors,
and the rest? We had tried keeping our church thatched
with grass for almost five years, and we knew from experience how little warmth and protection such a roof gave."

The Lindsborg pastor tells us that at the invitation
of Håkan Olson, pastor of Swedesburg, Iowa, he visited
that and sundry congregations in Iowa and brought home
more than $300 in contributions toward the completion
of his church. Gifts from churches elsewhere added to
the amount, which, together with a loan of $500 from
O. Stephenson of Swedesburg, aided the Lindsborg people
materially in completing their new church. Pastor Olsson
closed his account of the enterprise thus:

"To the delight of all givers it can now be announced
that our church is so far completed that on Saturday,
November 28, we could celebrate in it our first festival
and on Sunday, December 6, the first morning worship
with holy communion. That on these occasions there
were many joyful hearts in Lindsborg and copious tears
of joy flowed anyone can imagine who knows anything
about pioneer life and love to the church and the joy of
having a comfortable and appropriate house for the most
blessed of all occupations—the worship of God and communion with Him in His holy Word and sacraments."

The new church was an outstanding piece of work,
considering the time and place. It was a stone structure
of ample dimensions, 65 by 40 feet, second only to the
houses of worship reared prior to that time in much older
and larger Swedish Lutheran communities such as Chicago and Rockford. This sanctuary was dedicated Sunday, November 21, 1875.

EARLY PUBLICATION PROJECTS

At two different times while he served as a pastor in Kansas, Olsson's fertile mind was busy planning for the publication of periodicals. The second project was realized in 1873, in the form of a religious monthly entitled *Nytt och Gammalt*, which was published for a short time. The first we have seen nowhere mentioned, and small is the loss, for it did not materialize, the only trace of it being found in a letter among Olsson's papers. For other reasons the letter is interesting. It bears no date, but a phrase shows it to have been written in 1870. During his first year in America, Olsson is said to have taught English in his Sunday school, indicating that he had some prior knowledge of the language. This letter in his own handwriting—a draft with errors and corrections—if not his first, bears marks of being one of his earliest attempts at English letter writing, and it is faithfully reproduced partly to reveal Olsson's newspaper plan, but more especially to show how little difficulty he had with the new tongue. It reads verbatim:

"MESSRS. ORANGE JUDD & CO.

"I intend to publish a semi-monthly newspaper in the Swedish language Said paper should [deleted] will contain religious and political reading matter, and I wish also to have [deleted] give some informations to my countrymen in their own language of agriculture and horticulture. This latter I can not afford to do without taking information myself by means of American books and journals in agriculture and horticulture. Now I know You are publishers of very good books and journals in agriculture and horticulture. I am through my neighbour Mr. J. H. Johnson, postmaster of Lindsborg P. O., a subscriber for the American Agriculturist and I see in that journal very good materials for an abbreviated translation in swedish language. Also I have Mr. Warders book on Hedges, published by You, much needed to be translated for Swedes in an abbreviate form, as the Swedes are mostly settlers on the western prairies. As You might know, there are come to the United States a large number of Swedes during the last few years and most of these do not understand English. It would not pay to translate some agricultural books and journals in their whole length. The only way I see is to make some abbreviated translations in a newspaper. I am new in this country, just come from Sweden last summer. Therefor I am not acquainted with right of publishers I beg leave to ask You, if You would consider it as a violation of the copy right to translate in Swedish some parts of the agricultural books and journals published by You. Would You do me the favor of giving an answer and also by the same time giving me the authorization required for my purpose, I would be highly in duty bound to You. My opinion is, that, if You authorize me to translate some parts of your books, You will by and by have your reward, because by my references to your books my countrymen may be interested in buying them and reading them in full length.

"Here in Kansas are large settlements of Swedes. Yet they are poor, but I hope that they soon will be thrifty farmers by strenuous labour experience and also by taking notice of scientific farming. I hope You will helpe promote this aim. I trust the importance of the matter will be my best excuse for troubling You with it and remain

Yours truly,
O. OLSSON
Swedish Pastor"

We note, in passing, this Swedish clergyman's interest in scientific farming and his eye to the value of tree-planting in the prairie states of the Middle West, but without vesting him in any prophetic mantle as the seer of things coming to pass in our day.

The publishing enterprise started by Olsson in 1873 engages our attention for more substantial reasons. The little monthly religious journal, *Nytt och Gammalt*, published by him from April to the end of the year, while strictly objective and impersonal in content, reflects several sides of Olsson's character and interprets his attitude to a number of mooted questions.

This periodical was a 32-page paper with two columns to the page. The printing was done by the news, book, and job printing house of B. J. F. Hanna, publisher of the *Salina Herald*, at Salina, Kansas. For a Swedish paper put out by printers unfamiliar with the language, it was remarkably free from misprints, superior in this respect to most of the earlier and many of the later products of Swedish-American printing plants. For one thing the editor apologized—the use of roman type in a time when the German was so commonly used as to be called Swedish type.

In the first number, dated April 1873, the little new-comer made a modest bow to its elders in these words: "The publisher would like to say a few words to those who issue the older church papers of the Swedish Luther-an Church of America. . . . He fears that he might be looked upon as one who encroaches on another's office or uninvited enters another's field. He has no thought of crowding out or making superfluous any other church papers. It would be arrogant pride on the part of the newcomer to think himself a conqueror and to seek by force and intrigue to enter the domains of others. The publisher of this paper believes that his modest attempt may do some good without harming anyone. . . . There-fore, brethren, take me into your circle. Deal kindly with the beginner; do not use the power of the stronger to crush the weaker. We have a great area to defend, and the enemies are many. We need many fighters and many weapons—even youngsters may sometimes be of use in warfare."

The editor and publisher counted on his countrymen in Kansas and principally the members of the Kansas Conference for support of his periodical. Elsewhere, too, it was favorably received, as shown by many letters from pastors and other friends in various parts of the Synod, most of them reporting lists of subscribers. Some looked upon this undertaking as a rash adventure and expected the child would die aborning. Its own father was more hopeful, but dared not predict a long span of life. He had fears of its dying from starvation. In the very first issue of the journal, Olsson frankly stated that he guaranteed publication for six months only and would accept subscriptions for no longer term.

The program embraced seven departments, and in the first issue the following articles or series were started: A Sermon; Amplification of Luther's Small Catechism in the form of questions and answers; Life Pictures from the Ancient Times of the Christian Church; Contribution to the Defense of the Christian Faith; Questions of Church Polity. Later followed serial treatises on Repentance according to the Word of God and on the Doctrine of the Atonement. In all the articles one recognizes the pen of Olsson, clippings and reprints being conspicuously absent.

Eric Norelius, pastor at Vasa, Minnesota, gave the new paper a hearty welcome. Under date of May 5 he wrote: "I don't know why you needed to start out with an apology for your enterprise. You have no cause to be ashamed of your paper—and I say it sincerely. I wish I were able to write as directly to the point as you do. . . . You have doubtless been of the same mind as I and the brethren up here in Minnesota. We were not dissatisfied with *Augustana* and *Missionären* for what they are. We circulate them here as we did before, I think, but there was need of a local paper, and this led to the publishing of *Luthersk Kyrkotidning*. You must have felt the same need in Kansas . . . But an economic question confronts us. Inasmuch as our papers are much alike, it might be better to merge them. I for one would gladly do so on condition that the several regions be duly represented and that different views might be freely expressed whether or not they agreed with those of the editors.

"I wish you success in your undertaking. In my humble opinion, judging from this first issue, your mode of presentation is good, clear, and forthright. What you have said is Lutheran enough for me, and it gladdens my heart."

From Andover, Illinois, Rev. Jonas Swensson, another synodical leader, then serving as president, on April 29 wrote Olsson a sixteen-page criticism of the first issue. The letter, in a handwriting almost illegibly small, would have made a good-sized pamphlet. Swensson saw merit in the paper, but disapproved of it on the whole. He damned it with faint praise. His criticism was not a cold shower—it was an avalanche which might have buried a weaker man. Dealing as it does with the publicity situation in the Synod and the divisive forces at work at the time, the letter is in part pertinent to this record. Before launching his detailed examination of the journal, Swensson says: "That a periodical written in language easily understood and dealing with the questions you take up might be of great value I do not doubt. That people are given true knowledge in these subjects is important both for their own life and for the life of the church. Yet I fear you have not carefully considered the cost of such an enterprise. [Olsson *had* counted the cost] . . . The Swedish population in America is quite large in one respect, but when it comes to supporting Swedish papers, it is not very great. That is clearly seen from the many attempts to publish political papers, few of which have succeeded without other sources of support than subscriptions. The Swedish public shrinks still more in the matter of supporting and reading a church paper or religious journal . . . In another respect publishing such a paper entails great expense. I mean the editing. I do not see how you can find it possible to attend to your duties as the minister of a church and at the same time work out for every month an installment for each one of the seven departments of your periodical. All the subjects are of importance and require thorough treatment. My pastorate certainly does not leave me that much spare time. . . .

"There is another matter involved besides the question of cost. I have not liked and do not now like to see our forces scattered in so many directions. I have always believed, and I still believe, that we poor Swedes, as many as have the same faith and confession, ought to keep together in this country and work together in churchly matters. The scattering of forces causes weakness, but unity would give us strength. You say you do not intend to work for the division of the Synod. I have no reason to mistrust your word, but believe you sincerely mean what you say. But even different publishing attempts easily serve to promote division, although that is not their aim at the outset. Thus, quite some time ago there was started in Minnesota a Swedish newspaper containing both political and religious matter. But that paper got stuck in mud so deep that our Publication Society had to redeem it at great cost in order to drag its promoters out of the mire. Soon after, there came a request that the Synod transfer one of its church papers to Minnesota. It was not granted. Then they started their own church paper, and now, in spite of a unanimous resolution concerning our educational institution and the ingathering of a salary fund, the Minnesota Conference, not only by official decision, but through some tidbit in every issue of that paper, refuses to participate, and the division of the Synod is positively urged. . . . Now Kansas gets its own church paper. No one can prevent it, if Iowa, with its still greater field and many more of our countrymen settled there, soon launches its own conference paper, and the New York Conference, with a still larger field and still more people, if not more members, wants a church paper of its own. Thus we would soon have six church papers for those who belong to the same Synod. No one can stop them, but what about our common interests? Are those the means by which to further church fellowship and unity?"

Swensson expressed his conviction that if the synodical papers had been given more general support, they could have been made larger and richer in contents and would thus have better served their purpose. He admitted that fault was found with them, with or without cause, and that critics were many, but contributors few. Those who knew how to write he urged to collaborate in the organs of the Synod. "I must confess," he added, "that I have seldom done so. My duties have been too diversified for that, and my health these last years has been poor, so that may serve me as an excuse. Furthermore, I write a rather heavy style and am not much of a publicist." At the close, Swensson adds: "As for this letter of mine, you will understand that I write as a brother, at your request, and not in my capacity as president of the Synod. My aim is not to discourage you or set myself up as your master. I have only wanted to point to what seems to me not to go in the right direction. May the Spirit of the Lord guide us in all truth."

Whoever were the men back of the effort to split the Synod, either known to its president or suspected by him, Olsson was not one of them. There seem to have been others who imputed such motives to him and looked upon his paper as a mouthpiece of disruption, but Swensson appears to have been the only one to tell him so in blunt but brotherly frankness. At the time there was constant crossing of swords and clash of opinions in the Swedish press, both church and secular, and a sharp rebuttal of Swensson's charge might well have been expected. Instead, there appeared in the next issue of Olsson's paper this gentle reply: "To those who harbor such thoughts as to our intentions, the publisher would say that his sincere prayer is that by the grace of God he may be saved from giving joy to those who would gladly see the Augustana Synod disrupted, and that by the selfsame grace he may not be a child of sorrow to those who have the interests of that church at heart." Olsson was a man of peace, who heartily disliked newspaper polemics and partisan strife. In one controversy alone he drew his pen in battle, and then in defense of tenets that he held to be fundamental to Lutheranism and essential to true Christianity.

Olsson had an answer better than either counterattack or self-defense. In the July number appeared an article which is probably the strongest defense of the Synod and the ablest apology for its polity and organization published anywhere, the Synod's own papers not excepted. Two objectives seem to have been in Olsson's mind: to stem the outflow of members who called themselves Mission Friends and to discourage any movement from within toward the breakup of the Synod into district synods or independent smaller bodies. "It will no doubt surprise some of the older members of the Synod," he wrote, "to see one of the youngest undertake to publish his private views on its constitution. But it might also interest them to learn how one who was not with them from the start looks upon that which was accomplished before he joined them." After this modest note follows a brave argument for the Synod and an outspoken endorsement of its polity and its mode of operation. Enough to show Olsson's stand is here reproduced: "First of all we would say that both the constitution of the Augustana Synod and that of its congregations appears to us, just as they now are, to be a very beautiful and precious treasure for the Swedish Lutheran church of America. It seems to us that the congregations of the Synod ought therefore to cherish, preserve, and defend their constitution with the greatest affection. It is manifest to anyone studying it seriously and sensibly that the Lord guided with especial grace the men who laid down these principles for churchly order and government. The central thought in it all seems to be: *A free church bound only by the Word of God and the confessions of the Lutheran church*. These men seem to say, 'Now we are free, but we will let ourselves be bound by the Word of God in order to be one with Him and by the confessions of the earliest Christian and the Lutheran churches in order that we may be one in spirit with those churches, which we love and honor. What a glorious religious liberty to be free of obedience to the decrees of princes, the bulls of infallible popes, and the ordinances by which intriguing statesmen seek to throttle men's consciences. . . . We believe the Synod has taken a position where religious freedom and churchly restraint have joined hands and pledged themselves to work like brothers for the upbuilding of the kingdom of God.

"But mark well, we are dealing with a human work, and it would not occur to us to think anything perfect that men have said or done. We, too, find certain faults in this constitution, but these are such that, should we try to patch it with what we think right where it seems wrong, the holes might even grow larger."

In regard to the article on doctrine, not to be altered, Olsson's mouthpiece gave no uncertain sound:

"The church on earth is a militant body and must have a sure and definite war cry and countersign by which to distinguish those who are for from those who are against it. . . . As for human teachings and tenets, one may speak of progress and change from time to time. Divine truths and teachings, on the other hand, must be held eternal and unalterable. And here we have to do with God's everlasting truths revealed in His sacred Word, on which stands the Christian Church as on a rock. . . .

"Would not the Bible be sufficient as a Confession? If you look at the many factions within and without the various church bodies in this country especially, you will find that Holy Writ has been torn into a thousand pieces. Here is a little group; they have got hold of a portion of the Bible or only a few verses eagerly picked together in the process of dismemberment. These are shouting at the top of their voices, 'Here is the proof text; here we have found this teaching.' And so they go on propagating their favorite doctrine, thought to be embodied in the bit of Scripture they took with them. You know, there

is often such haste when new things are to be proclaimed
that the whole Bible is too much to carry on the teaching
mission, so just a part is torn out for that purpose. And
there we find another group or sect. They got hold of
another fragment of the Sacred Book, in which they have
found a teaching directly opposed to those propounded
by the first group. So we could go from group to group,
numbered by the hundred, and find each one having just
a small fraction of the Word of God. . . .

"This being the situation in the Church of Christ in
the world, it is imperative for a properly ordered church
body to have clear and positive confessional writings by
which it is bound and which it may lay before the public
and say, 'Here you see how we understand the Word of
God in that which concerns our eternal salvation. Compare our Confessions with Scripture. It is our firm belief
that they agree.' . . . Now you might ask, 'In holding
the unaltered Augsburg Confession to be a true summary
of the chief doctrine of Christendom, do you not condemn
all church bodies not adhering to that Confession?' If
you imply that the Augustana Synod by the doctrinal
article in its constitution seeks to usurp the judgment
seat of God and say in His stead, Depart, all ye that
do not confess the Lutheran doctrines, then you completely misunderstand us and put a wrong construction
on that article. In no sense does it imply a condemnation
of church groups of different persuasion—it has to do
only with a firm and positive belief in the truth of the
Word of God."

The objection raised that the doctrinal article at least
implies a cold gesture declining fellowship with other
Christians is shown to carry no weight. In the first con-

stitution of the church founded by Olsson there was a clause to the effect that this church, while adhering to the Lutheran confession, yet desired to maintain friendly and fraternal relations with Christians of other Protestant persuasion. In the synodical constitution for churches there was no such proviso expressed. But the implication was there, Olsson maintained. "We find no lack of charity there," he said. "When the Synod confesses that the Word of God, found in Holy Writ, is the only infallible rule of faith and regulation of life, it clearly extends a greeting of love and fellowship to all who make the same confession. This love is by no means extinguished by the further confession contained in the same article, although fellowship is limited in the degree necessary here on earth."

It will be seen in Olsson's later writings how firm a stand, as a churchman and a student and teacher, he took against the Roman church and its claim to stand for unitive Christendom. In the apology here examined, we find him taking an advanced position on the unitive character of Protestantism and making a plea for purely Scriptural Christianity as against arbitrary and fractional Scripture interpretation, emotionalism, subjectivism, hyperevangelism, and other types that were the mode of the day. Only in following closely the teachings of Christ and accepting that body of doctrine clearly implied in the whole of the gospel could the church be truly one— in this Olsson was one of the forerunners, by a space of more than fifty years, of the movement toward Protestant unity which has grown strong in recent times under the leadership of Archbishop Nathan Söderblom and others and which took organized form at the Stockholm

Conference on Life and Work in 1925 and was further advanced at the Oxford Conference in 1937. In Olsson's time church union was frowned on by most Augustana leaders as visionary, and to them the very term "unionism" smattered of heresy. Since then the synodical attitude on this point has undergone a marked change. The advocacy of church unity is no longer an ism. "Indeed, it is a commentary on the misinformed state of the church," writes Dr. Conrad Bergendoff, "that the very word 'unionism' is in such bad repute. Granted that some unionism is not healthy, certainly it is not a wholesome symptom when parts of the church glory in sectarianism and publish to the world that they will have nothing to do with any other Christians."

In the interest of good order, the Galesburg Rule of 1872, "Lutheran pulpits for Lutheran pastors; Lutheran altars for Lutheran communicants," is still generally observed, yet Augustana pastors and church members fellowship with Christians of other communions on occasion without scruples, and the Synod has taken official part in the Stockholm, Oxford, and Edinburgh Conferences. In the matter of favoring the unity of Protestant Christendom, it is now seen, Olsson was not in error. His only fault was that he was two generations ahead of his time.

Upon his return from the synod meeting held at Paxton, Illinois, the last week of June, 1873, Olsson reverted to the same topic in his comments on that convention appearing in the August issue of *Nytt och Gammalt*. He began by owning to "strong doubts" about the Synod at the time of his arrival in this country. These were his reasons: In many parts of Sweden the Synod was the

object of mistrust, chiefly among younger Christians, undoubtedly caused by letters from persons who on coming
to America formed vague and gratuitous opinions about
that church body before taking time to learn anything
about it. Furthermore, conditions in the new country
and the old were so different that anyone presuming to
understand and judge of everything here at once after
coming over must be either blinded by pride or misled
by ignorance. Experience, he admitted, is the best teacher, and he had been taught his lesson. An independent
congregation, even though purporting to be made up of
none but confessed Christians, had turned out much too
independent. This had prompted him to study the course
of the Synod with great care in order to gain first-hand
knowledge of its position as a church body. His confession of mistrust at one time he now followed up with a
declaration of complete faith and confidence in that body.
He said in brief: "Our first impression of the meeting,
and we say it sincerely, was a feeling that it is a great
gift and privilege to belong to this communion. We want
to say here that there are clear and positive evidences to
convince any sane observer that the Lord has chosen the
Augustana Synod as a church body through which to do
His work among our Swedish people in this country.
Now some one might exclaim excitedly, 'There you have
it! They want to make the Synod an infallible divine
institution with exclusive authority to stake out the way
of salvation for the Swedes of America.' If you, my
friend, are speaking in jest, we have nothing more to say
to you until you learn to speak seriously of serious
matters. If you think that way as a member of another
denomination, which to you is the right one, we would

say we have no time to waste in unprofitable dispute
with those who talk for the love of arguing. We only
desire to remind ourselves and others in the same fold
of the importance of being certain that the Lord works
through the church we belong to.

"True, the chief question is how we stand in relation
to the Lord Christ Himself, the head of the church. But
Scripture speaks of the church as the body of Christ,
and we can not be His members without being members
of His church on earth. If we love Christ, we must love
His church. You might say there is a great difference
between belonging to the communion of the faithful and
being a member of one of the Augustana churches.
Granted that not all, by far, who belong to the church
outwardly belong to the Lord Jesus as members of His
body, we admit a difficulty here which the mundane
church will always have to deal with. How can the true
children of God cordially love a congregation or a church
body, knowing for certain that it has many unfaithful
and godless members? Ask yourself this question: If by
grace you are a disciple of Christ, how can you love your
brethren in the faith when finding in them many vestiges
of sin and carnal desires? Just so we must look upon the
visible church of Christ. So, we think, we must also
regard the church body here spoken of—the Augustana
Synod."

The monthly periodical *Nytt och Gammalt* was issued
in six numbers from April to November 1873. Then, by
mutual agreement, all the periodicals published in the
Synod were merged into one, which was named *Augustana*. Into the merger went the two official organs of the
Synod, *Augustana* and *Missionären*, and the two inde-

pendent monthlies, *Luthersk Kyrkotidning*, published by
Norelius and his friends in Minnesota, and Olsson's paper,
designed as the mouthpiece of the Kansas Conference.
In his "Words of Farewell," Olsson, in explaining the
transaction, stated that the child of his bosom was not
dying of starvation; on the contrary, the paper had paid
its way so far, and there were resources in sight to carry
it through another year. But he yielded to the request
from official quarters. "The undersigned," he said, "looks
upon it as a duty prompted by love to discontinue his
little paper so as in a measure to help remove all obstacles
to the publication of one common church paper. He
realized that a larger and more general periodical, speaking for the whole Synod, should be a blessing. "To insist
on publishing our little paper would therefore be acting
contrary to the law of love."

By agreement, the Swedish Lutheran Publication Society, synodical publishers, was to compensate Norelius
and Olsson with two hundred dollars each. After due
consideration, Olsson declined the sum awarded. Doubtless with Jonas Swensson's criticism in mind, he wrote,
"The undersigned did not well consider that decision at
the time it was passed. After due consideration, he has
concluded that it would meet with objections should the
Publication Society pay good money for so new a paper
as *Nytt och Gammalt*. Hence he waives all claim to compensation for giving up his paper. He will on no condition
accept the offer made, but discontinues his paper without
any return. We have made this announcement public in
order to silence any possible disapproval of the aforesaid
decision." The new *Augustana* was to be issued semi-

monthly, and Olsson was chosen one of its editors, the others being T. N. Hasselquist and Eric Norelius.

After the merger of the four periodicals had been practically effected and Hasselquist had published the fact, affairs suddenly took a turn for the worse. The implications of his announcement were such that Olsson promptly severed all connection with the common enterprise and told him so in plain words. In his letter, dated November 8, he said:

"I really can not thank you from my heart for your last letter. You have thereby given me pain, yea, wounded me deeply. I too have human feelings. However, by your letter you have gained an advantage for the Publication Society. You may be sure that not one cent of its funds will come into my possession if I know it. I hereby positively refuse to accept either the two hundred dollars set aside as compensation for 'loss' or the three hundred voted me for editorial work. I am in earnest about this matter. You must not think this decision is made suddenly and in anger. My honor, small as it may be, demands it in order that I may escape the suspicions you seem to harbor against me and which others may put forth in more definite form. If, dear Uncle, you who love me can go so far, what will not others do? You consider that the society has done me a kindness of incalculable value by taking over my little paper. You also believe its affairs were in such desperate plight that I had to come to the Publication Society as a beggar, beseeching them to save me from utter ruin. On the contrary, the affairs and prospects of my paper are at present, humanly speaking, such that I have every reason to be confident for the near future. But I would rather not speak of this.

I will gladly, by the grace of God, humble myself, but when an untrue and debasing act of humility is demanded —well, then I think it is in order not to bow too profoundly before men. . . . I shall abide unswervingly by any promise to cease publishing my little paper at New Year's. As to the other decisions made at the Chicago meeting, I deem you to have been the first to break the agreement while acting on the society's behalf, hence, I shall deem myself freed from all obligations to the new paper, except the duty to do all I can to circulate it.

"Do not think I have hereby canceled the friendship and love I cherish for you personally. If I may still be embraced in your affections, it will be a joy to me. . . .

"I had abandoned myself to fond dreams of brotherly collaboration in the new paper; yes, I even had thought seriously of accepting the call to Moline in order to be close by. But on reading your last letter I was rudely awakened and felt myself surrounded by ice-cold reality, all of which gave me a sense of downheartedness and profound sorrow. Henceforth let all this be forgotten. I promise not to touch upon it again on condition that you do not publicly express such suspicions of me as are unreservedly uttered in your letter. I am writing Norelius, informing him of my decision to withdraw from this sorry affair."

This would seem to have put an end to the literary co-operation of the two men before it was begun. And yet Olsson's name appeared with those of Hasselquist and Norelius when the editorial staff of the reinforced *Augustana* was announced. It would be hard to learn why from the published announcements, but in a badly faded letter of November 26, Olsson's own explanation to Hasselquist can still be deciphered: "If I am to have anything further to do with the new paper, it will be only on the specific condition that the Publication Society rescind the decision to pay me two hundred dollars for my paper and that this action be publicly announced. If this is done, I shall gladly work for the new paper by writing for it and rendering other services. . . . When that action is revoked, all is clear between us. My affection for you is not quenched, thank God, no, nor even lessened by the difficulty between us just referred to. I am willing to forgive and forget all such differences, and I have the hope and assurance that you will do the same."

Jonas Swensson's words about the Publication Society pulling private publishers out of the mire were fresh in Olsson's mind, and he explained to Hasselquist that he could not afford to have his publication and himself repudiated in that fashion.

In his reply (December 2 and 4) Hasselquist stated that he had been completely misunderstood; that his announcement had been written in haste—"as is everything I write"—; that, since the wording could be misconstrued, he would do his utmost to set the matter right by following his announcement with a clarifying statement in both *Augustana* and *Hemlandet*. The explanation, a copy of which was enclosed in the letter, ran thus:

"From certain words in the foregoing announcement someone might now or later conclude that the two publishers of *Luthersk Kyrkotidning* and of *Nytt och Gammalt* had sustained losses on their publications and consequently were anxious to be rid of them. To forestall such a misunderstanding I, the undersigned, desire to explain that the proposal to combine our papers came from me

alone, but was embraced with interest by the aforenamed
publishers to promote a good cause, because they as well
as I saw the need of uniting our forces. Since the publishing of a paper always entails financial worry, or at
least the trouble of collecting subscriptions, I cited that
fact as one reason for the merger; but I am now able to
say that the two papers have done well financially; hence,
the motive for combining them was none other than the
desire and hope that in the new form the four papers
would be more widely read and all the more useful.

T. N. H."

The misunderstanding between the two men might
have seemed to have arisen from an act of petulance on
Olsson's part had not their differences been resolved in a
way to put the matter in a different light. Olsson never
compromised where personal honor was concerned; no,
not even, as in this case, where no reflection would have
been cast on his good name. He was too sensitive to
tolerate even the appearance of evil report. An ordinary
man might have accepted the stipulated sum as his just
due. But in this case the allied publishing concerns were
not dealing with an ordinary man. There were some harsh
words in Hasselquist's letter of explanation: "Now I will
tell you openly and before God, who knows my thoughts,
that you are utterly unjust to me from first to last."—
"My conscience tells me that in this matter I am inno-
cent of all the things you charge me with."—"I cannot
recall that even an enemy has painted me such as you
make me out in your letter."

And yet it included an apology and ended on this
conciliatory note: "If I have trespassed against you,

Brother, it was done entirely without my knowledge. For not a syllable of what you said about my plans is true. Now it remains for you to settle this matter so as to be able to answer for it before God. But I long to embrace you with brotherly love more intense than ever before and salute you with the holy kiss. If this difficulty, which so unexpectedly arose between us, is removed, I hope that from now on the murderer of souls will not find it so easy to tear us apart."

It seems that a suggestion by Hasselquist to call in some of the brethren to settle this difference proved needless, for a reconciliation between the two men was soon effected which knitted closer than ever before the bonds of friendship between them. From 1874 on, Olsson and Hasselquist became close co-laborers for more than fifteen years, and we have found no evidence of any serious misunderstanding between them during all that time.

The mind of Jonas Swensson must have been set at rest. This was doubtless true of any other men in the Synod who may have thought of Olsson as a disquieting factor and his monthly messenger as a wedge designed to split off a block to form a district synod. For in his brief career as an independent publisher, Olsson had kept his paper free from polemical matter and destructive criticism. One looks in vain for one word of adverse comment on the Synod. On the contrary, he had declared his loyalty in two unreserved endorsements of the Synod's doctrinal position. He had expressed his belief that it was the one church body especially ordained by God to serve the Swedish element in the United States. He had pointed out the forces that were at work, if not actually splitting the Synod, chipping off large fragments on all sides. He had begun a series of articles to enlighten the many souls who were perplexed by the new interpretation of the Atonement, thereby incurring the enmity of some of his own church members and of the dissenters from many other Lutheran congregations. When, at the close of the year, Jonas Swensson, president of the Synod, passed away, he had first seen what he thought to be disintegrating factors removed and the bond of unity knit stronger in the form of one church paper instead of four. But even so, all was not peace in the Synod. Fanned by the Waldenstromian teaching, the fire of dissent kept spreading among the churches, and for the next decade Olsson was foremost among those who fought the flames. He vindicated himself as one of the strongest forces for the conservation of Lutheranism among his countrymen, meanwhile working for the progress of the Synod along the lines of education and general culture.

PLANS FOR NEGRO AND INDIAN MISSIONS

The missionary spirit was strong in Olsson. Very early, as we have seen, his heart was set on fitting himself to go out as a gospel messenger to heathen lands. When his superiors advised against it in view of his frail health, that dampened his zeal only for a time. He did not cease to look for a way to open for him to serve God in foreign parts. When he first planned to come to America to serve his own countrymen here, it was with the distinct purpose of combining that service with work among the Negroes.

After the emancipation of the Negroes had been safeguarded in the United States through the outcome of the Civil War, many warmhearted men in Sweden thought the time ripe for starting missionary work among the freedmen. The Fatherland Foundation favored such an undertaking and made overtures to the Augustana Synod looking to co-operation. "Out here we will participate in the foreign missions of the Foundation as far as we are able," Hasselquist had pledged in 1868. "Many prayers are offered up for the beloved brethren in the new East African mission field, and among us that work is being followed with eager attention and great interest." But he made this reservation: "A mission among the liberated Negroes in this country has indeed been spoken of among us, but in view of all our other activities, I

114

dare not think of our starting such a mission unless the Lord should open a door and command us to enter. But should the means given the Foundation for that purpose be sent here, they would at least be put at the disposal of some Lutheran mission among the colored population."

Olsson was among the first proponents of Swedish Lutheran missionary work among the American Negroes. As early as April 1867 he had been invited by Hasselquist to come over and join in the work of the Synod. This call he considered seriously for months and finally declared his willingness to come should the Lord remove certain obstacles. His letter to Hasselquist reveals his plan:

"One of the main reasons why I should like to go to America is that I would want to work a part of the year among the Negroes. Would you kindly inform me whether a proposal like this could be carried out? I desire to be stationed in some Swedish Lutheran congregation in the West, but on condition that I might go to the Negroes for a part of the year. Kindly look with Christian charity on me if I am suggesting a foolish project. My heart goes out to these people. Yet, with a wife and two small children, I cannot see how I could make my home among them altogether. I am able to pay my own fare to America; might even buy a little home for myself, if not too costly, so that I could use part of my salary from the Swedish Lutheran church served to pay for my travels to the Negro missions. I wonder whether such a congregation would be content with a pastor who would not live with them all the year round. Would the Swedish Lutheran Negro mission be opened in some near-by state, so that travel would not be so expensive as to make my plan impracticable?"

The proposed Negro mission did not materialize, although in response to appeals in Sweden, by P. A. Ahlberg, among others, contributions to the cause had begun to come in. The reason for this was doubtless the Synod's lack of men and means to devote to that cause, as Hasselquist had intimated. At his school, Ahlberg had even begun to teach English to his divinity students in preparing them for such a mission, but as a number of them later became pastors in this country, his labor was not entirely wasted.

After Olsson's arrival in America, his missionary interest embraced also the American Indians. It was imparted to some of his brethren, who gave him their support.

The Synod in 1874, doubtless on Olsson's initiative, instructed its mission board to make inquiries with a view to opening a mission station among the Delaware Indians and other half-civilized tribes in the Indian Territory and, should the outlook for so important an enterprise seem good, to send able men there as missionaries. The matter was put off for almost two years.

In March 1875, Norelius, as president of the Synod, informed Olsson of his selection by the mission board as the official investigator. "For my part," said Norelius, after asking him to make the trip, "I am free to admit that I cannot see how we could now undertake mission work among the Indians with the limited working force we have. Besides, it might well be questioned whether it were right to start such a mission while the field among our own countrymen craves all our attention and we have far from enough men and means to cultivate it. But after all, it has been so decided, and we must do our best in carrying out the decision."

In May 1876, Olsson was finally able to make the journey. Via Topeka he went to Chetopah by rail and then rode forty-five miles over country roads to reach the headquarters of the chief of the Delaware tribe, Charles Journeycake by name. The gentleman put him up for the night of May 26–27. The chief was himself a Baptist pastor, and Olsson was well entertained in his home. He had a rather neat house surrounded by a garden. There was a reed organ, which one of the chief's daughters played quite well. She and the others in the family also sang. Olsson sang to them and accompanied their singing on the organ, and he found it "truly touching to be permitted to sing and play together with these Indian children." At morning devotions the old chief read Scripture in English and offered prayer in his native tongue. The visitor spoke serious words of farewell and left this Indian home "with deep emotion," we are told. Of the tribe, 218 made up the Baptist flock, with their chief as pastor. The mission among them had been started some forty-two years before. Their public worship was conducted in the Delaware Indian language, which was mostly used in daily intercourse, although many spoke English well. The tribe comprised about one thousand souls, equally divided between two settlements or camps twenty miles apart. The chief favored the establishing of a Lutheran mission station at the second camp, of which he himself was unable to have full religious oversight. But the Synod's emissary thought best to begin work among a tribe where the Word of God had

not yet been preached. The chief then suggested the
Pawnee tribe, promising to go with the missionaries and
introduce them. Olsson learnt to his sorrow that the
Delawares had made no provision for the training of any
of their young men as spiritual teachers, and that the
American Baptists had left them entirely to themselves.
The old chief spoke of this with regret.

In his report to the Synod, after narrating the events
of the trip, Olsson made a fervent plea for Indian missions, supporting his written report with direct advocacy
from the floor. The report leaves no doubt as to where
Olsson's heart was in the matter of missions. The document is of interest as a fragment of church history as
well as of the life of the man. In its essential part it reads:

"As to the advisability of our beginning a mission
among the Indians, that is for the Synod to decide. But
the need is manifest, since so many tribes are still without the Word of God, and even the work among the
Delawares would need spiritual freshening, as I clearly
saw during my stay with them. Mr. Journeycake deeply
deplored the apathy of the American denominations,
which lay very little stress on their mission work among
the Indians. I have a letter to deliver to the Synod from
this chief requesting us to open a mission there. Those
Indian agents who take the hardships of the Indians to
heart also complain bitterly against the various church
bodies for their neglect, leaving the heathen in our own
land to dwell in complete darkness. I have also a letter
from the superintendent of the Indian agency of the
entire Indian Territory assuring us that the Government
will not hinder but rather encourage missions. Chief
Journeycake expressed his positive conviction that now

is the right time to start mission work among those tribes not yet served with the Word of God, because they have now begun to settle down, and it is of the greatest importance that they come under religious influence in the period of transition from their nomadic to a more civilized mode of living. I am also expecting a letter from an experienced Presbyterian missionary working among the Seminoles in the southern part of the Territory, who may have information of importance to give us.

"After my conversation with informed persons, it is evident to me that an Indian mission must necessarily start with a children's home or boarding school, where the young would receive religious instruction and learn useful trades. This would call for the establishment of a little mission colony to make such a mission of real value. (Of this I will give my opinion orally before the Synod.) As far as I have been able to find, the Lutheran church does no mission work whatever among the Indians. To me it seems significant that our Synod's churches in Kansas lie so close to this mission field that a lively communion might be established between our congregations and the new churches among the heathen, God granting that our work would live and thrive. May we deal prayerfully with this matter. Should the Synod altogether lack men for this work, it will find in me one who, by the grace of God, is willing to go. But let the whole matter be submitted to the Lord's will."

Olsson's pleading moved the Synod to instruct its mission board to start a mission among the Pawnee Indians once suitable men could be found. All contributions to foreign missions not earmarked for special purposes were ordered set aside for this particular work.

The board found a missionary in Rev. John Telleen, who made further survey of the field, but started no work. Three Indian youths recommended by him studied for a time at Augustana College with the missionary calling in view, but they left no trace in the synodical records. In 1877 Telleen advised that work be started among the Comanches; the same year a committee went to Washington asking that the Synod be given an Indian agency of its own; in 1878 the mission board sent its chairman to investigate, and he, too, selected the Comanches; Matthias Wahlstrom, a divinity student, was sent as Indian missionary in 1879, but he soon returned owing to war between the Comanches and some neighboring tribe. Thus, year after year the board reported no progress, and by 1883 it said simply this: "The board during the past year has not been able to extend its work to the poor Indians."

Besides the religious motive, there may have been historical or sentimental reasons for singling out the Delaware Indians as the objects of a second Lutheran mission following the first one in the Swedish Delaware Colony about 240 years earlier, but obstacles in the way of an Indian mission seemed too great and the means too small, so the "Dreamer from Wärmland" saw one more of his dreams consigned to oblivion. The first rude awakening had come when his ideal church of saints began to break up.

IX

PUBLIC OFFICES

To follow Olsson in his activities apart from his office as pastor of the local churches in the Lindsborg and Fremont settlements, we go back to his first years in Kansas. We find the young clergyman soon after his arrival taking part in public affairs. McPherson county was organized in 1870, and Lindsborg was the county seat for three years, until the honor went to the town of McPherson. Olsson was elected the first superintendent of schools in the county. His experience as schoolmaster in his former parish in Wärmland was greatly in his favor, leaving only the use of the new language to be acquired. The new superintendent doubtless outdid any of the pupils in application to his studies, judged by his earliest letters in the English language. Not much is known of his work of school supervision, most of which must have been in the line of routine.

A form of promotion came to him as a public official when he was elected a member of the Kansas legislature. He served his first term in 1871, and his constituents sent him back to Topeka for another term. That was the extent of his political career. Though new to the country and unfamiliar with conditions and public policies, Olsson made his influence felt and his service fruitful. It is known that two bills sponsored by him were enacted into law. The one, known as the Herd Law, put a stop

to the trespass and depredation on the fields of the settlers
committed by the Texas cattlemen, who drove their
herds, numbering thousands of heads, over the prairies
in total disregard of the rights of the homesteaders.
Salina, one of their shipping points, was reached by a
trail following mainly the course of the Smoky Hill River
from the southwest. Large herds were often driven
through the settlement around Lindsborg, passing close
by Olsson's home and doing damage to crops on his farm
and those of his neighbors. Up to that time, farmers
seeking redress of grievances had no recourse under any
specific law, and their protests and law suits were of no
avail until implemented by this statute.

Another law fathered by the pastor-legislator was
designed primarily to protect railroad laborers from ex-
ploitation by conscienceless contractors. Newcomers in
large numbers working in railway construction gangs were
often cheated out of their pay by various sharp tricks
worked by unscrupulous bosses on their "greenhorn"
employees. Pastor Olsson maintained on the best of
authority that the laborer is worthy of his hire, and his
bill was passed, holding employers of labor to a stricter
accounting. Nowhere in his writings has Olsson indicated
any taste for political life or coveting of its honors or
emoluments. Yet, while in public office, he made his
service count. Always a spokesman for the common
people, he took it that since it was mostly farmers and
laborers who sent him to the legislature, it was his clear
duty to make their interests his own—a theory of government as sound now as it was then, even if less practiced
today.

With all matters of importance locally, Olsson, as the first citizen of Lindsborg, had more or less to do, and he often spoke the decisive word. When in 1872 there was a sharp contest for the postmastership, Olsson sent a strong appeal to Washington in behalf of John Ferm, then serving. It read in part: "The people generally desire no change in the management of our postoffice. A young man by name of P. Nelson . . . is desirous of having the postoffice removed to his store. We have heard that he has circulated a petition among his special friends for the removal of the postoffice. He sells whisky openly against the will of a majority of the people. . . . Most of the people here would feel very sorry in case the Department should remove our postoffice to a place more like a saloon than anything else . . ." Nelson failed to obtain the office, which was held by John Ferm until October 1875. For his good offices in behalf of his friend, Olsson was rewarded not long afterward when John Ferm, who was a prominent member of his church, withdrew and joined the group of Waldenstromians who caused the dissension in the Bethany church. Four days later, at the request of friends, Olsson wrote the Honorable Mr. Hutchinson, founder of Hutchinson, Kansas, inquiring what security he gave purchasers of town lots that they would get valid deeds when their contracts expired; also what provision was made for tree planting. The Lindsborg town site had recently been laid out, and he took evident interest in safeguarding the rights of the property owners there. He also inquired about mail routes, a matter on which he had written to the Senator. The projected rival town of McPherson is referred to thus: "Some parties are now going to start a town in the center of our county."

Lindsborg had no railroad, and its merchants had to have all their goods hauled from Salina, a distance of more than twenty miles, while the farmers thereabout were compelled to make the same long haul. A group of men of which Olsson was one sought by all fair means to induce the Kansas Pacific Railroad Company to build a spur or feeder from Salina to Lindsborg. Twice in 1874 and again in 1876 Olsson wrote Robert E. Carr, president of the road, with a view to inducing him to realize the plan.

The first letter was a well-reasoned fourteen-page argument for the building of the road, pointing out every advantage to accrue from the enterprise both to the Lindsborgians and to the railway company. The second was accompanied by a map showing a roadbed already graded by a company which had abandoned the project and a right of way which could be had for the asking. Facts and figures were set forth with reference to the freight business of the proposed road, and these Mr. Carr was invited to put under the test of his business sagacity and larger experience. There were no fast freights in those days, and it seems this particular railroad Carr moved very slowly. Having had no reply from the Kansas City headquarters for fourteen months, Olsson addressed the railway magnate again, advising him that railroad meetings were being held in McPherson County and that the people were determined to have an outlet for their products at all hazards. If he did not act soon, the business of the Smoky Hill Valley would very likely be lost to his road. The letter ended characteristically: "It may look foolish and as mere child's play to you that a poor preacher undertakes to write to you in reference to such business. I have lived with my [deleted] the people here from the beginning of the settlement and feel interested in the welfare of our community, and I therefore dare to do even foolish things, hoping to induce others to do what is wise and good for us." At all events, Lindsborg got no railroad until 1879, when the Union Pacific came through; Olsson's efforts had been in vain, yet they should be set down to his credit for the zeal for the welfare of his community thereby attested and for the purpose of showing in one more instance that this village parson, later reputed to be an impractical dreamer, was alert to everyday affairs and both willing and able to cope with practical problems.

It is worthy of note that when Olsson was elected county superintendent of public instruction in 1870, he had just acquired citizenship and had been a resident of the county scarcely a year. His term of office was cut short when in the following year he was elected representative from McPherson County in the Kansas legislature on the issue of securing protection for the settlers against the incursions of the cattlemen. When in order to take his new office he had to resign the old, the man appointed to the superintendency proved unfit for the office.

An incident from Olsson's term of service in the legislature showing that the business of lawmaking was with him a sacred civic duty was related by Dr. Peter Henry Pearson of Upsala College shortly before his recent death. At the first session of the legislature, the members, in adopting the order of business, did not provide for the

opening of the legislative day with Scripture and prayer.
To the pastor-legislator this was a grave oversight. He
insisted on a reconsideration, and when the matter was
taken up again, Olsson made such a fervent plea that a
place was made for devotional exercises in the new order
of business. Until very recently, this informant adds, the
portrait of Olsson, as the first superintendent of schools
in McPherson County, hung in the superintendent's
office in the county courthouse. It seems to have been
removed without motive or warrant.

In 1873, while in the legislature, Olsson sought to
make Lindsborg the permanent county seat after it had
been established at McPherson. But as Lindsborg was
located close to the north line of the county, his plan met
with objections. These he tried to overcome by having
a tier of townships cut off and added to Harvey County
on the south while a similar strip from Saline County
was to be added on the north. The bargain was agreed
to by the southern neighbor, yet the plan miscarried
when the Salina people succeeded in having the proposition, fair though it seemed, defeated in the legislature.
In every way, it seems, Olsson looked out for the interests
of his constituents, most of these interests being central-
ized in the Lindsborg community. Even after he left
Kansas, he had the welfare of Lindsborg at heart, as is
shown by private letters and public writings.

X

SYNODICAL INTERESTS

During Pastor Olsson's seven years in Lindsborg, that community, with the church he served, was the apple of his eye. He gave it all that was best in him, and when called to another field of labor, he parted from it with the profoundest regret. In after years he continued to think of Lindsborg as his real home, to apostrophize it in his writings on every suitable occasion, and to long for the time when he might retire from his life's work and come back there to await the setting of the sun. His esthetic eye saw beauty in the smoky-blue hills and the sunlit expanse, soon checkered with fields and studded with groves and farmsteads. No scene could have differed more from the picturesque environments of his childhood home in Wärmland, yet this is how the plain impressed him when he saw it again in 1878: "That man O. O., as you may know, is especially in tune with Kansas and the Kansas folks. The truth to tell, there are hardly more beautiful regions to be found anywhere in America than the Swedish settlements in Kansas."

Almost twenty years after leaving Kansas, Olsson wrote: "I have often bitterly regretted that I left my first earthly home in America, for there I thought I had full divine and human right to live, because I had had a part in breaking ground in the wilderness and making it a home."

Fifteen years after having sat in the Kansas legislature Olsson wrote a little passage in praise of the Homestead Law which testifies to the pioneer pastor's attachment to the soil while it throws further light on his attitude as a representative of the plain people, the common folk who had made their homes on the Kansas prairies. "What," said he, "is the pioneer's first thought when he strikes out through the wilderness with nothing but toil and trials, hardship and deprivation before him? What is he thinking of? He has a home in mind; his sure hope is for a home of his own. Throughout his days of toil, an inner voice says, 'There is my very own home, where I can rest.' Is not that the true purport of that American statute known as the Homestead Law? We all know what that means. A finer law was never enacted on this earth. Or name me a country that can show such an act, a law of love and mercy to the poor. This is the brightest star of all on the star-spangled banner. When I see as in a vision all the Swedish settlements I have visited; when I see all the little homes my beloved countrymen have built with labor and hardship but with a recompense of love from God in that they all have their own homes, then my heart leaps within me for joy, and particularly when I look at all this in the light of history, knowing as I do that centuries ago the laborers in Europe, the most civilized continent in the world, were all slaves— yes, slaves and nothing more."

The fame of the pioneer preacher on the southwestern frontier had been carried to other parts of the Synod, and the stronger congregations were beginning to bid for his services. He received and declined a number of calls to other fields. At New Year's, 1874, shortly after the death of Jonas Swensson, president of the Synod, Olsson was called to succeed him as pastor of the church at Andover, Illinois. The same month a similar call came from the congregation at Chisago Lake, Minnesota. Olsson was constrained to decline both calls. His reasons in each case were cogently stated in his reply to Andover, dated March 19, after that church had followed his declination with a second call. "Briefly I may inform you that the spirit of partisanship is causing such a storm in my little congregation here that it seems in immediate peril of being torn to pieces. Furthermore, we have begun to build a new church right in the midst of the storm. I have been here from the beginning when we were only a few, and it would be impossible for me to desert my flock in this time of strife. I must remain at the watchman's post God has assigned to me. . . ."

"I do not begrudge the Andover people the best one of our Synod's pastors," wrote Rev. J. S. Benzon from Omaha, "but with all my heart I wish they would not take you away from us, for then this Conference [Nebraska then belonging to the Kansas Conference] would suffer as great a loss as befell the Illinois Conference when Jonas Swensson passed away." Another of the brethren, Rev. J. Seleen of Randolph, Kansas, made this comment in a letter to Olsson: "It is indeed a self-sacrifice on your part to have declined all the profitable calls extended to you since you came here and to have stayed out here and shared the poverty of the people, although they have often, no doubt, proved ungrateful. But, dear Brother Olsson, have patience; do not leave the congregation, do not leave our Conference; conditions are bound to improve in both spiritual and temporal matters." Such was the spirit of the men stationed at the outposts in those days.

Central Kansas had a drought and a grasshopper visitation in 1874, and many of the Swedish settlers were reduced to the necessity of asking for help in tiding over the disaster. Through Olsson's efforts relief came to them from many sources. The appeals for aid made by him, both in private letters and publicly, brought in considerable money and many carloads of corn and other farm products from more favored communities. How far Olsson went in extending private charity to his parishioners in their hard early years in Kansas is not known. His meager salary, never more than five hundred dollars a year, did not all go to the support of his own family. His home was a humble as most others in the settlement; articles of wearing apparel would often find their way from the parsonage to some needy neighbor, while the pastor himself went about in attire that we would now call shabby, or at least unseemly for a man of the cloth. Traditionally the parson's bag has no bottom; that seems to have been true also of the flour barrel in the Olsson home, but in a very different sense, for it would not stay filled when bread was lacking on some poor settler's table. The survivors in the Olsson family could tell much of their parents' open-handedness if there were further need of such evidence. When all has been said of the benevolence that was so notable a trait in Olsson's character, the best yet remains in the Scriptural words so consistently lived up to by him: "Let us not be weary in well-doing. . . . As we have opportunity, let us work that which is good toward all men, and especially toward them that are of the faith."

Carl Johan Nyvall, Olsson's friend and yokefellow in the lay missionary movement in Värmland, in 1875 made his long contemplated visit to the United States, starting from Sweden in September and returning the following spring. Nyvall was not one of those who sought to widen the chasm that was then opening between the new-evangelicals and the established church. He still had hopes for a solution of the differences between the more conservative evangelical element and the adherents of New Evangelism, also called "free friends," most of whom accepted Waldenström's leadership and teaching. "In those days when for or against Waldenström was the criterion of faith and intolerance was rampant on both sides," says David Nyvall, in the work cited, "it must be said to the credit of my father that it was as odious to him on the one side as on the other."

At all events, Nyvall did not want to appear partisan. On this trip he fraternized with Augustana and Mission Friend pastors and preached in their churches without discrimination. Norelius, then president of the Synod, wrote to Olsson from Moline October 16: "Nyvall came with us from Galesburg and has been with us during our proceedings here. He preached in the Moline church last night. It was good, plain, and edifying. He declared most positively that Christ died for us—in the place of sinners. I cannot understand how he can be an adherent of Waldenström." Ten days later he wrote: "I hope you will soon be on good terms with Nyvall and that, when all is said and done, he will be our good friend. If so, let the Kansas Conference call him as a traveling missionary for their large field. When he becomes fully one of us, as I hope he will, he might be ordained. . . . If Nyvall joins with us, he would doubtless be of great usefulness. The man's seriousness and uprightness appealed to me. I am speaking, of course, from a casual impression; the facts might be different. If, however, his appearance in Moline was a disguise, then I maintain that he would be a master hypocrite, but it does not seem possible to believe that."

On his itinerary, Nyvall reached Kansas in October, having been invited to Lindsborg both by Olsson personally and by the group of Mission Friends there. His declared purpose was to remain impartial, to deal with his former friends on equal terms. Could this be done where these had so recently been divided into two hostile camps? At Lindsborg he faced the real test. Two letters exchanged between Olsson and Norelius tell the story, that of Olsson showing his old friendship with Nyvall still intact, while the reply by Norelius clearly reveals the fact that the leaders in the Synod were extending the hand of fellowship to him as to all that had not deserted to the heterodox camp.

"I must tell you frankly that your attitude toward Nyvall puzzles me," was the blunt statement with which Olsson began his inquiry as to what, in the view of the president of the Synod, would be the proper way to deal officially with his visitor. The letter, dated October 27, reads further: "We pass thundering resolutions against pulpit fellowship. You invite Nyvall without a question to preach in our churches. Nyvall is a sincere and, in private, a zealous defender of Waldenström's teaching as conforming to the Word of God. You have no doubt read Waldenström's recent Good Friday sermon. More recently I have read published letters in which he positively denies that Christ died *in our stead*. . . . Christ came to make us spiritually alive, not to suffer condemnation and death for us, he goes on. Now, my dear Brother, you will realize that, should I follow my natural inclination, I would eagerly and most sincerely invite Nyvall to preach in my churches, for he has been my best friend on earth, and I am still intimately devoted to him. But the question arises: Would I do right, would I as a shepherd of souls be faithful to my official vow [oath of office], if I asked him to preach, knowing from conversations with him that he holds Waldenström to be a great instrument in God's hand and his teaching to be the clear Word of God, and that he is spreading his sermons and writings. True, Nyvall is now, as he always was, a hearty and lovable man, amenable in all things, retaining in his preaching a great deal of the old truth. But give me your advice, for I need it. I cannot understand you, but I will not put my own judgment above yours. I do not want a fight with you in addition to the controversy with the Waldenström faction in which I have been involved. I will gladly follow your advice and example, peculiar even though they seem to me.

"Yes, I mean every word of it: Give me your advice, and I will take it in love. You know that the old doctrine of Atonement is dear to my heart, and that I abhor Waldenström's sophistry; but if you think one ought to compromise, then tell me so."

From Norelius' reply of November 4, which ran to some length, these excerpts are made: "You ask my advice, but I must first give you an explanation. I shall therefore relate to you fully the story of our fellowship with Nyvall in Illinois, so you will not get a wrong conception of the matter.

"Nyvall came to Galesburg while we were there attending the convention of the General Council. He preached one evening in Anjou's church. . . . It was said that Sanngren warned him not to go to Rock Island and Moline, but he went there nevertheless. I had only a few words of conversation with him, in the railway station at Galesburg, so that my opinion of him is not based on any personal acquaintance or intercourse. I must also admit that it takes me a long time to establish full confidence in any person. I asked those who had known Nyvall in Sweden and who talked with him, including Pastor Wallin of Knoxville and two students, Boman and Evald, what they thought of him now, and they said: Nyvall is the same man as before; true, he has great confidence in Waldenström, but he does not understand Waldenström's teachings thoroughly. This estimate seemed to be corroborated by the discourse I heard Nyvall give one evening in the Moline church. I thought then that he must be like so many other followers of Waldenström—they do not really understand what Waldenström teaches—and that when he should meet you and you two would have an opportunity to talk thinks over thoroughly, he would be convinced that Waldenström is in error. Just that was my thought, for the man seemed to me quite frank and sincere. . . .

"I own to having nourished a rather strong hope that this man would find his way, and it was in this hope that I wrote you. I was not so sanguine as to think this would happen at once, nor did I mean that you should without question place your church, or rather your pulpit, at his disposal and immediately accept him as orthodox; but I did think, or at least hope, that when you two got together and could discuss doctrines thoroughly, he would get on the right track.

"Yes, I have noticed the latest steps taken by Waldenström. It was just what I had expected; quite consistent, but terrible. We certainly cannot tolerate any of these heresies in our pulpits or congregations. If the man defends these heresies, it is clear that you cannot admit him to your pulpit. If he came here, I should ask him whether he believes and defends such teachings as Waldenström's, and if he does, I would not for all the world let him preach. The fact that Brother Carlsson permitted him to preach in Moline is no precedent for you to follow for you must take the circumstances into account. Nyvall came from Sweden as a colporteur of the Fatherland Foundation, and before there was anything to prove him a Waldenstromian, clearly he could not be turned away unheard. . . . I think I express the unanimous sentiment and advice of the brethren when I say: Should you find anyone, even the dearest of friends, to be an adherent of Waldenström's with full knowledge and intent, you cannot as a Lutheran pastor favor him or permit him to work in your congregation. But I am convinced that even among these partisans there are sincere souls who, while following the crowd, have not yet relinquished the true doctrine, and these must be considerately dealt with in order that they may be brought back into the right road."

Thus, it is seen that Nyvall, coming as a colporteur and emissary of the Fatherland Foundation, with which Augustana had always had intimate relations, was well received by the Synod's men. The reception in the Illinois Conference had been very cordial, its president, Erland Carlsson, having invited Nyvall to speak on a Biblical text before he himself preached the conference sermon. The Kansas Conference, in session when Nyvall came to Lindsborg, expressed pleasure at his presence and gave him the privilege of the floor as advisory member, like the visiting pastors from other parts of the Synod. And now that Norelius, its president, had so advised, Olsson had no misgivings about welcoming his old-time friend.

Many changes had taken place, however, between the spring of 1869, when these two men parted in Värmland, and the fall of 1875, when they met again in Kansas. Prior to that farewell, Nyvall was "thoroughly Lutheran in his views," as shown in the biography by his son, who later records his father's change of attitude in these words: "It is at this time that my father in his free-church contemplations turns to Waldenström. At the annual convention of the Fatherland Foundation at Stockholm in 1869, where the great free-church questions stood out strongly in the foreground, he met Waldenström. . . . Father was deeply concerned about those questions, which implied nothing less than a laymen's activity comprising not only the preaching of the Word but also the administration of the sacraments and a rejection of an unconnected clergyman's right to function. He seeks advice and guidance. How natural, then, that he should turn to Waldenström, whom he already revered as a great light and loved as a witness to divine truth almost without a peer. Three years later, the free church concept to my father has acquired a wider meaning, not to be confined within the trammels of orthodoxy, although he himself is still in essentials unquestionably Lutheran in all respects, still far from separatistical."

In a farewell letter to his friends just before his departure, Nyvall deplored the controversy among them on the question of the sacrament of the altar, deeming the bitterness of their strife just as terrible as the alleged eucharistic misuse in the state church, but he had no idea of how far the separatist movement had gone among his like-minded countrymen in America.

"It is surprising," says David Nyvall (p. 312), "to find in that survey not a word said about the division among the free-church element in Sweden owing to doctrinal differences caused by Waldenström's new teaching on the Atonement. We find that up to the very hour of departure my father urges a general confederation with Fosterlandsstiftelsen. Strange to say, it must have been just this visit to America which opened his eyes to the presence of divisive elements which cut deeper than even the sad contention over the holy communion which divided his friends at home. To his astonishment he found this division so marked and bitter in America that it threatened to frustrate his expectations for a successful tour. True, he knew of friends there who could not or would not join the Augustana Synod; but he could not have been aware of the fact that his friends in Kansas were themselves divided. At all events, he did not realize the implications of such fierce partisanship in the new country."

Nyvall's real destination was Lindsborg, but the president of the new Mission Synod, J. M. Sanngren of Chicago, pastor of the oldest church of the Mission Friends, made up a preaching itinerary for him, and thus Nyvall,

without knowing it, was diverted from the road that
would naturally have led to Augustana. Incidentally, he
attended the dedication of the new college building in
Rock Island on the fourteenth of October, but as a
stranger and a spectator. Olsson, whom he most longed
to meet, was not there. "And a still greater disappointment was that when at last the two met in Lindsborg, it
was not as it used to be. There was something that had
forced them apart in the interval. . . . How my father
felt at meeting his former Jonathan would better be told
in his own words: 'The following day, and then as often
as I found time, I paid Olsson a visit. I heard him preach,
which gave me joy and edification. We talked about old
times and new; we read the Word and prayed together.
I cannot think but that he, like myself, felt something of
tender brotherly love. But because of the aforesaid partisan strife and for the reason that I could not share his
views about P. W. [Waldenström] and his writings, he
told me he could not invite me to preach to his congregation. I tried to take this coolly, but my feelings anyone
can understand who knows how intimately Olsson and I
had formerly lived together.' At length the situation
grew intolerable to my father, who asked for 'a conference with Olsson and his church council, which was
granted.' Then he had an opportunity to explain his
attitude, and thereby matters were righted insofar that
he 'was asked to preach at a Conference held November
17th and was even made an advisory member,' as had
been done at the great festivities in Rock Island and
Moline; but he could not but notice such mistrust on the
part of some of the ministers that he 'felt little inclination
to take part in the discussion.' "

From Olsson's letters among the Norelius papers we gather further details of Nyvall's notable visit of which Olsson wrote in advance: "Now we are daily expecting a guest from Sweden who was my best friend on earth. He is now a fervid adherent of Waldenström. He has been called over here by the Mission Friends in order to lay at his feet all that he finds here of Christianity and Christians."

The Kansas Conference met at Lindsborg, and the new church edifice was dedicated Sunday, November 21. Nyvall was present throughout the meeting, and he took part in the dedication and in the celebration of the Lord's Supper, not, however, before he had met with Olsson and his church board and agreed to preach in accordance with the Lutheran confession. Nyvall also stated that he had found nothing in Waldenström that differed from the teaching of the Scriptures except his denial of Christ's vicarious suffering and death, which Nyvall did not subscribe to. This according to a letter dated December 14. But on February 21 he mentions having received a saddening letter from Nyvall who "still holds W— to be sound in doctrine." Lest Nyvall might seem to be misjudged by his friend, his own explanation of his attitude may here be noted. It was given directly and at some length to Norelius in a letter dated at Lindsborg November 8. From it these passages are quoted: "I was born within the Lutheran church, as you know, and by pressure from other confessions I have been compelled to do a little searching of the Scriptures, and then I found, for the comfort of my heart, our Lutheran doctrine to agree most accurately with the Word; hence I have no intention of deserting it. . . . However, I was unable to agree with Olsson, in his paper, against W——m [Waldenström], but wrote and told how richly God had blessed us in our homeland through this man's sermons and writings; and this made the Mission Friends here eager to have me come. So I came at their call. . . . One thing more, as long as the Mission Friends tolerate me, I will proclaim the Word among them." The chasm between the two church groups was, however, too wide to be straddled, and Nyvall's well-meant effort to reunite them was fore-doomed to failure.

About Christmas, Nyvall visited Lindsborg again, when he encountered one of the Kansas snowstorms. "But there were other storms worse than that. He sensed beforehand 'what was to be expected there on account of renewed strife occasioned by letters of his that P. W. had caused to be published.' Father owned to having 'offended and grieved Olsson by writing injudicious letters to him.' In reply he had received 'a sharp, serious letter, from which he inferred that the way about to be opened to him was now closed'. . . . Father closes his account of that visit with these words: 'I felt great relief, joy, and encouragement after I had talked with Olsson and we had been reconciled. True, I could not undo the offense my letter had given him; only confess my sin. He forgave me, and we parted in peace' " (*op. cit.*, 315).

XI

CHAMPION OF LUTHERANISM

The schismatic movement which in the decade of the 1870's transplanted many thousands of Lutheran believers from the Augustana Synod churches to independent congregations which eventually formed three new church groups—the Mission Covenant, the Swedish Congregationalists, and the Evangelical Free Church—had its roots in the movement in Sweden first known as New Evangelism. Begun as a liberalized Lutheranism, it departed step by step from the teachings of the Church of Sweden as the leadership passed from certain of her eminent clergymen to laymen not less devout but certainly less firmly grounded in Christian doctrine. In the high name of liberty of conscience, these latter propagated many arbitrary views, and they made a virtue of dissent from the "dead orthodoxy" of the established church of the realm and disloyalty to her priesthood, the great number of whose members were alleged to be "spiritually dead." From a movement making for revitalized Lutheranism, it thus developed into a trend away from the Lutheran church. Its leaders became the left wing of the Evangelical Fatherland Foundation, which stood for sound but also more practical churchmanship, and these withdrew when they could not take the Foundation with them out of the Church of Sweden.

In the early seventies, Peter Paul Waldenström came

to the fore in this free-church movement as a preacher and a writer. He interpreted Scripture in his own way, disregarding recognized religious authorities and often taking bold and flippant stabs at them—including Luther —as having taught religion from the head, not from the heart. His first book, *Om försoningens betydelse*, was a new venture in Biblical exegesis. It was a rationalistic interpretation of Christ's atonement amounting to a denial of the work of the Mediator between God and man attributed to Him by most Christian confessions. The dissenters thought they saw a great light; they accepted Waldenström's interpretation without question, all but a few, with minds of their own, like C. J. Nyvall, who did not at once surrender. Even these, however, yielded by degrees, and soon Waldenström claimed thousands upon thousands of adherents to his views. He became the accepted leader of this group of Christians, and their tenets came to be known as Waldenstromianism. Little known as it is among theologians outside the Lutheran church, it is hard to say what standing this new school of Bible interpretation has with churchmen of other confessions. It was not countenanced by Swedish theologians. The book brought forth numerous refutations, including that by Chr. Möller of Denmark and those by Bishop Lars Landgren, Dr. Peter Fjellstedt, a noted Bible commentator, and Pastor G. E. Beskow of Sweden. The latter published two books in answer to Waldenström.

The Lutheran view of Christ's redemptive sacrifice, presented in "The Lord as High Priest" by Beshow, was scouted by Waldenström as "a doctrine which in our opinion is the most unscriptural and therefore the most dangerous."

Of the doctrine of man's justification through the imputed righteousness of Christ, Pastor Ekman, another leader of the New-evangelicals, in a book endorsed by Waldenström as being founded on the Scriptures, had this to say: "Hence it must be clear that the purpose of Christ's work was an actual righteousness within us. . . . With an *imputed righteousness*, heaven can never to us become a true heaven." This new theology Beskow characterizes in these words:

"Thus, Christ's righteousness, *earned* for us and *imputed* to us, is positively rejected. They go so far as to contend that Scripture knows of no such righteousness. They make bold to call that righteousness *unreal* and to say that one who has no better justification to rely on would find no bliss in heaven itself. These are plain words. Now we understand one another, and it should be clear to every one what the new doctrine teaches about the justification of sinners before God. We can not but see a great peril to our Swedish Zion in these new teachings as they attack one doctrine after another, . . . each time *making Christ lesser*, no matter how often His name is used."

Olsson was a most zealous and vigilant champion of pure Lutheran doctrine. This brought him into sharp conflict with the groups from Sweden who from the New Evangelism of the Fatherland Foundation type went still farther to the left and in the United States successively formed three or more religious groups. This led to his controversy with Waldenström when that man became the recognized spokesman for the Mission Friends on both sides of the Atlantic and to Olsson's estrangement from his close friend Nyvall when the latter, after long hesitation, finally accepted Waldenström's teachings and became one of the recognized leaders of the group.

Olsson's uncompromising opposition to this schism, which sprang from the very movement in Sweden in which he had been a force, can hardly be understood without some knowledge of the origin of the American branch of the Mission Covenant. From a book entitled, *Missionsvännerna i Amerika*, by C. V. Bowman, we reproduce in part that historian's account of the very first meeting of Mission Friends, held in the Immanuel Lutheran Church of Chicago in July 1869. Bowman says:

"That some of the representatives of the Mission Society did not always show due deference during the discussion, but on the contrary were guilty of much that was unseemly, this they later realized and admitted. Especially a former student from Augustana College, it was said, made a vicious attack on the teaching and life of the pastors. After his irritating talk, he took his hat and left the church in a huff. When he was gone, some one exclaimed in a broad Värmland brogue, 'We must excuse our young friend for being a little too Lutheran.' At that point Pastor Carlsson took the floor, declaring that if that was the sort of men the new mission societies were to put into the field, the churches would most likely be closed to their workers. This disturbing and unpleasant episode was disapproved of by the Mission Friends. Several took exception to the improper conduct of the student and sought to exonerate the society. On the other hand, the Lutheran pastors took part in the discussion with calm self-control and showed unexpected consideration for their opponents. . . . This memorable and interesting mission meeting came to be of very great significance not only for the society already formed in Chicago, but for the entire field, for thereby it was made generally known that now there existed a freer spiritual movement than the Augustana Synod."

The same writer tells us that the Mission Friends in Chicago had not thought of separating themselves from the Lutheran congregation, yet they worshiped separately on Sunday mornings, built their own "mission house," or church, soon after, and before long they planned to constitute themselves as an independent Christian congregation, prompted more especially by "believers recently arrived from Sweden who, not yet members of any church, longed to celebrate the Lord's Supper together with the children of God." Opinions differed for a time on this last point, but it finally came to this: The first society of Mission Friends unanimously agreed that "if the society was to attain its purpose, it must also in the matter of Holy Communion assert its independence of the Lutheran clergy." The first communion was then celebrated in the mission house, conducted by J. M. Sanngren, a lay preacher, Erland Carlsson, their pastor, being given no part in the services. "By the step thus taken, the group factually declared itself to be more than a mere mission society; it had proclaimed itself a Christian congregation," says the historian of the church group here formed.

In other places where the Mission Friends established their early communions in the 1870's, the procedure varied according to local conditions, but the spirit was the same. It was admittedly a breaking away from the

Augustana churches on the alleged ground that they were too much like the congregations of the Church of Sweden and that their pastors were not all spiritual, therefore alleged to be unfit to preach the Word and administer the sacraments. The seceding groups virtually claimed to be true children of God, one and all, in distinction from the other church members, and their mission societies, not always known as churches, were patterned after so-called Communion Societies in Sweden, which held Holy Communion of no effect if administered by a worldly-minded pastor or if partaken of together with other than converts.

It was against this un-Lutheran movement that Olsson spoke out with great force and conviction, more particularly when these dissenting groups quite generally added Waldenstromianism to their other tenets. He knew personally, by trial and error, that a "pure" church on earth was not possible, and as a Christian scholar he felt it a duty to expose teachings and practices held to be both unbiblical and contrary to the policy of the Lutheran church and the Synod to which he belonged. Certainly no just charge of partisanship and unwise zeal can be laid against a churchman who, seeing an exodus of members from his own church body going on year after year, sought by all the powers at his command to stem the tide of deserters. The new views of the church and of the Christian religion itself propounded by a number of lay preachers and the strange interpretations of Scripture by Waldenström in Sweden were in his opinion erroneous and ought to be fought to a finish. "No one carried on this fight more ably than did Olsson, and thereby he did more than anyone else to save the unity of the Augustana Synod," said Dr. S. G. Youngert in his evaluation of Olsson's life work.

Some have minimized this doctrinal controversy, making Olsson out as only another champion of abstract orthodoxy, moved by overzealous partisanship. This is misjudging both the man and his motives. Let those who charge his action to mere partisan zeal look farther, and they shall find that the battle raged around one of the central teachings of Christianity, which was being arbitrarily revised. Should leading churchmen of Sweden or of the Augustana Synod be deemed partial or prejudiced, the case of Waldenstromianism might be taken to a nonpartisan judge. In the heat of the controversy, well along in the seventies, Professor G. Fritschel, a German Lutheran theologian having no connection with Augustana, after a study of Waldenström's teachings, published his conclusions. His verdict was summarized in these words: "The very kernel of Waldenstromianism lies in this, that thereby the bitter suffering and death of our Lord and Saviour Jesus Christ is robbed of its content. It tells us that nothing happened at that time for the redemption of the world and for the earning of our salvation. That takes place in the heart of man at the moment of conversion, it is claimed. At this very point we see the great unbridgable gulf separating Waldenström's teachings from the accepted Christian faith. Here it appears how completely he has broken with the ancient Christian truth. It is actually a terrible mutilation of the chief articles of the Christian doctrine and a complete reversal of Christian belief. It is another faith, another gospel than that taught in Scripture, which this new apostle proclaims." (*Augustana*, 1879, p. 452.)

The movement vitally affected the Augustana Synod, larger or smaller groups withdrawing from quite a number of its churches year by year. At the 1874 convention, its ministerium set aside much time to discuss "The Biblical Implication of the Atonement." Chosen to report the discussion, Olsson wrote a very full report which ran in several issues of the synodical paper. From his first contact with this movement he had opposed it and sought to stem the defection. He preached and wrote thorough and scholarly discourses in refutation of Waldenström's interpretation of the Bible in general and his doctrine on Christ's atonement for sin, a teaching which was embraced by many as shedding new light on the way of salvation, but which he showed to be known in church history as an old fallacious doctrine based on misreading of a number of proof texts out of the original Greek arrayed in its support. His writings on the subject were not in the nature of abstract theological apologetics so much as they were simple presentations for the common reader, written in a devotional spirit and with a view to establishing the people of the Synod in the faith common to the great Christian churches on this point. He despaired of convincing Waldenström himself and of winning back the dissenters who avidly accepted his interpretation without question—this, curiously enough, after having positively asserted the right of each one to do his own interpreting of Scripture and renounced the authority of older teachers in the church as well as the teachings of their present pastors. The trend was to discard Christian *doctrine* and stress Christian *life*, while overstressing the religious insight as well as the sainthood of the individual Christian. In the exaltation that goes with certain forms of religious revival, it was forgotten that the new teachings were "doctrine" in the same sense as the old, only less firmly supported by conviction, experience, and proof. Olsson was, as elsewhere shown, a believer in the right of private judgment and independent thinking along religious lines, but in this controversy he stood squarely on the age-old doctrine of the ecumenical church and held that touching the Atonement Waldenström was clearly in error. The words of a recent writer apply here: "To suppose that, thinking or experimenting independently, I can arrive at significant truth seems to me to represent an absurd overemphasis upon my own insight and upon the wisdom of my own generation." (JOHN COLEMAN BENNETT in *The Christian Century*, February, 1939.)

Again and again, in the course of the argument, Olsson showed that conversion could not have its source in the human heart, as was maintained by those who called themselves the "free friends." He held this to be a poor and insufficient ground on which to rest one's hope of salvation and deplored the emotional element in the movement, which obscures and minimizes God's part in His reconciliation of sinners with Himself and makes man's own effort the decisive step in conversion. There can be no question that Olsson's position was impregnable, standing as he did on the accepted interpretation of Scripture on the point at issue, in contrast to Waldenström, whose views were unsupported by any Christian teachers except the Socinians and at least subject to grave doubt. From their day to this, the Lutheran church has never compromised on the doctrine of Redemption. At the present time, leading churchmen in Sweden are making this same question the subject for profound study and research, resulting in a number of new works in this field and deepened insight into the meaning of the Atonement on the part of both clergy and laity. Nowhere have Olsson's views been found at variance with the position taken by these Christian scholars. On the contrary, many parallel passages might be quoted showing remarkable agreement both in thought and in expression. In an analogy drawn from the relation between a father and his children, for instance, Archbishop Eidem, in his book, *The Suffering God*, stresses the truth that when a child has sinned against his parent, it is not the child's love that leads to repentance, but the father's, a love that suffers, yet will not abandon the sinner, who is still a child to be won back. If Olsson's position had to be stated in a few words, this simple illustration by the present primate of Sweden would serve the purpose very well.

In the United States, the group of believers that withdrew from the Swedish Lutheran churches was split up into factions which became known under many different names. Its adherents called themselves variously Free Friends, Mission Friends, the Free Mission, and they eventually formed four distinct groups with no very distinct gradation in their professed freedom from ecclesiastical trammels. Thus there is, in addition to the Mission Covenant, the Swedish Congregationalists, and the Evangelical Free Church, even a group designated as the "Free-free" Mission Friends. It was against the whole movement, call it what you will, that the leading men of the Augustana Synod put up a conservative opposition. The assumption that Waldenstromianism was the only aberration among the new lay preachers and their eager followers would be wide of the mark. For a fair statement of what this struggle for "freedom" in Christian faith and life implied and how it degenerated into license and often sank to the lowest forms of fanaticism and religious excesses before the wiser heads called a halt, we turn to one who himself was a leader of one of these groups. The following is reproduced from the "Reminiscences of J. G. Princell" published by his wife Josephine Princell at the request of the Swedish Evangelical Free Church. One need have no fear that Princell had any bias in favor of the Augustana Synod, having been excommunicated by the ministerium of that body. Under the head of "Various Doctrinal Views Held by the Free Friends" (Chapter IV, p. 175 ff.) we read:

"They held general mission meetings at various places . . . and while rather peculiar things were in evidence, yet the meetings were good. . . . At most of the larger meetings later on, one or several prophetic topics would be discussed. Meanwhile many were converted, and many Christians were awakened to a warmer and more intimate spiritual life and to expect Jesus' coming from heaven.

"But not always or everywhere was a Christian mental balance maintained in all these things, beautiful, pure, and true as they were. The times were no doubt fraught with excesses. At the meetings people became very much excited, overjoyed, and happy, the preachers not least. Well and good, but when it turned to mental intoxication, so that people shouted loudly and fell to the floor overcome by their feelings, then this brought them much opprobrium from the unsaved, who openly mocked at those who were lying by the platform, rolling from side to side, shouting, laughing, or weeping in turn. There were preachers who now began to propound the doctrine that nothing was genuine and spiritual that did not come with noise and storm.

"Much was taught that was good and right . . . yet they sometimes went to extremes, deeming it sinful to have curtains at the windows, carpets on the floor, paper on the walls, etc. . . . In the earliest days of the Free Mission, people went farther in their zeal than was proper, making it a sin to wear a wedding ring, forbidding the carrying of a watch chain, and condemning as vanity such articles as collars and neckties. To deposit money in a bank was to do wrong. Thus many sensitive consciences were bound. Of course these things were nothing new; the same thing had happened before, as instanced by the Montanists who appeared at the close of the second century. That sect was founded by Montanus, who taught that the Millennium was then about to be established. His followers held that they alone of all Christian believers were inspired and led by the Holy Spirit. . . . At their divine services they went to such excesses as were common, and still occur here and there, among the Free Friends, such as, fainting away, shouting, and setting up real howls; and all this they alleged to be the work of the Spirit. . . . This is not a unique phenomenon in the history of the church, for whenever the calm development of the Christian congregation ordained by God is in any way stopped or interfered with by some extraordinary movement, it has recurred in all its characteristic phases. To suspect all learning that calls for brave and serious exertion, to despise all literature, to take an inimical attitude to art, science, and general culture, to abandon all orderly ways of life, in short, a crude, odd, and disgragreeable outward appearance, used as a cover for another sort of vanity than that of this world, and a one-sided stressing of deprivation, combined with prediction of terrible judgments of God—these are acts and phenomena often met with in church history."

For characteristics of the movement so vigorously opposed by Olsson, we have drawn from two sources which may be relied upon not to have exaggerated its shortcomings. Neither Bowman nor Princell could be suspected of overdrawing the weaknesses of the group to which he belonged and whose history he was recording. For cumulative evidence one might draw from *Chicago-Bladet* and other papers which in the thickest of the fight laid on valiantly with weapons varying from legitimate theological arguments to specious fallacies and abusive epithets. From the original assumption that the Church of Sweden was a "dead church" it was easily argued that the Augustana Synod could not be a living one; hence it must be an abortive offspring. In the opposing camp the standing terms for Augustana pastors were consequently "false shepherds," "dead preachers," "dead dogs." Olsson tells us somewhere that the last was a pet name often applied to him, adding his expectation to meet in glory even the brethren who were so unkind but expressing his preference in this life for fellowship with less self-righteous folk, who were willing to leave final judgment with God.

While terms of abuse were often hurled in this fray, the main battle was fought on a higher plane. That is not saying that the contestants did not sometimes make their arguments pointedly personal. In his *Reseminnen*, describing his visit to America, the elder Nyvall spoke of men and conditions in the Synod in words which could hardly go unchallenged. Olsson made a reply none the less forthright for coming from an old friend. After having had Augustana churches opened to him as a representative of the Fatherland Foundation and as a positive Lutheran by his own testimony, Nyvall, it appeared, had accepted Waldenström's views. When Olsson pointed this out in a published refutation of those views, Nyvall complained of this as a grievous personal attack. A careful reading of both the book and the answer has not given the impression that the latter is more personal than the former. The difference, if any, lies in this, that Olsson names the men whose acts and views he criticizes, while Nyvall leaves his most pertinent comments unaddressed.

Olsson was fully aware of some of the sinister trends in the religious thinking, or lack of it, among these new groups. He knew what Princell knew—and deplored at a later time. After his having studied the movement "all last fall and winter," as he told Hasselquist in 1873, and then followed its development year after year, the following characteristics were as clear to him as an outside observer as they were to Princell and others within the groups: (1) An emotionalism as extreme in spots as that of the Holy Rollers; (2) vagaries in the interpretation of the prophecies; (3) fanciful chiliastic expectations and a false assurance of Christ's early coming again; (4) perverted ideas of holiness, ranging from Puritanism to the perfectionist belief in absolute sinlessness ("Many pushed the doctrine of sinlessness to the point where they found themselves sunk in mud"—PRINCELL, p. 178); (5) the synergistic view of salvation and the idea of earning righteousness by works, self-denial, and sundry outer observances; (6) deprecation of human intelligence and educational institutions; (7) belief in immediate personal inspiration through the Holy Spirit.

What Princell, writing in 1885, said of the Montanist and other extravagances revived among some Mission Friends recalls this warning by Olsson several years before:

"Whence comes the credulity by which a great many Christians embrace old soul-destroying errors when these appear in made-over attire? If these credulous Christians knew, as they might know from church history, what boundless desolation these same errors have caused in times past, they would not hail with delight every new wind of doctrine that blows. He who has seen the destructive effect of the storm that follows is astounded to see the signs foreboding the next one and takes all possible precautions to protect himself from the peril. Next to the Word of God, there is no more effective means than the history of the church by which to identify the prince of darkness when disguised as an angel of light." (*Augustana*, 1881, p. 252.)

Several years before that, at the request of his students, Olsson had exposed the chief fallacies of Waldenström. In his treatise, *Reformationen och socinianismen* (The Reformation and Socinianism), it is shown that the new exegete was tinged with the rationalism of Socinus and his sect, which flourished in Europe in the sixteenth and seventeenth centuries. The doctrine acclaimed as his was not new. What Waldenström taught, the Socinians had taught two hundred years before. *The view that salvation was secured by Christ's suffering and death they declared to be false and pernicious.* So did Waldenström, and he wrote book after book to prove his point. They taught that the guilt and punishment of one can not be borne by another; hence Christ could not obey or suffer for others. So Waldenström held. They maintained that Christ delivers man from the bondage of sin by keeping him from committing sins; that justification consists in this, that God treats believers in Him as righteous, without any imputation of Christ's merit, and they declared the latter theory a human fiction. And these things Waldenström adopted and taught as his own interpretation of the Bible. But, as the Encyclopaedia of Religious Knowledge has later stated the case, "In the Socianian theory Scriptural and unscriptural elements strangely meet. It was the real forerunner of modern rationalism and in this consideration lies its chief claim to prolonged attention."

At this point it may be noted that Olsson's attitude has been misjudged by George M. Stephenson in his work, *The Religious Aspects of Swedish Immigration*, where he says: "In the fall of 1876 he became professor in Augustana Theological Seminary, in which atmosphere of excessive orthodoxy he was betrayed into writing an attack on the new-fangled doctrine of the atonement and on the 'free church' element among the Swedes" (p. 286). The facts recorded here do not warrant so light an aspect of the religious movement which stirred the Swedish immigrants more deeply than any other and which, but for Olsson and Hasselquist, would have left the Augustana Synod defenseless and taken a much greater toll from the Lutheran church. Far from being betrayed into an attack, Olsson had studied the movement years before on his own initiative, and had written a refutation of the new doctrine as early as 1873. His *defense* of Lutheran doctrine against the *attacks* of the dissenters was the most earnest and conscientious piece of work in his whole career. When, in a footnote on Olsson's treatise of 1878 (published in Stockholm, 1880), this critic says "an attempt is made to identify Waldenstromian doctrine with the Socinian 'heresy'," he ignores the deadly parallels drawn by Olsson from the two very similar doctrines.

Stephenson, however, at once follows up this criticism with a kinder and more correct estimate: "But Olsson was too generous-hearted to be suited to the role of 'hammerer of heretics,' and he lived to regret this attack upon his former teacher at Uppsala. We have his own words as authority for the statement that with the passing of every year he favored union more—*the bête noire* of the Augustana Synod, with its Galesburg rule." It is true that Olsson modified his attitude toward the Mission Friends later but not until they had found their bearings and the sober element had prevailed in the forming of the Mission Covenant in 1885. In discussing a possible rapprochement between the Covenant and the Synod, Stephenson says further: "Like the Mission Covenant in Sweden, with the passing years the sister church in America has become more institutional, and as a result the verbal warfare between it and the Augustana Synod has practically subsided. Not a few Mission Friend preachers in America and Sweden have sought and obtained ordination in the Augustana Synod or in the Church of Sweden. On both sides of the water this situation is due partly to the fact that an organized body carries greater prestige than one without organization."

We know that Olsson clasped hands with his former antagonists after some of their differences had been composed. He visited E. A. Skogsbergh in Minneapolis, one of his opponents, in a spirit of Christian fellowship. He received C. J. Nyvall as a guest in his home when the latter visited America a second and a third time. About 1888, he asked some of his brethren, in effect, "Must we forever remain apart from these other Christians who, after all, confess the same Lord as we?" Overtures looking toward uniting the Covenant and the Synod have sometimes been talked about, but they have never been made. Nevertheless, when individual pastors of the Covenant have asked to be admitted into the ministerium of the Synod, no obstacles have been raised to bar them, and the *odium theologicum* of past years no longer attaches to their fellowship.

The nearest approach to effecting a more cordial understanding officially endorsed by both sides was made in 1915 when the Synod extended a friendly hand. A resolution then adopted sought to "pave the way for a better understanding among the Swedish church bodies, especially between the Augustana Synod and the Mission Covenant." Nothing came out of this move, owing to an unwarranted suspicion that it would be the first step toward organic union. Speaking for the Covenant, the weekly *Missions-Vännen* curtly said that body "had never thought of any approach to the Augustana Synod," but *Augustana* (1915, p. 530) maintained that a better relation was desirable, adding: "We believe this to be a desideratum with many Mission Friends, both pastors and congregations."

XII

FIRST TOUR OF EUROPE

In the early part of the year 1879, Olsson, suffering
from impaired health, was compelled to ask for leave of
absence in order to rest from his duties as professor,
preacher, writer, and, not least, solicitor of funds, in the
hope of building up his strength and refreshing his spirit.
"I had long cherished a wish to undertake an extended
tour during which I might rest from preaching, study,
work, and worry," he explained. "Feeling my powers
very much reduced, I took this as a sign from the Lord
that I ought to rest for a time." He decided on a trip
to Europe.

On March 18, Olsson left Rock Island after bidding
farewell to the student body at the morning devotions
in chapel. Their chorus and band had serenaded him
the evening before, and the divinity students now accompanied him to the railway station in a body. After visiting the C. P. Holmbergs in Chicago and another good
friend, Pastor E. A. Fogelström, in Brooklyn, he embarked for England March 22, on the "S. S. Erin" of
the National Line.

He was now on his way, leaving behind him the
burden of routine work and the cares that infest a teacher's day. But did he? "I was not looking for adventure.
The trip was a serious one for me. I was not traveling
for pleasure," he told his friends at home. We may well

believe it, for his very first message from abroad was— an appeal in behalf of Augustana College, pleading for the payment of its debt by collecting the prescribed but not forthcoming 25-cent fee, this to be carried out through an envelope system. It may be noted in passing that this plan was proposed by Olsson fifty years before such a system for the collection of church dues was adopted by the Synod. On Palm Sunday the traveler visited Charles H. Spurgeon's tabernacle in London and heard a sermon by that noted divine. "But what has the 25-cent fee to do with Spurgeon's tabernacle?" In answer, he tells us that the Pastors' College, a seminary of one hundred students and requiring $20,000 a year, was being amply supported simply through collection boxes placed at all the doors of the tabernacle. He goes on to say: "Then I thought, would it not be well to have such savings chests placed in our churches? Each communicant might use a little envelope, write his name, put in a quarter and drop it in at any time when attending church. . . . Long before visiting Spurgeon's tabernacle I had given much thought to some such method, and when I there found it used to so great advantage and with so little trouble, my former idea came back to me. . . . With a sense of sadness I wonder whether our churches have already grown so fine that they would be thought disfigured by plain wooden boxes at the doors, bearing the legend: FOR AUGUSTANA COLLEGE AND SEMINARY."

During the passage across the sea, Olsson, immune as he was from seasickness, could spend the days leisurely, resting, writing, or philosophizing, according as the mood prompted. Pipe dreams were banned from the outset, for in going second class (which then meant by smoking

car) from Chicago to New York, our tourist, till then a
moderate smoker, was thoroughly cured of the habit by
a Duke's mixture of fumes which, to "Uncle" Hasselquist's great delight made Olsson a recruit for the college
Anti-Tobacco Society. *Augustana och Missionären*, 1879,
p. 340, is proof in point.

On shipboard he put down some of the impressions
received in passing through cities like Pittsburgh and
New York. His reaction at seeing the congested workingmen's districts in the industrial cities was one of disgust and sadness. The following observations, typical of
the man, we find recorded in the first travel letter:

"My old antipathy to big cities began to grow, and
my sympathy for the poor workingmen to deepen, especially when I saw Pittsburgh. Oh horrors, what workers'
quarters in these factory towns! Of course the workingmen's shacks are located in the worst hollows, with smoke,
dirt, and mire without limit! What are five years of living
on the prairies, with a dugout for a home, and with bed-
bugs for tenants and rattlesnakes for nearest neighbors,
compared to a whole life lived in these wretched hovels?
On the prairie, even the poorest has at least fresh air and
God's glorious sunshine for nothing when he comes out
of his sodhouse. Oh, for a summer morning on the plains
—how it makes one forget all the hardships of pioneer
life! If, therefore, my voice should reach the young men
of the cities, who think it a mighty fine thing to spend
their leisure time walking the streets all dressed up and
with cigars in their mouths, I would call out: "Young
man, throw away your cigar; buy a spade; go west with
the guidance of God and yield your heart to Him; put
up with a few years of hardship and deprivation; and

when you have put your dwelling in order, ask a God-fearing lass to be the wife of a free yeoman of the soil who humbly serves God alone and, though working in the sweat of his brow, need not truckle to the proud over-lords in the cities. But what if they should all leave the cities? No fear; there is not so much good sense in the world; don't be afraid that those miserable cities will be depopulated. . . . When I saw New York, it warmed my feeling for country life still more. Living in the big cities looks to me like prison life."

From London, Olsson sailed for Germany and re-mained for some time at Carlsbad, on the Tepl River, near the picturesque mountains of Bohemia. "Why I headed for Germany," he explains, "was partly because I wished to stop at some health resort, but mostly be-cause I wanted to see that land of culture and of 'Kultur-kampf,' and especially of the Reformation." He had not traveled far in Europe before he made this confession: "One thing I may say at once: after what I have seen and heard in England and Germany, I love America more than ever before; in the glare of royalty and imperialism I was made a stronger and more convinced republican than I ever was, so now you may hail me as a citizen of the United States, heart and soul. Yes, from my heart I thank God for our American form of government, and," he adds, "especially do I praise the Lord for the religious freedom we enjoy in the United States. The time of state churches is past, and for that we may well sing, *Te Deum laudamus*, even though many beloved men in Europe are still striving to maintain that which must ultimately fall."

Observing how almost all his fellow travelers, the

women in particular, intoxicated themselves with the reading of novels, Olsson made this comment: "It is the ungodly novel that is the worst and most dangerous enemy of morality and true Christianity. After the women have turned infidels, one may be sure that there will be an end to the home, the church, the republic, and all. As for religious novels, I will testify that I positively disapprove of most of them. When we have so much of true and real history, of biographies, and the like, why should we not put truth rather than fiction into the hands of our young people? True, the novel is generally written in simple, easy, and pleasant style, so that the very reading of such has a fascination; history, on the other hand, is often written clumsily, tediously, and too learnedly— the more's the pity. What foolish learning, that will not let the truth be presented in simple, childlike garb, without pedantic disguise! I detest such scholarly claptrap, but admire historians such as a Merle D'Aubigné."

To the coincidence that Olsson was in London when the annual rendition of Handel's great oratorio, "The Messiah," occurred we owe the early introduction of that masterpiece of religious music at the colleges of the Augustana Synod, first at Augustana College and next at Bethany College in Lindsborg. Arriving in the world metropolis late Friday afternoon, April 4, he lost no time in preparing to attend that performance, to be given in Exeter Hall the same evening by a chorus of about seven hundred, directed by Sir Michael Costa. He rejoiced beforehand at this opportunity and went into raptures while the sacred work was being sung, as may be gathered from his own comment:

"Please understand me, this great musical work by

Handel has a special significance for me as being one in
which the highest musical art on earth has been employed
to magnify the cross and the blood of our Lord Jesus
Christ. . . . Had I missed the event at Exeter Hall that
night I could hardly have made up for the loss, yet, what
was this singing, though grand, to the song in heaven?
What is one evening compared to an eternity? . . . I may
well wonder what my old mother will say when she sees
me enjoying the music of violins. For she made me
destroy a fiddle I procured in my boyhood because I was
bound to learn to play. Yet, when the violin is used in
the service of God, it is a wonderful instrument. Just
think, if we would begin playing the violin at our school—
would not our dear friends condemn us as altogether
godless? Some of them are on the point of deserting our
school because of our band instruments. But stop and
think how the human voice is being used in the service
of Satan, and yet one does not destroy one's voice upon
becoming a Christian, but rather begins to sing praises
to God with the very voice with which one served the
kingdom of darkness. So also with the instruments. . . .

"I will not even attempt to describe it all, for that
were beyond my power. At times I was so carried away
that I scarcely knew myself. Well, my friends may smile
at my childishness. Let them smile. But I don't know
what sort of man he would be who had no feeling for
beautiful spiritual music. Among other things sung were
the names of our Saviour given in the ninth chapter of
Isaiah: Wonderful, Counsellor, Mighty God. When the
great chorus and the full orchestra intoned these words,
I was so thrilled through bone and marrow that I feared
the shock would be too much for me." He goes on at

some length describing the letter and the spirit of the oratorio and its rendition, closing with the words, "That evening in Exeter Hall will, I may well say, remain the most beautiful memory of my tour." The value of this one experience of Olsson to the Synod and its institutions will be accounted for in the proper place.

After viewing St. Paul's Cathedral, he commented: "As a memorial fane, St. Paul's is magnificent and awe-inspiring; as a church, it is, like so many large churches, a failure. Imagine the enormous sums spent on such memorials used instead to erect true sanctuaries for worship and the preaching of the Word. That church and state in England are built into one structure is seen the moment one enters this cathedral. It is a question how long the mortar will make the bonds endure."

In taking his leave from the school, Olsson was supposed to have thrown his official cares to the winds. He put an ocean between himself and his field of labor, but he was unable to take his mind from the interests that had engrossed him at home. While at Herrnhut, Saxony, he was gravely concerned about the issue of a number of matters to come before the approaching synodical convention in Chicago. In his "Greeting to the Augustana Synod," written during attendance at the general synod of the Brethren at Herrnhut, he could not refrain from expressing his views on what to him were the most vital questions pending. His observations of the many winds of doctrine then blowing through the churches of Germany moved him to stress the importance to the Synod of "holding fast to the Word of God through pure and unadulterated teaching, and yet keep the peace, not, as do the otherwise worthy Missourians, constantly assault-

ing other believers, hitting right and left and shouting
their battle cry: Pure doctrine! One must distinguish
carefully between defensive and offensive warfare in the
kingdom of God. We are called to attack the ungodly and
unregenerate with the sword that is the Word of God;
defend the truth we must, even against Christians who
by the machinations of the Deceiver are become partisans who seek to rob us of the pearl of great price—
divine truth; but as soon as the need of such warlike
defense ceases, we ought to use all the grace and power
God grants us for building within our God-given domain.
Oh, let us not forget what is the heart and center of
Lutheran doctrine—Christ and the redemption of the
world through His death."

Against weak and inane preaching of orthodoxy, on
the other hand, he warned: "Will it come to this among
us, that we lose simplicity and preach sermons which,
though very pretty and correct, yet fail to draw the sap
of life from the vine to the branches, because the preacher
lacks the true and simple faith. Pardon me, dear brethren, for saying so; by the grace of God I am aware of
my own frailty in this respect. We are in danger; the
way is narrow, and narrowest for the minister. Likewise
my wish and prayer to God is that we may never carry
with us into the pulpit the ragbag of human learning to
empty out its tawdry contents before a pitiable audience.
Learning is good and needful, even secular learning, but
in the pulpit there is room only for a humble disciple
of Jesus."

The members of the Synod were admonished not to
be unduly troubled over the school indebtedness still
unpaid. From the headquarters of the Moravian Breth-

ren he informed them that this little communion had
many educational institutions for which it had often gone
deeply into debt, yet, strong in faith, its small churches
had overcome all difficulties during one hundred and
fifty years. He advised against mutual jealousy as between the schools at Rock Island and at St. Peter and
counseled the exercise of brotherly love in order that the
two institutions might help rather than harm each other.
He prayed that the Synod might be of one mind in
changing its constitution, overruling a suspected interest
on the part of the Minnesota Conference in forming a
synod of its own, and that ways might be found to keep
the Synod one body, yet to leave its various parts the
freedom of action required for efficiency in church work.
"Is it not noteworthy," he wrote, "that the communion
of Brethren, although scattered over the world, is held
together in one Synod? A remarkable example indeed."

The Synod was to act on a proposed new Catechism
for the religious instruction of the young, worked out by
Hasselquist, Olsson, Erland Carlsson, and others. Intensely interested in the outcome, Olsson cautioned
against accepting the new Catechism adopted in Sweden
and urged careful and unhurried consideration of the
draft submitted. "My work on the committee is of small
worth; the thing of real value is a positive, fresh, full-
toned confession with respect to the fundamental doctrines of Christianity; and being *free*, why should we not
speak out so that our children may hear what has been
harped and piped? The Swedish Catechism has caught
a cold from the winds of the times and sounds hoarse."

It would be hard to say whether this message carried
more weight with the Synod than Olsson's personal pres-

ence would have done, for his personal influence in synodical affairs was already notable; but the minutes of the proceedings of that convention show that his views on most points at issue prevailed. No fault was found with him for not having been able to remove the entire debt resting on the Synod's school. A revised constitution for the Synod was adopted, leaving due powers in the hands of its constituent Conferences, no split or secession resulting. And, lastly, the Synod's own version of Luther's Catechism was adopted. Olsson closed his message with words characteristic of his humility and lack of self-assertiveness: "My illness has caused me profound sorrow and regret, making me, against my will, a liability to the school during the past year. Should there be any man to put in my place, the brethren need not hesitate to do so. By the grace of God, I would not take it amiss, although the call to teach compelled me to leave a dearly beloved congregation." Only to this part of Olsson's message from abroad the convention paid no heed.

From each of the historic Luther places, the traveler sent letters of greeting. In Luther's chair at Wittenberg, on June 16, he penned this message to the Synod in general and to Augustana College and Seminary in particular: "Let us, strong through the power of Christ Jesus, unswervingly hold fast to the pure doctrine as Luther taught it out of the Word of God by the guidance of His Spirit." The next day he was at Wartburg, enraptured by the beauty of its environment and the historic treasures of the old castle. Seated at the table where Luther worked on his translation of the Bible, Olsson wrote: "Let us diligently study Holy Writ, for that is the sum of all theology," adding later, "You would hardly believe how lavishly the wonders of God's creation have been heaped in the lap of this place. The cross above, on the castle tower, verdant nature below and all around me—if anything could make me a poet, this would have done so. But—impossible! Yet in my heart I praise the Lord for the Light of the Word spread anew over the world from this magnificent stronghold."

At Worms, at Augsburg, and in the Coburg Castle, Olsson reveled in Reformation memories and memorials as only an ardent Lutheran theologian could do.

In Hermannsburg, while visiting the famous institute for education, missions, and charity which was the creation of Th. Harms, Olsson wrote, after attending a festive event: "During the addresses and the intercourse I naturally thought of Rock Island and our rather well-behaved, but sometimes naughty and tricky youngsters. . . . The beauty and simplicity of Hermannsburg, oh, how they appeal to my rustic mind! I have always held this against the dear old fathers, that they placed our school in a large town. When in another chapter I shall describe the exterior beauty and surrounding quiet here, I hope to do so in such a way that we all would like to gather at our school, pick it up and carry it away to Andover, Lindsborg, or some other rural locality, where the farmers are not all too close-fisted. But no, my friends, I do not want to tear up things—indeed not. It is not my purpose to be unkind to our dear city folk, but that I love the country more than the city, that fact I can never conceal." Augustana remained in Rock Island, but the suggestion of a school in Lindsborg was more than a fancy. The thought of the teacher was materialized by one of his students two years afterward.

From Dresden, Olsson wrote to Hasselquist April 12, with the impressions from the rendition of "The Messiah" in London still fresh in his mind: "Never shall I forget that evening, and not until in heaven will I be privileged to hear greater music. . . . Now there remained for me only one more desire in a musical way—to hear J. S. Bach's oratorio of the Passion. And, dear Uncle, what do you think? Even that joy was vouchsafed to me." Upon his arrival in Leipsic on Maundy Thursday, the traveler found that that very oratorio was to be rendered there on Good Friday evening.

"In my simplicity, I prayed the Lord to grant me the strength to attend. I did, and though utterly weak, I hardly felt my weariness. . . . In London the orchestra and chorus were more powerful, but believe me, Uncle, Bach's chorales, interspersed in his oratorio, these are, in a word, *heavenly*. In them the evangelical chorale of the Lutheran church has found its unexcelled utterance. And then, the masterly organ interludes—there the harmonic art has scored its greatest triumph. In my simple way, I believe nothing on this earth could excel that organ music. . . . Should any wonder that I wanted to be in Leipsic merely to hear a piece of music, I would forgive their faultfinding and say in my own defense that it is the joy of my heart to listen to the gospel of the cross and that to me the most precious of all sermons is that gospel sung and played. As did Bach, no mortal has ever been able to proclaim in music the message of the cross. I least of all know how to describe his celestial music— for so it truly is. Yet I have a sense of appreciation of such music, far as it surpasses my ability to understand."

On his way to Leipsic, the historical scholar made this comment on passing rapidly through Elberfeld and vicinity, notable in church history: "While my train speeded through these regions, especially along the Fulda River, noted in the history of missions, I thought of St. Boniface, that Christian hero of the Middle Ages who penetrated forests and wildernesses to bring the Word of God to the wild, powerful Germans. Why, indeed, do the higher schools devote themselves so eagerly to the study of slaughter and bloodshed while the heroes of peace are mostly consigned to oblivion? When a man is constrained by love for Christ to force his way through the midst of wild tribes in order to convert them by the gospel of peace and make of them a Christian people— that I call true heroism. What would even the powerful people of Northern Europe be today if the medieval missionaries had not risked life and all to Christianize the migrant barbarian hordes from Asia? May we be given grace to educate at our school in Rock Island heroes ready to sacrifice temporal comfort and worldly fame, brave enough to endure the threats, the attacks, the derision of our modern savages in bearing Christ's message to the people of Christian lands which are about to become, or already are, paganized. God grant that we may bring up Christian champions willing also to go out to the dark heathen lands where the gospel messenger has to sacrifice everything for Christ's cause. How we are shamed by those medieval evangelists, we who have a clearer gospel light and yet are so loath to sacrifice, renounce, and suffer! A Boniface, an Ansgar, and a thousand others, who had very little of the gospel light, gladly gave their powers and their whole life to the work among

pagan races. Think of their parsonages, their means of
travel, their meager comforts of life! Little enough it
was! We pastors have every reason to repent in sack-
cloth and ashes when we recall how we too often look
after the things that are seen. This is not said to scold
churches that are so favorably situated as to provide a
fair and decent living for their pastors, but I would remind us elders and particularly the young men who have
entered, or are about to enter, the holy ministry that,
by the grace of God, we must guard against presuming
on great temporal comfort and a good living in our
preaching of the gospel. It is bad enough if a clergyman
becomes selfish and arbitrary, indolent and haughty, but
no better when church members in general who are well-
to-do grow so miserly that they would have their pastor
a ragamuffin struggling to make both ends meet. May
I be forgiven for indulging in such reflections in passing
through the mission field of old St. Boniface."

A glimpse of Weimar, "a little town claiming to be
the Athens of modern times, the capital of German culture, philosophy, and belles lettres," gave rise to these
comments, characteristic of Olsson as a Christian scholar:
"Here the two great poets of Germany, Goethe and
Schiller, loved to dwell, here rest the bones of these idols
of the German people. One may exalt the genius of these
men; even a Christian may have cause to admire the
wealth of beauty, the many high and noble thoughts and
sentiments found in their writings, yet the truth is, to
the German nation they glorified paganism more than
they did Christianity. It is equally true that he who
would take these men as his guides in life and in death
walks in darkness and knows not where they would bring

him. The love of Christ, which surpasses all knowledge, was not permitted to rule the heart and life of these men; hence there is in their works no power or savor from on high. One walks as in a flower garden in reading their artfully wrought poems; then finds the flowers artificial and the words of these masters, after all, devoid of spirit and life. . . . One can not without profound regret take note of the idolatry of their great poets practiced by the Germans. I remember with utter disgust the ludicrous show lay and learned folk in Germany made of themselves during the Schiller commemoration in 1859. I shall never forget the disagreeable impression made on my youthful mind by a Schiller memorial sermon preached by that great theologian Kahnis on Advent Sunday that year in the Pauline church at Leipsic. Well may we value the beauty of human thought in the words of the poets, yet— beware of rushing, body and soul, into the bottomless marsh in pursuit of a will-o'-the-wisp."

At Leipsic he lost no time in visiting the simple monument to Johann Sebastian Bach erected in front of the Thomas school, where Bach was a cantor and a teacher of music. There he goes into ecstatic reveries over the man who "in his life and his music made such a beautiful confession of Christ the Crucified." His thoughts at this shrine he summed up in the words: "Of Bach's music it must be said in the fullest sense that it is a confession indeed, *the Confession of the Lutheran Church set to music.*"

In a later account of his visit to Spurgeon's tabernacle in London to hear that eminent preacher, the traveler made this typical apology to his readers: "I suppose you will take me, an orthodox Lutheran, to task at once for my eagerness to hear a Baptist clergyman.

Must I write an apology for so doing? No, I will not apologize; I will only say what I have often said and what has always been my attitude: Every one who from the heart believes in Jesus as the Son of God and the true Substitute of sinners, he is my friend and brother in Christ. In other words, to him who sincerely believes and confesses the sum of the law and the gospel I heartily extend the hand of fellowship. Yet, in so doing I am so strict a Lutheran that I will not yield one iota of Lutheran doctrine, and such is my love that should one of my brethren in Christ of some other confession seek to win our people over to his teaching, I would tell him: "Fare thee well. I trust we shall meet in heaven; but the difference in our confessions compels us to stay apart in our work here below. The Lord will at last test the work of each and judge between me and thee. Should anyone term that an odd sort of fellowship, very well, let him do so; I know where I stand in this matter. Should any among us be unstable and want to do without a confession, I cry to them out of the depth of my heart, Hold fast, in the strength of our Lord Jesus hold fast to our old positive confession of faith, or you will drift like flotsam on the waves and land no one knows where."

This was Olsson's impression of Prague, where he spent Ascension Day:

"I wandered about all day in the history of the Hussites. Oh, how it stirs one's emotions to see the rich historic memorials in Prague! I will not dwell on them now. Today, however, I have seen Catholicism in its glory and its horror. Oh, Luther, how great you were by the power of God! I have stood in the hall where the Thirty-years' War began, in the frightful hole where the Hussites and others as state prisoners perished from hunger; I have witnessed the magnificent worship (of God?) in St. Veit's Cathedral; I have seen the skeleton of Nepomuk, the great saint, etc. etc."

Upon his return from Europe, Olsson wrote into his story of the tour the following farewell to Leipsic, which throws added light on his experiences while a student in the mission intitute in that city: "Before leaving Leipsic, I desired to see once more the mission house where I had spent a year and where I had to fight such bitter spiritual battles, within and without, that I expected nothing but disaster to body and soul. Those struggles and the studies and cares of that year broke my health and strength for the remainder of my earthly life. Some may want to know now why I left the mission institute at Leipsic. Then let me say briefly: To try to make a lively young *läsare* from Värmland feel at home in Leipsic during the years 1859 and 1860 was like teaching a fish to swim on dry land. Of course my youthful ignorance must bear a good part of the blame. But of the mission institute I am bound to say that orthodoxy without an intimate, childlike life in Christ is a wretched thing indeed. . . . I left that institute, not as a runaway, but with due permission and after proper arrangement with my unforgettable father, Doctor P. Fjellstedt. In the year 1879 I saw once again the mission house in Leipsic and looked back upon my former struggles and sins and recalled the Lord's unspeakable mercy upon me. How inscrutable are His ways! Taking it all in all, I hope the Lord will pour out His blessing richly upon the Leipsic Mission, and with that I take my leave of that city of learning."

XIII

PROMOTER OF HIGHER MUSIC

If the vacation trip to Europe by Professor Olof Olsson of the Augustana Theological Seminary was valuable to himself, it proved still more profitable to the Augustana Synod. His impressions and observations while there gave rise to two outstanding activities in his home church, the hospital and deaconess work, elsewhere accounted for, and the cultivation of higher music by oratorio societies and conservatories.

Not long after his return to Rock Island and to his chair in the seminary, Olsson went quietly about, interesting students and other young people of the community in the forming of a chorus capable of rendering great musical works such as he had heard while abroad. Carl Swensson, one of those students most keenly interested, wrote this recollection years later (*Vid hemmets härd*, p. 342): "After his return from Europe—I think it was in the fall or the spring of 1880—he talked with Lieutenant Joseph E. Osborn about the beautiful Messiah oratorio. His thoughts and words bore fruit in action. The Messiah [in part] was given that summer at the commencement. Thereby a fire was kindled which is still burning in Rock Island, in St. Peter, in Lindsborg, and in Wahoo."

In January, 1881, Olsson's plan took more concrete form through the organization of a large chorus named the Augustana Oratorio Society. After regular rehearsals, in which Olsson took part with great enthusiasm, often playing the organ score to aid the singers, the oratorio was rendered in the large First church of Moline, in neighboring communities, and at Chicago.

Carl Swensson, who had become Olsson's successor at Lindsborg and who started a small academy there in the fall of the same year, was powerfully influenced by Olsson's enthusiasm. In less than a year, he had enlisted the interest of the church choirs of the vicinity, and early in 1882 a large group of singers was rehearsing the same oratorio. At Eastertide that year "The Messiah" was rendered at Lindsborg for the first time. In a short time this chorus turned out to be the finest embodiment of Olsson's idea, outdoing the Rock Island chorus in numbers and in the excellence of their Messiah festivals.

Toward Easter of 1882, invitations came from Minneapolis, Omaha, and other distant places with requests for the oratorio society of Rock Island to render Handel's great work in their localities. Olsson saw that it could not be done: it would cost too much to send a large group of singers so far. Although he had to decline all such requests from distances that were prohibitive, Olsson improved the occasion by urging the formation of local oratorio societies wherever groups of churches made such concerted action possible. In an "Open Letter" to lovers of oratorio, published March 15, he said:

"For my own part, I consider spiritual song and music to be that pure and very precious nard with which we even today ought to anoint the feet of Jesus so copiously that the whole church of God, yea, all the world may be filled with the odor of this ointment. Even though the cost might be more than three hundred shillings (dollars) for each music festival, this money would not be wasted. But there may not be many in our churches who approve of this interpretation of John 12."

Besides the economic objection, he pointed out a number of others. At that time and stage of development many church members had conscientious scruples about the use of certain musical instruments. Hence Olsson was obliged to make a lengthy argument in defense of their use. In the course of this apology for the use of an orchestra in support of the oratorio chorus, he wrote: "One obstacle in the way of our society is the need of certain musical instruments. If we were concerned with singing only, there would be no such difficulty, but it so happens that in Handel's and other oratorios the singing is to be accompanied by various instruments. These are objected to by many sincere Christians, and far be it from us to mock at tender consciences. Those who have been used to seeing certain instruments employed only for sinful purposes find it hard to believe that the same ones may be used in the service of God. Of a man long fettered by Satan, it is hard to believe that he may be released, and if conversion actually takes place with an old hardened sinner, one doubts its sincerity. This is true of certain musical instruments. Certain stringed instruments in particular are dangerous and detestable while used in the service of the devil, but become most delightful when employed by skilled hands to produce sacred music. In order to prevent all manner of misuse, many Christians insist that every instrument except the human voice and the church organ ought to be broken to pieces and thrown away. Indeed, many in the Reformed churches will have nothing to do even with the organ. But, alas, how frightfully even the human voice has been misused in the service of sin and Satan! If, then, we were to discard everything that has been or may be misused, what would there be left of ourselves or of all that God has made? . . . It is not without cause that I deal at some length with the question of what instruments we use in connection with our Messiah chorus. The utmost skill ought to be combined with a sanctified mind in the handling of such musical instruments; indeed, only a master and saint ought to play the violin if it is to produce the tones of sacred sweetness of which it is capable."

Still another difficulty pointed out was the lack of appropriate assembly halls where oratorios could be rendered. "We do not want to be driven to theaters and ordinary halls to sing 'The Messiah.' Then our society might easily be taken for a common theatrical troupe— the worst dishonor that could befall us. My desire is that our concerts and music festivals may become in fact divine services. . . . Again, I see no essential difference between charging admission and receiving a collection. One as well as the other ought to be done in true fear and love of God."

In this connection the father of oratorio singing in the Augustana Synod outlined his plan thus:

"If I could, and were permitted to do so, I should organize a new society within our church. It would not be a secret one—mark well. It would not bear my name. The requirements for entry should be: first of all, a devout Christian attitude and a sincere will to sacrificial service; second, a good voice for singing or proficiency on some musical instrument. The members would dress in ordinary garb, but with the stress on simplicity for both men and women, so as not to yield to the decrees of luxury and fashion. Then one would be spared the pain of seeing some make a display of themselves. The members would devote themselves to the Word of God and prayer and, besides their duties, to the cultivation of Christian song and churchly music and to charitable work among the sick, the poor, and those in misery. Thus it would be possible to render the glorious oratorios of Handel, Bach, and other masters at the great festivals of the church. Thereby the lost masses in the big cities might be attracted and admitted free of charge so that the gospel might be preached to them between choral numbers. In this way we would be able to render the musical works of the church with spirit and life in the highest form of musical art.—These are some of the fancies that haunt me as I lie awake nights tortured by severe headaches. Those who will may laugh at my dreams . . ."

But these were no idle fancies. His dream had already come true. At the very time of writing, Olsson's plan was taking concrete form. In that very "letter," he was able to announce the first Messiah concerts at Lindsborg and in surrounding churches, to be given at Easter.

"I am well aware," he wrote, "that in *Augustana* I am not supposed to mention Kansas, much less Lindsborg, but if the interdict is ignored for once, I hope to be pardoned. I only want to say that the church choirs in Lindsborg and its neighboring congregations are to begin the coming Easter season by singing several selections from "The Messiah" of Handel and that the singers are all young people of these congregations."

If the synodical mouthpiece restrained him from boosting Swensson's new school and other enterprises, Olsson was not to be hampered in his zeal for promoting the highest type of church music. He was heart and soul for the work started at Lindsborg by Swensson and did all in his power to aid him in making the first performance of "The Messiah" at Lindsborg a worthy one. He brought the college orchestra with him from Rock Island to accompany the Kansas singers and presided at the organ himself on that historic occasion when "The Messiah" was first sung on the prairies of Kansas. In recent years, Bach's great work, "The Passion of St. Matthew," has also been rendered. Of this, too, Olsson wrote from Germany after having heard it with rapture.

The yearly Messiah Festival at Bethany College has become an institution. The chorus has grown into a permanent community organization of upward five hundred singers. Around this chorus grew a large conservatory of music with an excellent college orchestra. These factors have given the college and town high repute; its musical activities have brought Bethany its national reputation and have carried its name abroad. People come from near and far to attend the Easter week music festivals, at which the foremost artists deem it a privilege and a distinction to appear in the solo parts. In the *World Almanac* the Messiah Festival at Lindsborg has been recognized as one of the great musical events of America. Thus Olsson's idea took root in the community he founded, and his love of immortal music may almost be said to pervade Lindsborg as its dominant spirit.

At his own institution, Olsson saw the art of music of the same high type flourish more or less for almost two decades, largely under his cultivation and care. The oratorio society founded by him maintained a high standard of musical culture at Augustana College which has endured down to the present time. Since April 12, 1881, the date of its first rendition of "The Messiah," that oratorio has alternated with other great musical works at the annual concerts given. It was rendered twice in Moline the following year and once at a noteworthy Luther festival at the college in November 1883.

With that festival Olsson had much to do—it was in fact his idea, carried out under his personal direction. No hall large enough to house the expected audiences being available, one had to be built. He conceived the idea of putting up a large structure on the slope of the college hill, which would form a natural amphitheater. With this advantage, a temporary concert hall with a capacity of nearly three thousand was actually built for $1,800. This unique building, named Jubilee Hall, served during the Luther Quadricentenary celebration as assembly room by day, concert hall in the evenings, and hotel by night. Here, on the 7th and 8th of November, the Oratorio Society gave two really grand concerts before audiences which taxed the capacity of the hall both evenings. On the first evening, "The Messiah" was rendered, on the second a number of Wennerberg's "Psalms of David" were sung. The chorus, under the direction of Joseph Osborn, sang to the accompaniment of Gustav Stolpe at the organ (an instrument built for the occasion), and the college orchestra reinforced by an orchestra newly formed at Bethany Academy. To all who took part, the festival was an inspiring event; moreover, it proved a financial success, the concert receipts of $1,400 taking the bulk of the burden off the shoulders of Olsson, on whom the pecuniary responsibility was laid.

In succeeding years the chorus rendered such works as "The Creation," by Haydn, "Elijah," by Mendelssohn, "The Daughter of Jairus," by Stainer, "The Woman of Samaria," by Bennett, "The Holy City," by Gaul, and others. Handel's great oratorio was not given annually, as at Bethany College, where it has been sung more than one hundred and fifty times; nevertheless the best musical traditions have survived at Augustana as at Bethany from Olsson's time to our own. In recent years, the rendition of "The Messiah" at Christmas has been made an outstanding musical event. Surely his spirit would rejoice, as it did at the hearing of Bach's Passion oratorio at Leipsic in 1879, to know that this masterly work, which Olsson deemed the highest form of earthly music, has been taken up and is now being sung by the choruses of the two institutions whose musical life he fathered and fostered.

In a historical sketch of "Oratorio Work at Augustana College" (*Augustana Bulletin*, March, 1906) Netta C. Anderson, an Augustana alumna, gives this estimate: "I doubt that Dr. Olsson even dreamed, when he gathered together the first chorus, that the movement would live and grow through all these years. It is indeed a heavy debt of honor and gratitude the college and the community at large owe to this noble man; for who shall calculate how far-reaching his influence has been and shall continue to be felt in bringing us to an appreciation of the best music."

The idea underlying the establishment of a conservatory of music at the Augustana institution of learning may also be traced to Olsson. The same year oratorio singing was introduced, he publicly expressed the desirability of having a permanent orchestra, a trained chorus, and a professor of music at the institution. We quote his words on this point: "If ever there was a place for an orchestra and a good chorus it is at a divinity school. There the great works of Handel, Bach, and other masters ought to be most thoroughly studied. In their sacred compositions there is more genuine theology than in many a heavy tome of Biblical exegesis and theological treatises. Had our congregations the correct conception of the matter, they would forthwith engage a competent professor of sacred music at our institution."

It remained for Prof. Olsson to discover the man for the place. From Longmont, Colorado, where he had pastoral charge during the summer vacation, Olsson wrote Hasselquist (August 23): "Director Stolpe is living in Denver without any chance of supporting himself. I think it is wrong to let a man of his attainments waste his time here and suffer want besides. I have heard him on the piano, and in my opinion he is a master. He is a man of sober Christian and firm Lutheran views and is a devoted churchman. Now I would inquire whether he might be engaged as instructor in music at the school. Should Director Stolpe come to us as a teacher, the students would find in him a man who by his superior accomplishments would gain their respect. While with him in Denver one day, I asked to hear selections from all the great masters I could recall. I did hear a long succession of noted and most difficult compositions, all played from memory, including selections from Em. Bach, the performance of which was certainly no child's play."

Gustav Stolpe, the man in question, was an organist, pianist, violinist, and director of music from Sweden who had come to the United States for a concert tour in 1881. The enterprise did not prove a financial success, and thus a musician of great skill was available to Augustana just when the institution needed such a man. He was called as professor of music that fall on recommendation of Olsson at whose suggestion he also became organist of the large First Church of Moline in 1883.

The next step in the promotion of musical art at Augustana was taken in 1886, when a conservatory of music was privately established. The ground work had already been done by Olsson in connection with the oratorio chorus and the professorship. President Hasselquist, himself a singer, held that "the cultivation of the art of song ought to be a required subject throughout the institution." Due to the efforts of the two theologians and music lovers, the new music school was incorporated with the institution in 1887, with Stolpe at its head. This outstanding virtuoso and composer was connected with the school for more than a decade. Some of its best musical traditions date from his time, and Olsson's enthusiasm for sacred music in its highest form is living still in musical activities which recently have gained for Augustana national reputation as a musical center.

When in the year 1887 a hymnal in the English language for the Augustana churches was first contemplated, Professor Olsson was chosen to head the committee elected to work out such a book. His colaborers were to be Pastor Nils Forsander, Mr. John A. Enander, and Professors C. P. Rydholm and S. M. Hill. Except for the last named, these contributed nothing to the book that was eventually produced in 1901. Work was long deferred to await a proposed revision of the Psalmbook of the Church of Sweden on which to draw in producing English versions of favorite hymns. No revised book then forthcoming—it took fifty years before it was adopted— the Synod in 1895 decided to go on with its project. The theological faculty was commissioned to prepare the proposed book. Olsson, remaining as chairman, directed the work now taken up in earnest. He called into service men of the college faculty, including C. W. Foss, A. O. Bersell, P. M. Lindberg, V. O. Peterson, and E. A. Zetterstrand, and drafted others living near the college, clergy and lay, among them Albert Rodell, Emil A. Edlen, John Jesperson, John Telleen, and the present writer. This committee worked with a will—if one ever did. In the heat of summer, these men met weekly, were assigned hymns to turn into English, by the sweat of their brow, and brought in the results such as they were. The scripts were read, referred, revised, resubmitted, re-examined, rejected, or re-revised. Within the year quite a number of the best loved Swedish hymns and gospel songs were put into English dress. The work went on, a new volunteer lending his hand and pen now and then. After several years of accumulation, much of what is best in Swedish hymnody had been translated, and that element in the new compilation was thought to be adequately provided for. Professor Foss shared with Olsson most of the work on the hymnal project, and to him much credit is due for the finished work. Not only was he a skillful translator himself; the work of most of the other translators was made acceptable by his revision. He was appointed to edit the material, and in 1901 Olsson could report to the Synod the completion of the hymnal, a book of 355 hymns, about fifty of which were from the Swedish. Although a temporary book of worship, it is worthy of note here, not only as largely Olsson's work, but more so as the first book of its kind in the English language that drew in any considerable measure on the rich hymnodic treasury of the Church of Sweden.

Olsson had a part also in the production of the first English church manual of the Synod. In 1897, a committee of six began work on the translation of the Swedish church service into the English of our present church book. Dr. Bartholomew, who acted as secretary and who later was chosen to see the new church book through the press, tells us: "While Dr. Olsson was not officially a member of the committee, he was often present at its meetings and participated in the discussions, so that nothing found its way into the new book without his knowledge and sanction. He had an important part in arranging the music for the altar service. At a meeting of the committee October 9, the secretary was instructed to ask the faculty of the conservatory, through its president, Dr. Olsson, to take in hand the arrangement of the music for the new church service book. As a matter of fact, the musical part of the service was largely the work of Dr. Olsson and Dr. Stolpe. Subsequently this sub-committee on music was requested to arrange the same music for the Litany as that given in the Swedish service, and to see that the music for the *Agnus Dei* be printed both as it is in the English and in the Swedish service." From this it appears that Dr. Olsson had much to do with the making up of the new church service book.

XIV

FATHER OF BENEVOLENT INSTITUTIONS

About Easter time, on his European tour in 1879, Olsson had made a short stay at the Lutheran deaconess institute at Dresden, capital city of Saxony, the homeland of the Reformation. There he received "unforgettable impressions while visiting the rooms where sufferers from every kind of sickness were tenderly nursed, body and soul, by kind deaconesses." Moved by his recollections from that institution, Olsson during the following two years repeatedly pleaded with the Synod to found a deaconess institute and hospital. To all appearances, his was the very first public appeal for starting charity work of this kind within the Augustana Synod. It appeared in *Augustana och Missionären* for March 17, 1880, and as a first step toward the founding of the Augustana Hospital and Deaconess Institution in Chicago in 1882 it engages our interest. Under the head, "A Remarkable Bible Commentary," Olsson wrote in part:

"Herewith I would warmly recommend a Bible commentary, an explanation of the Gospels in particular, which is better, clearer, and more forceful than those of Luther, Rosenius, Fjellstedt, Gezelius, Starke, or any other that we love and value highly. . . . 'Oh,' you may say, 'that must be one he himself intends to write, and he is conceited enough to boast so highly of it!' No, my friend, I do not plan to write it, so you may calmly listen to the announcement. It is to be a peculiar work indeed. And, what is still more peculiar, every one who reads this, who is a member of an Augustana congregation, is earnestly and sincerely invited to take part in the writing of this commentary. Thus, we will be too many authors to have our names on the title page. We mean to have at least fifty thousand contributors. 'But,' someone remarks, 'all this is foolish and puzzling. Why not tell us at once what your idea is with this new book?' My friend, yet a few words, then you will learn what kind of commentary I have in mind. If you had lived at the time when the Lord Jesus walked visibly here on earth and had looked for Him, what outward signs, do you think, would have shown you where He was? Where you would have seen multitudes of sick people, halt, blind, maimed, possessed, wretched persons, lepers, cripples, there you could have been sure to find Jesus. . . . But tell me, what does this mean, that our Saviour during His earthly life devoted Himself almost entirely to the sick, the possessed, the poor, those in misery? Would it not have been better if He had preached constantly and given spiritual advice? Ought He not to have been busy writing books, especially works against unbelief and unbelievers? Just think what powerful refutations of error and unbelief He might have written! But mark well, He did not touch a pen. . . . His works of love were the most powerful proof of the truth of His teaching, His tender care of the unfortunate gave stronger testimony against infidelity than any written words. *Believe me for my work's sake*—thus He challenged the doubters. . . . Woe unto us Christians, who talk much and use big words, but when it comes to deeds done out of love to the Lord who redeemed us with His blood—what do we do?

"This brings me at last to the point I want to make about our interpretation of the Scriptures. Even though some may consider me foolish and unreasonable, I am bound to mention what has long been a burden on my heart. May I be forgiven for not being able to keep these thoughts back any longer. They will out, whether or not they will do any good. This matter is brought up, I assure you, without any intent to call attention to myself. I know, too, that I am not alone in pondering this thing. What thing?

"*As a church we must very soon have a deaconess institution in connection with a hospital. That is to say, our Synod must start some such work without delay. . . .*

"It would indeed be doubly gratifying to belong to our church body if we had such an institution. . . . There is no exposition of the Gospels more potent than a Christian hospital. The Christlike charity Christian people show to their suffering fellow men is a sermon straight to the heart. Now I think you know what kind of Bible commentary I have been speaking about. . . . Perhaps my appeal will go unheard. You may say, 'We have our schools and our orphans' homes; let that suffice as our commentary on the Word of God? Well may we rejoice over the part we have in working for Christian schools and children's homes—let us provide well for them—but as gospel interpretation that is not enough."

The writer explained his project further by urging first a central institute, which, if the enterprise prospered, might in time lead to the establishment of similar institutions in the states where members of the Synod were most numerous. These latter, he wrote, ought to be integrated with the principal one. As a central location for this, he suggested Chicago, where there would be need and suffering aplenty and which would therefore be a suitable place for our first large-scale institution of charity.

Olsson would not let his project rest. At first he planned to meet with interested persons in Chicago to discuss his plan. Failing in this, he wrote on the subject again, calling a meeting in the Moline church November 6th, in connection with the Reformation festival at Augustana College. There was already a sprinkling of small gifts toward the realization of the enterprise. The meeting took place as announced. Olsson himself made an address showing the charity work of the apostolic church to have been the fruit of true faith, while that of the Middle Ages degenerated into work-righteousness. The speaker pointed to the revival of the true life of faith through the Lutheran Reformation and its resurgence after the age of rationalism. Then faith again bore fruit in the form of pure charity, as exemplified in the founding of the first deaconess institute by the Protestants. This, he urged, should be the model for the institution he now proposed. The first step toward organization was taken in the appointment of a committee of seven headed by Olsson. The committee was to solicit and receive money, look for a site that might be purchased or donated, make inquiry about land held for hospital purposes in Chicago by Rev. W. A. Passavant of Pittsburgh, and ask for two experienced deaconesses from an institute in Stockholm.

On January 26, 1881, an article by Olsson in *Augustana* put the question, "Where Is Our Hospital to Be Built?" He felt encouraged by the decision of certain brethren of the Minnesota Conference to found such an institution in their state. Having learned that the brethren in Chicago desired larger representation in the committee, he encouraged them by all means to take the matter seriously in hand, explaining that the members from Rock Island and Moline would be glad of their co-operation since they already had their hands full in looking after the interests of the school. He warned them, however, against the selfish assumption, damaging to the project, that Chicago was the only possible location for the proposed institution. He considered Rockford, Illinois, another desirable location, and on visiting and inspecting a proposed site near that city he found it excellent—but too costly.

We next hear from him in the synodical paper (March 30) shortly after the Illinois Conference had endorsed his project, giving official approval by making the acting committee its own and adding an eighth member. Encouraging as this was, Olsson still confessed to a profound disappointment. The substantial contributions expected from the well-to-do had not been forthcoming; only the mites of the poor and a few small sums. He wrote: "It was not our intention that the poor should shoulder the burden of supporting this institution. From the first I had thought this work would appeal particularly to those who have possessions they ought to give away, but who want to see visible evidence that they are given to the Lord's cause. . . . I believe those who will listen at all to the Word of God and the voice of conscience will have to agree that a hospital among us would serve God's cause and hence we ought to work for it with all our might." This, his fifth appeal, he closed with a suggestion that "first we ought to pray God to select a man who would devote heart, soul, and body, and all his mind and powers to this cause," adding the hint that, as in England "The Messiah" of Handel was used by the composer himself and others to bring in money for benevolent institutions, so "we might here use the same spiritual ways in an attempt to thaw out many hearts which are frozen by indifference to the Lord and to the sufferings of mankind."

On May 11, Olsson reproduced from a Lutheran paper the story of how Lutherans in New York City had just organized to begin hospital work. Quoting in full the appeal there made, he added the comment: "Even if there is no clink in our treasury, we cannot let there be silence in our paper. Sooner or later we will no doubt wake up to the need of a hospital for our people. . . . I wonder how many among us would take the trouble to make a list of persons who would pledge one dollar or more per year for a hospital. I wonder whether anyone of us will live to see the day when it may be said: Praise God, now the Swedish Lutheran church in America has an institution for the care of the sick!"

Meeting in Moline October 28, the committee authorized by the Illinois Conference decided upon Lake View in the city of Chicago as the location of the projected institution, this in the form of a recommendation subject to the action of the next conference convention. While awaiting the decision of the Conference, Olsson visited churches in Minnesota shortly before Christmas 1881. Of this visit he wrote in his paper (he continued as associate editor until July 1882) under date of February 1:

"It happened as I thought and said: Minnesota got ahead of Illinois in starting a hospital. The Minnesota Conference now has a neat little home for the sick, well situated by picturesque Lake Como, near the city limits of St. Paul. The property, comprising ten acres of ground, a large dwelling, and several farm buildings, was acquired for the sum of $6,000. . . . Brother Montén is now engaged in soliciting fifteen hundred or two thousand dollars for remodeling the dwelling and equipping it for hospital purposes. The ingathering already foots up to twelve hundred dollars. I had the pleasure of pulling this load a little way up the hill. . . . It gave me great joy to see this neat-looking house by Lake Como, which, I have reason to hope, will soon be converted into a real home for the sick. For some time I have longed for the day when a Christian hospital would be founded within our Synod." Olsson's article contains a warm-hearted appeal for funds for the new Minnesota institution, with a plea for the future hospital in Lake View appended. Thus it appears that the institution at St. Paul was not only founded at Olsson's initiative but benefited from his personal efforts in the raising of funds.

When the Illinois Conference met at Chicago the following February, the recommendations made by the committee were adopted, whereby definite steps were taken toward founding the institution precisely as Olsson had planned. He was made one of the seven members of the first board of directors, the others being the three Chicago pastors, Erland Carlsson, C. B. L. Boman, and M. C. Ranseen, and three lay members, C. P. Holmberg,

G. A. Bohman, both of that city, and John Erlander of Rockford. On February 13 (1882) the board drew up and signed the charter for the new institution, which was named The Deaconess Institution of the Swedish Evangelical Lutheran Church, but known as the Augustana Hospital. It was founded on a site bought from Pastor Carlsson, and in his house, which went with the purchase, the hospital was opened later in the year. Olsson was to follow up negotiations with Pastor Bring with a view to securing two deaconesses from the institution in Stockholm. Nothing came out of this phase of his plan, however, since the new hospital was all that the Conference could carry for some years to come and a department for deaconess work was not realized. In the course of time the little institution begun at Chicago in 1882 grew in size and usefulness, and as one of the city's foremost institutions of its kind the present Augustana Hospital bears eloquent testimony of the one who fathered it. This man was Olof Olsson.

That part which was to apply to the proposed deaconess institute was eventually dropped from the corporate name of this institution, yet the idea survived. Intimate letters were exchanged between Olsson and Pastor E. A. Fogelström from time to time during the years following, as posthumous papers show. When the latter, in 1890, while pastor of the Immanuel church of Omaha, Nebraska, there founded the Immanuel Hospital and Deaconess Institute, now the official deaconess institution of the Augustana Synod, it may well be that in this good work he was prompted by his friend and fellow enthusiast and that thus Olsson's idea again came to life and bore fruit.

At the request of the board, the founding of the hospital in Chicago was made public by Olsson, who connected the news story with still another ardent appeal in behalf of the institution that was to be. He was, furthermore, chosen by the Conference to solicit the funds that the project called for. His duties as a teacher and as a pastor—that summer he was to serve a church in Colorado—left him little time for this task, so he had to beg off as traveling solicitor, but he continued to promote as best he could in other ways the new undertaking. His interest in these charitable institutions never relaxed, and it may be truly said that each one of them was a child of his brain and his heart, the fruit of his prayers and of his love and sympathy for his fellow men.

XV

SOLICITOR FOR AUGUSTANA COLLEGE

Just before and at the time Augustana College and Theological Seminary was being removed from Paxton, Illinois, and established at Rock Island, in 1874–75, the institution was in great financial distress. A per-capita fee of twenty-five cents per year, voted by the Synod toward its support, was but indifferently paid in, causing the deficit in the college treasury to mount higher year by year. To provide much-needed funds for the maintenance of the school, the Synod first sold *Hemlandet*, its general weekly newspaper, for $10,000, in 1872, to the Chicago firm of Enander and Bohman, and two years later disposed of its printing plant, book store, and publishing rights for $17,000, the purchasers being the firm of Engberg, Holmberg, and Lindell, also of Chicago. The $27,000 realized by these transactions and payable in installments brought in an average of $2,000 for the next few years, yet by the year 1878 a debt of more than twenty-seven thousand had been incurred.

Then the authorities concluded that time for effectual measures was at hand. Professor Olsson, who had taught in the seminary two years and had come to live permanently in Rock Island only one year before, was put in charge of a general ingathering. He had a facile pen, a resourceful mind, and what was most needful, a courageous enthusiasm for the cause of education.

197

A campaign paper named *Skolvännen* was started to serve as his mouthpiece. It was published once a month, or nearly so, which would be a leisurely mode of appeal in our day, yet it had its effect. As solicitor, Olsson was given two students, J. H. Randahl and Carl Swensson, as office assistants; otherwise, it appears, he carried on the campaign single-handed. *Skolvännen* was filled with appealing articles, almost all from Olsson's pen. Writing or speaking, the solicitor referred to himself as the "Beggar Boy," a title in which he took great pride as having been officially conferred on him by an institution of learning.

Most of the appeals were in a light, cheerful, chatty vein—"childlike and good-humored," Hasselquist, the president of the school, called them. Now and then the arguments were earnest, insistent, importunate, the prayers of one consumed with zeal for his cause. But Olsson always urged giving in the spirit of love—painlessly, not, in the damaging phrase, "till it hurts." He asked for large gifts, then repented and begged for small ones as being the greater blessing. And the response was mostly in the form of little contributions, many of them given at some sacrifice. Children sent in their candy money or other allowance; one person gave a gold chain that was a cherished keepsake; a farmer offered to ship a 400-pound hog; an orphaned girl, bedridden for eleven years, sent a dollar—the price brought by her father's ear rings and her mother's wedding ring. Besides writing, Olsson traveled, preached, and prayed in behalf of the school. One specimen of Olsson's arguments for the support of Augustana College taken from *Skolvännen* was this:

"It is well known that our fathers in Sweden gave to the universities of Uppsala and Lund many large landed estates which were to belong to them in perpetuity. These are rented out, and the university bursars need only to call on the tenants when in need of money. It seems to me that our school in Rock Island, on the whole, has as many tenancies as Uppsala and Lund, or more. Haven't you heard of them? Well, let me tell you, every farmer in the Synod is a tenant of one of the properties of our college and seminary. I have taken a copy of the abstract of title. . . . 'Ha,' some one exclaims, 'these Augustana preachers are fixing things up as they were in the Middle Ages, so the land will be under the control of the church and nobody will have any say about his own property.' Yes, dear friends, this is the very theory we preach: *The earth is the Lord's and the fullness thereof.* And when we have to do with those who are His children, we are quite certain their earthly possessions also are the Lord's and have been devoted to use for His kingdom."

In December, Olsson could report a total of $16,790 in cash receipts from the campaign carried on mainly through the few numbers of *Skolvännen* published by him. In number twelve, issued in October 1879, he could announce that the Synod had relieved him of further concern with the finances of the school by allocating the remainder of the school debt to the constituent Conferences. How much credit was due the aggressive solicitor and his campaign paper for the seventeen thousand and more paid in to the institution during that fiscal year is a matter of conjecture. It is hard to see, however, how the little school with mounting deficits could have continued much longer without the very substantial sum

raised through Olsson's energy and power of appeal. That
was the opinion of Hasselquist, president of the institution, as expressed in official reports, and of Norelius as
stated in his history of the Synod. This was the second
time the educational institution of the Synod was rescued
from threatening financial disaster. The first was five
years before, when the board of directors saved it from
impending bankruptcy by selling the synodical publication business, including the weekly *Hemlandet*, for the
benefit of the school.

Skolvännen was discontinued in May 1880, after fifteen numbers had been published. It was revived in 1883
to further the raising of funds for a new college building
and again in 1887 to supplement that ingathering. Spo-
radic issues appearing in 1894 to promote the general
interests of the school did not bear Olsson's name or the
stamp of originality that marked all writing over the
familiar "O. O." signature.

In the jubilee year 1883, the four hundredth anniversary of Luther's birth, when a plan was launched to
erect a new classroom building—now known as "Old
Main"—, Olsson was again drafted to head the campaign
for funds. The first step was to prepare for an appropriate
festival to be held at Rock Island in commemoration of
the great Reformer. That work, too, was largely left to
him, and it was no perfunctory task. An assembly hall
had to be built, large enough to hold the large audiences
looked for and to shelter many of the visitors. Programs
with a number of speakers and much music had to be
drawn up. A jubilee chorus had to be assembled from
surrounding churches to render works by Handel, Bach,
Haydn, and Wennerberg. A week of rehearsals at the

college called for the housing and keep of many of the singers. Provisions for the feeding of the expected multitude were solicited from congregations far and near. In addition, Olsson issued an anniversary book, entitled *Luther-Kalender*, the contents of which were largely from his own pen.

The so-called Jubilee Hall was built on the slope of Zion Hill south of the present Gymnasium and Auditorium building, the incline providing a natural "gallery" with rude plank benches seating two thousand or more. It had to be large but cheap, with low walls and a vast area of shingled roof. Many of the older pastors remember when it was built. They were young students then and willingly pushed the wheelbarrows and wielded hammer and saw under Professor Olsson as construction boss. (Compare KARL A. MARTIN, *Från Östervåg*, p. 80.) No thought could be given to architectural style, and while gratified at its completion, he was not proud of the structure. Built for an emergency, it was made to serve as college gymnasium and occasionally as a festival hall for almost ten years. For the history it helped to make as the stage of the first large-scale Reformation Festival at Augustana, the building and its various functions may well be described here in Olsson's own words:

"In the first place, the festival building where we are to assemble is so simple as not to stand the gaze of any but plain folk. The proud would only scoff at it, and that they may do to their heart's content, just so they stay away from our festival. In erecting our assembly or jubilee hall, we had to economize on lumber so as to keep the cost down as near one thousand dollars as could be done. . . . When our wealthy farmers build their barns,

they even adorn them with little steeples and paint and
decorate them one way or another. Our jubilee hall has
no tower; neither will it be painted unless some kind
friend should stumble on a happy thought and send us
the wherewithal to paint the hall red. I wonder where
that honorable gentleman resides. But how does the
structure look? Like a barn? No. Like a church? No.
Its appearance is altogether indescribable. But at least
it has a regular roof of shingles, so visitors need fear
neither rain nor snow; and good solid walls, so that with
a couple of gigantic stoves we will be able to temper the
cold and make the concourse of visitors comfortable. At
night most of the building will be turned into a huge
bedroom for the men. The ladies will be accommodated
in private houses and in our class rooms. Mattresses are
being made from coffee bags and filled with straw. That
is all the bedding we furnish. Hence our guests will have
to bring blankets, shawls, and whatever covers they can
find." (*Skolvännen*, October 1883.)

In planning the musical program for the jubilee,
Olsson's experience from the renditions of "The Messiah" two years before stood him in good stead. Through
his efforts and partly under his personal direction, a large
chorus was brought together and drilled for the occasion.
Neither did the members of local and neighboring congregations and other visitors fail to meet his wishes in
the matter of food supplies, for the guests ate their fill
at fifteen cents a meal while in Rock Island.

This notable Luther Festival took place November
7–8, the exercises well-nigh filling the two days. Olsson
himself made one of the seven addresses, and he was often
at the organ or the piano during the musical renditions.

Sacred concerts were given both evenings, when the festival chorus rendered "The Messiah" almost entire, two Bach numbers, one selection from "The Creation" by Haydn, and eight of Wennerberg's "Psalms of David." In Olsson's opinion the occasion called for music of a high order, and with his artistic taste he was seldom satisfied with any but the best. Elsewhere he characterized the works of these masters as "tonal sermons and homilies." When the commemoration was over, he modestly limited his comments on the program to a sentence: "*Skolvännen* had too much to do with the festival to say anything further about it here."

Luther-Kalender, the memorial publication of 1883, written or compiled by Olsson, was published with two objectives in view—an ideal and a pecuniary one. The first he explained thus: "It is a sad lack on the part of our people—forgive me for saying it—that they have so little appreciation for history and historical events, especially for church history and the memory of God's great wonders through His church on earth. Have we cut off our connection with both secular and church history by leaving the land of our fathers, so beautiful and so rich in historic memories? If we saw off that branch of the church on which we are sitting, we will fall, it is hard to say how far." In the second place, this work of his was designed to bring in something to the building fund that was being raised.

With the Luther anniversary festivities serving as a springboard, Olsson and others threw themselves into a campaign which yielded money enough to warrant the school in starting to build. But even with the aid of an unsolicited donation of $25,000 from Mr. P. L. Cable of the Rock Island railroad, only the exterior of the building could be completed. For several years it stood there with doors and windows boarded up, dark and cavernous within and looking none too reputable from without. Who had failed it is not easy to say, but to all appearances the enterprise was a failure.

Then for the third time Olsson was drafted for service as solicitor for school funds. *Skolvännen*, after an interval of four years, again appeared. The editor was the same man as in 1878 and 1883. Other leaders in the Synod had written time and again about its needs and financial perplexities, but no other man, it seemed, could make the popular appeal that Olsson did. In the twentieth number of his special mouthpiece (April 1887), he spoke again in behalf of the school. Taking the Synod folk into his confidence as before, he wrote:

"*Is it necessary?* What? This very question: Is it necessary to make an ingathering for the new college building at Rock Island once again? Judge for yourselves, dear friends. Here that building has been standing now a long, long time without windows, without doors, and entirely unfinished within. Railway trains and street cars pass it daily with masses of strangers and of our local citizens. All are looking and pointing their fingers at this new but old structure which the Augustana Synod has reared but, as it seems, never intends to complete. What kind of church body can it be that takes care of its oldest and foremost educational institution in that fashion? If that is love, surely its affection is of a very peculiar kind. Should a congregation build a church and then let it stand for years with nothing but walls and roof, what would you say of such a congregation?"

The announcement that more than thirteen thousand dollars had been raised by the foregoing effort was made in these cheerful words: "That so large a sum could be gathered for our common institution at Rock Island in such hard times and with so little toil and trouble is indeed cause for hearty thanksgiving." It was estimated that fifty cents from each adult member of the Synod would finish the building, and in article after article Olsson now sought to kindle the interest and zeal needed to bring this about.

This time a sad chord sounds through all of Olsson's appeals. "Dear brethren," he writes, "I would gladly do our school some kind little service, but it is almost impossible for me to write. My sorrow smothers my words." His beloved wife had died suddenly a few weeks before, and he was steeped in profound grief; yet he had added to his teaching duties this extra task—to him not a burden but a labor of love. Listen to his pleading:

"Oh, to have the power to instill fifty cents worth of love in the heart of every church member! Can the Lord do this? Will He? If there were real heroes of prayer among us, we would surely receive this gift from Him—for it must be His gift, or it will amount to nothing. Shall we for once be one people, with one heart, one soul, united in support of our common institution? Could our daughters in St. Peter, Lindsborg, and Wahoo [the schools of the Conferences] possibly oppose such a feast of love and unity?"

The charge that pride was back of the scheme and that the new building was needlessly fine is answered thus: "If you belong to a congregation with many church-goers, but a small, low, and stuffy sanctuary, where the air grows so thick one is in danger of suffocating, would it be a matter of pride to build a new, roomy edifice with plenty of space and fresh air? Why go to church if the air is so unwholesome and fetid that one is stupified body and soul in trying to listen to the Word of God? Much better then stay at home and sleep in bed! . . . This is true also of a school building. Now we are able both to erect and to finish and equip a more sanitary building at Rock Island—if we want to do so. Then, let us not be so humble as to let wind and weather have the new building all to themselves while we ourselves are still sitting in the little old crowded rooms."

Another well-aimed argument followed: "What good purpose is served by erecting new, fine churches if we fail to educate pastors capable of preaching in those churches and caring for souls in those congregations? The future of our entire Synod depends, under the grace of God, on well educated ministers. If we will not assume the cost, then let us discontinue our work at once."

This first appeal by the heart-sick solicitor ended with a pathetic plea: "*Skolvännen* ought of course to be in very good spirits, but no one can be merry and lighthearted to order. If the hearts of our dear friends were moved by true love and pity, they would hasten to send each a half-dollar toward finishing our building and thus relieve from all writing and worry about money matters a man whose heart is torn to shreds by grief and bereavement. I would not write; I would pray. In sorrow nothing avails but silent prayer."

All that spring, summer, and fall, until October, Olsson wrote, traveled, talked, and preached in behalf of the college and seminary, with which he had been connected for eleven years and as whose chief spokesman he was looked upon wherever he appeared. We say *preached* with a stress, for in his many sermons, on visitations to the congregations in all parts of the Synod, he rarely neglected to emphasize that education is vital to any church body and that Christian schools and theological seminaries are the peculiar instruments with which God works to propagate His kingdom. This time he was intimately associated in the work with Pastor Erland Carlsson, who had assumed the position of business manager of the school to help put the ingathering through and to complete the building. Half of the money needed had come in by fall, and work on the interior was well advanced when Olsson laid down his task. His health was failing, and he felt compelled to give up his chair in the seminary, his resignation to take effect at the close of the academic year, in June 1888. His plan at that time was to retire to a little home of his own and take his rest—for a year at least.

XVI

BEREAVEMENT AND CONSOLATION

From his youth on, Olsson was never in robust health. This fact at times put limits to an activity that was nevertheless greater and more varied than that of most men in positions of leadership and trust. On his second "begging trip" for the school, in 1884, he tells us, he was often so worn down with talking and traveling that many engagements had to be canceled. Again he had assumed a like task in lieu of vacation after a year's teaching and lecturing and under the added burden of a great bereavement when his beloved wife Anna was taken by death. He bore up under the loss with the fortitude that Christian faith alone can lend, and went on with the work assigned to him as long as his strength lasted. It has been said that Olsson's feelings sometimes ran away with his better judgment. Be that as it might at other times, in this most crucial test it was not so. He did not resign his professorship until his health was badly impaired. To this condition other causes may have contributed, yet the most likely one was overwork.

The death of Mrs. Anna Olsson on March 18, 1887 (the published obituary erred in stating that the burial took place in September 1887) ended a most happy and congenial marital union which had lasted through weal and woe for twenty-three years. Sensitive and contemplative soul that he was, Olsson mourned her profoundly, but with the serene hope and certitude that goes with Christian faith. His own description of her passing away is preserved. Without invading the sanctity of the scene, so much may be revealed as shows the beauty of a Christian deathbed, such as this, and the full-hearted mutual devotion that pervaded the union it dissolved. Olsson himself did not deem his account too confidential to be given to a friend of Mrs. Olsson who had been employed in their home in Lindsborg for six years. His letter to Mrs. Anna Berg, of Lindsborg, April 3, 1887, reads in part:

"In the morning of the day of her death we awoke about 4 o'clock. She came over to my bed, and we talked almost till six, when I arose. Among other things, we spoke of which one of us had most to forgive in the other. I said—and say it yet—that I was most at fault. She said, 'No, the faults have been mostly mine.' Then we most heartily declared to one another that all was forgiven, just as we had always done in speaking of these things. 'Anna,' I said, 'I shall—I will love you in my latter years more fervently than ever before.' So I felt, and so I feel now. She was glad and grateful, as always, for kindness and love. Thus we parted that morning, glad and happy. . . . At the supper table she ate and was cheerful like the rest of us. I was away that evening until about 10 o'clock. Hearing she was then awake, I went to her bed and asked how she felt. 'I feel faint,' she answered. This was not uncommon with her, and I gave her the usual medicine. I sat a long while at her bedside to wait upon her. When all was quiet, I sought my own bed and went to sleep. 'Come,' she called suddenly, and I got up and sought to make her comfortable.

Soon she ran into my room and sat down in a sofa. I tried to cool her temples with water. A moment later she exclaimed, 'I am dying,' and uttered a short prayer. 'Jesus is here,' I assured her, again and again. She looked at me with clear eyes, but said nothing more. Her face paled, but she breathed lightly as I laid her down. Soon all was over. Not a moan, not the stir of a limb—truly, this was falling asleep."

Sometimes, in supreme moments such as this, men's hearts are opened, permitting a glimpse into their innermost soul. Some of the thoughts that surged through the mind of the devoted husband and father as he stood at the deathbed, he put into words:

"The darling of my youth, the beloved one who had filled my wedded life with temporal bliss—now she is gone from me and our dear children. . . . All the past seems like a short dream. . . . Many a time as we talked together, she told me how that when she married me she thought she got an angel. My poor, dear little Anna, how sadly she was disappointed! What she got was just a poor sinful man. And yet, he was one who with all his shortcomings desired to follow his Saviour. Oh, to be without sin, completely holy! Now, by the grace of God, I ought to become truly heavenly-minded. In heaven is my Lord and Saviour; my faithful Anna is there, and there are our four little ones. There, by God's grace, I desire to be with my other four. Would that I were a heavenly being!"

His wife's death inspired Olsson to much thinking on immortality and the life to be. The result was a little book of meditations published under the title *Det kristna hoppet* (Christian Hope). It abounds in beautiful thoughts on the life hereafter, interspersed with ideas that to many seemed too fanciful and earned him his reputation as a mystic. Gustaf N. Swan, the writer, critic, and literary collector, deemed this a remarkable book in many respects. In *Olla Podrida*, a series of essays on Swedish literature in America, he says of it: "The author deals with the subject of the association of the survivors with those departed and their reunion in a better world, quoting also Lavater, the German thinker, on an episode in his own life. The book attracted no small attention, and it is related that certain of his ultraorthodox brethren purposed to charge the author with heresy at the next following meeting of the Synod. . . . If anyone now remembers or reads that book, it is mostly because of the less flattering reputation thereby gained for it." The fact that the matter was never brought up on the Synod floor is probably sufficient proof that the charge was not well founded. At all events, devout readers shared with its author the comfort he sought to derive for himself from speculation as to the state of the dead and on things to come in the kingdom of the blest. His quotation from Lavater recalls the fact shown in his writings and attested by his students that Olsson read the works of that scholar and shared some of his views. The two men were alike in more ways than one, it may be noted in passing, should anyone look for a reason for this spiritual affinity. They had in common great depth of feeling, especially on religious themes, and remarkable fluency of fervent and persuasive discourse, based on genuine depth of conviction; poetic and picturesque conception and mode of expression; a mystical turn in their theological thinking; extraordinary personal influence, giving each a large following. Both men were consulted as spiritual advisers by thousands, either in person or by correspondence. The parallel does not hold throughout, for the popular eighteenth century preacher was erratic and bigoted to a degree and laid himself open to the charge of superstition and hypocrisy, while Olsson, the outstanding Augustana preacher of his time, was tolerant of all views not patently unchristian, but fought ignorance, deception, bigotry, and error with tongue and pen to the last. Lavater wrote a work to further the knowledge of mankind and love to men, and the writings of Olsson everywhere manifest his sympathy for the poor, his fellow feeling for the toilers, his love for the common man.

XVII

AN INTERVAL

The Galesburg meeting of the Augustana Synod in 1888 marks a cloudy interval in the life of Olof Olsson. The very convention which heaped praises upon him for his past services as a teacher of theology and voted him a sum of money to be raised by a synod-wide ingathering in gratitude for the extra services rendered by him for the good of the synodical institution of learning left a pain in his heart which took much time to heal. While that action and the resolution of thanks are duly recorded, the published proceedings show no trace of that procedure in which some of the brethren of the clergy sought to put Olsson the theologian out of their way for good and all. It was not a set trial for erroneous teaching, but the attacks made on Olsson in the secret session of the ministerium aimed to make out the Synod's most militant champion of Christian doctrine as a heretic.

The assailants of Olsson's position as a theologian were chiefly Pastors S. P. A. Lindahl and P. Sjöblom. Indirectly and in his absence, it has been stated by persons present, these men, in questioning candidates for the ministry, sought to worm out of them statements as to Olsson's instruction which, they alleged, were dogmatic errors. When, after a lengthy examination of one of the seminarians, Olsson came into the room, one report has it, he exclaimed, "Brethren, be merciful! If it be me

you are examining, let this man go." After learning what
some of the charges or suspicions against him were,
Olsson is said to have made a brief defense of his views
on the points challenged. The opposition did not come
out in the open, choosing to make veiled insinuations
rather than preferring precise charges. The "dangerous"
views for which Olsson was blamed were, according to
various sources, those on relations between the living and
the dead, eventual reunion in the world to come, the final
restoration (apocatastasis), and related thought problems.

In his book on Christian hope, published shortly
before, Olsson had touched on these matters, supporting
his own speculations by Scriptural proof, but not to the
satisfaction of the ultraconservative theologians such as
his present antagonists. That book was not deemed
worthy of announcement or review in the Synod's own
paper. Hasselquist personally announced a new book of
his own, but made no mention of Olsson's. This is explained by the fact—of which the writer has found ample
evidence—that Lindahl was in practical control of *Augustana's* editorial policy for several years while Hasselquist
was still the editor. Both as president of the printing
house that leased the paper edited by Hasselquist and as
chairman of the college board, Lindahl had the means
whereby to make his authority felt. With all their influence, however, the men who launched this attack were
powerless to control the Synod's action. It had implicit
confidence in the man whose doctrinal position was under
fire and gave him a vote of thanks. The resolution
passed on the floor of the Synod after the interlude in
the ministerium reads:

"In view of the resignation of Prof. O. Olsson, be it

Resolved, (1) that although the Synod most earnestly would have wished to keep this faithful and greatly beloved teacher in the place filled by him for so many years, yet it can see no way, considering his unalterable request, but to accept his resignation, in the hope, nevertheless, and with sincere prayer that the Lord may restore to him health and strength to serve our communion and, if it be God's will, give the Synod an opportunity to restore to him the office he has filled with faithfulness and zeal; (2) that the Synod tender Professor O. Olsson heartfelt thanks for the faithfulness and love shown in his work for the development of our educational institution and pray God's richest grace and blessing upon him and his children."

The ingathering ordered by the Synod for Olsson's benefit at this crucial point reached a total of eighteen hundred dollars—a comfortable cushion against financial worry at a time when he was at a loss where to turn. On September 13, Olsson wrote (*Augustana*, p. 455):

"I do not know how to express the gratitude I feel toward all those who have so kindly contributed to the collection taken by the churches in my behalf. . . . I had announced in the last issue of *Skolvännen* that under no circumstances would the Synod be at any expense on my account. When I heard about the ingathering, I was nonplussed and knew not what to do. I greatly feared that, no matter what I did, this thing would cause ill will. I had to keep calm and leave it all to God.

"Early last spring I expressed to some friends my wish to seek rest somewhere in Germany, knowing, as I do, of quiet and inexpensive retreats there, suitable for those who need rest for body and soul. Instantly the accommodating journalists got hold of this bit of news and published it far and wide. I was very sorry when I read about my plans in the papers. It will now be said, I imagine, that I have grown rich in the service of the school, so I can take a pleasure trip. I find myself in a state, physically and mentally, where I need complete rest from preaching and even from visiting and talking with friends—but of this I can not convince my most intimate friends, much less the readers of our newspapers. . . . I was bound to be misunderstood.

"This summer, when I found conditions in Lindsborg such that my property there could not be sold, I was about to abandon my whole vacation plan and leave myself utterly in the hands of God. It was then these unexpected collections came as a complete surprise. But now the year was too far gone for me to think of starting on a tour. With profoundest gratitude, I will, however, use this money for a vacation tour next year. How I shall repay all these dear friends for their gifts I know not; that I would gladly do so, I assure them. Once again—*most sincere thanks from me and my children.* I read through the lists of givers with prayer, supplication, and thanksgiving.

"Since I am not likely to attend another meeting of the Synod, I beg herewith to say a hearty farewell in the Lord to all brethren and friends whose faces I shall not look upon again in this life. Cordial greetings to all those who pressed my hand that first evening of the synod meeting in Galesburg. A special greeting to the brethren who saw me to the station the next morning, more particularly the brethren of my last class at the Augustana Seminary. All the young brethren with whom I have associated while at the institution in Rock Island are dear to me, but the members of the last classes I remember best of all—I can see them whenever I will. The parting from them at Galesburg is unforgettable. I looked upon it then, and do so now, as my farewell to the Augustana Synod.

"At home in our Father's house of many mansions we shall meet again. To brethren and friends, my farewell in the name of the Lord, and most heartfelt thanks for all the proofs of your affection.

"Your fellow servant in Christ,

O. OLSSON."

Carbondale, Osage Co., Kansas, Merrill
Mineral Springs, September 13, 1888."

About this time, Bethany College at Lindsborg was submerged in debt, and its president, Pastor Carl Swensson, was leaving no way untried to keep the school afloat. It was only natural that his friend, who had again and again brought financial relief to Augustana, should lend him a helping hand in an endeavor to do as much for Bethany. After having built himself up physically during the summer, partly by a séjour at the Mineral Springs, Olsson, who could not for long remain inactive, felt strong enough to proffer his services to the hard-pressed college. The help of so experienced a solicitor was gladly accepted, and Olsson was soon engaged in this voluntary task. In this work, undertaken purely for the love he bore his old Kansas friends, chiefly his former parishioners in Lindsborg and their pastor, Olsson did not escape the criticism of persons in Rock Island who without regret saw him leave, but looked askance at his work in

behalf of a school in which they thought they saw a
dangerous rival of the central educational institution of
the Synod.

A close-up view of Olsson while at work that winter
for Bethany College has been given by the late Dr.
Gustav Andreen, a member of the Bethany faculty at
the time. What here follows is in the main his own account.

When Olsson came to Lindsborg that fall to help save
Bethany financially, he at once launched a publicity
campaign to advance this cause. Among other things,
he drew up a comparison between Swensson and Count
Zinzendorf, the great leader of the Moravian Brethren,
who had met great pecuniary difficulties in promoting
the work of his church.

One Sunday morning, Olsson stepped into the sacristy,
where Swensson sat ready to begin the services, and
stated abruptly, "I will preach *today*." Taken by surprise, Swensson could not but give his consent. That
Sunday Olsson preached a powerful sermon. His text
was, "The last shall be first . . ." Toward the close, he
turned to the matter of the campaign and told the Lindsborg people that if the required amount—over sixty
thousand dollars—was to be raised for the school, they,
the home group, would have to subscribe at least twenty
thousand. The good Lindsborg folk felt that during all
the years since the school was founded in 1881, they had
been the ones to furnish most of its support. At this time
they were willing to bear their just share of the burden,
in proportion to what the other congregations assumed.
This would have meant upwards of seven thousand
dollars. Now Olsson suddenly demanded three times that

much from Lindsborg alone, and he insisted that this amount be subscribed before any other congregations be approached. That of course set the whole town talking. We all objected, we all argued, and—in the end we all yielded. Psychologically Olsson took the correct stand. Without such a heroic effort on the part of the Lindsborg people, the whole plan would have failed. Now, by God's guidance, through the instrumentality of His servants Olsson and Swensson, it was carried through to success, and Bethany was saved.

We have Dr. Andreen's word for it that it took the united efforts of the two men to pry the little school from under a debt of something like eighty-five thousand dollars and set it on a fairly safe financial footing.

Olsson's work in behalf of Bethany College had afforded him a period of relief from the mental agony inflicted on him by the Galesburg episode. For a full year from the date of his "farewell" letter, little is known of the grief that darkened his life at this time and onward with little surcease for no one knows how long. Indeed, some have thought they saw signs to show that he was not quite the same man after that dread ordeal for a soul as sensitive as his. Yet on this point even his own children hesitate to speak.

Of his mental suffering, however, Olsson spoke out in plain words to his friends. One might almost say his *one friend*, for in no one did he confide so intimately as in his yokefellow of the past few months, Pastor Swensson of Lindsborg. In letters sent him from Europe late in 1889, Olsson spoke his mind and revealed his heart. Here no words could tell the story better than his own. From Kornthal, Württemberg, he wrote on August 26:

"Long ago I ought to have thanked you for your kind and encouraging letters. I must confess, however, that every issue of *Augustana* contradicts the glad hopes you inspire. Oh, if you could only know how terrible that paper now appears to me. But I ought not to speak so, for I myself, as you know, became a mighty and intrepid fighter when, after much hesitation, I joined the Augustana Synod. Thus I have helped to shape a church body in which I now find myself homeless, a church whose honored leaders are afire with unquenchable fanaticism. Just now I was reading Lindheim's "Schreckensjahre," a story, and a true one, of the time of our orthodox witch trials. There I read: 'One must take no compassion upon witches; to persecute and torture them is to serve God.' That statement *Augustana* might well apply to me and to those who may derive from the Word of God some hope for His mercy on poor, miserable men. I say this, not to complain, for why complain about the unavoidable, but to show you how impossible it would be for me to accept an office of any importance in the Augustana Synod. You yourself must see how impossible it would be to think of R. I.; likewise the presidency in Lindsborg. Dear Brother, I am sincerely thankful to you for your words of sympathy and hope, for I know you mean it; but kindly do not say another word along this line, as it would only exasperate *Augustana* the more.

"Yesterday I had a letter from Mariedahl about my being called there. It is certainly very kind of them to be thinking of me. But a call to serve *two* congregations I dare not accept, owing to my feeble health. Hence that door is closed. My greatest concern is for my children. They feel most at home in R. I. They now know

I will no longer serve at the institution, and with that they are satisfied. If possible, I should like to build a little home between Moline and Rock Island. Then they would have a home where they like to live.

"Possibly there is so much freedom of conscience in the Kansas Conference that it might engage me as traveling missionary. The salary attached would suffice for the support of my children. For myself I will not need much when I cease buying books. If I then traveled ten months of the year, there would be one month in the winter and another in the summer to spend with my family. That is all a heretic could expect. When I read of what my brother heretics in former days had to put up with, I am ashamed to live in the peace and comfort that is really mine. Some time in the future doubtless there will be born, even among the Swedes, a church communion in which a true Christian may live in peace even if he is unable to subscribe to Weidner's Dogmatics. I cherish the silent hope that the Mission Synod may at least pave the way for such a body.

"Now I pray the Lord in my humble privacy for such a measure of health that I may, for a few more years, be of some help to my children. Yes, it is still my joy indeed to proclaim the gospel of grace. My heart is constantly afire with a zeal for guiding poor souls to happiness for time and eternity. . . .

"Waldenström wrote me a kind little letter from Salina. It gave me great joy. Through Carlson in L—g I sent him a reply. Convey hearty greetings to our friends in Lindsborg. Regards to Pastor Carlsson and his family from me and mine. In calm expectation of God's mercy, "Your affectionate

O. OLSSON."

A month later, September 26, he wrote again from Kornthal:

"You do not know how deeply grateful your letters made me. It is your nobility as a man and a Christian that captivates me more and more. It is a pity that we should have had that strife over Bethany. I trust you forgive me—I sincerely pray for your forgiveness—and that the matter be completely forgotten. I will never touch on it again, publicly or in private. Now I withdraw entirely from the public eye, except in this one respect that, should anyone want to be my publisher, I plan to have published a somewhat comprehensive book of travel, done as carefully as I can, and containing a special dissertation on religious liberty. This last I pledged myself to do as I stood at the Huss memorial on my recent visit to Kostnitz, but to do it objectively and with no reference to the Augustana Synod. This, then, is to be my simple testament to my brethren, not in revenge, as my writings have already been interpreted, but as a help to lighten the burdens of the brethren who shall come after us, so they need not suffer the agony I have endured for the past few years in a church body shackled by its confession. I have also visited Stenthal to stand at the grave of dear old Oberlin and to see his church and his parsonage. How indescribably interesting! A short trip into Switzerland brought me as it were before the very *throne of God* at Uetleberg near Zürich. Such another morning hour I shall never again experience—not until I actually stand before the throne of the Lamb. It is no sacrilege, I assure you, if I apply 2 Corinthians 12. 1–5 to the scene there witnessed. It was mainly in behalf of *Framåt* that I made these extra trips.

Now, dear Brother, you must not think it meanness in me if these newspaper correspondences cease. There are several reasons for this my decision, known to you without any argumentation on my part. What I have left of travel recollections which are beautiful at least to me might accrue as a wee bit of a fund which I owe it to myself and my family to conserve."

After a grateful reference to a call tendered him by Mariadahl and a neighboring church in Kansas—which he would have gladly accepted but for lack of strength to serve two congregations—and a bitter comment on the recent inquisition, Olsson makes this commitment:

"If in any way you are able to arrange it so that a poor, unnoticed rural pastor is relieved from the duty to attend synods, I shall be thankful to spend my remaining days in quiet obscurity as pastor of some country or small-town church in the Augustana Synod, if they will let me, and thus end my days in peace. Should I be expelled for heresy, I shall even so pray God for grace to take it calmly. . . .

"Visit the Tyrol, where Robertson was when his spirit broke the iron shackles of Westminster, then tell me whether you have not there seen a Father far above all that bear the name of father in heaven or on earth. You call me an idealist. May that be so! What is the true ideal? It is to see God under His countenance and have one's soul released from all human bonds so as to live in free communion with the Word, which is at least as wide and great as God's creation."

This letter reveals a curious idea conceived by some of Olsson's friends and communicated to him by Swensson. It seems that those friends ascribed Olsson's ill health to lonesomeness, melancholy, or some such cause, and in their great solicitude for his welfare they offered the kind suggestion that a remedy might be found in a remarriage. This well-meant advice was promptly and rather curtly declined in these terms: "The remedy you and several other kind brethren prescribe for the sick man (and the visionary, I take it you mean, although you are too kind to say it outright)—from that I pray God to save me. To love a *second time:* just as impossible as to know what love is! Enough of this, dear Brother; I do not expect to live long enough for that. . . . Give my regards to the well-intentioned friends who offered that kind advice and tell them that they understand my case as little as I understand them. Could I ever add to our other sorrows that of giving my children a step-mother and leave behind me a widow? May my dear Father in heaven preserve me from so doing."

The pastoral call tendered was declined by Olsson, who planned to spend a year in Europe. He felt unequal to the demands of a joint parish, requiring double service and much traveling back and forth. He feared the parish-ioners would fail to understand the limitations ill health had placed upon his physical strength and his mental powers as well. "They say they will be kind," he wrote. "Yes, I know what they mean: they would try to be satisfied with what I might be able to give them. But I know they would not understand my condition. I know they would think it an easy matter for me to ride my circuit and preach day in and day out. How could I expect the common folk to understand when not even you and my other friends take into account that the mental collapse of my brother-in-law, the death of my wife, and many other events have left me totally crushed in body and mind."

Two days later the traveler unburdened his mind in another long letter to Swensson, who kept him well informed on events at home and to whom in turn he confided his innermost thoughts with implicit trust. This exchange of private letters, therefore, is of value as the frankest revelation of Olsson at a crucial period in his life—even more revealing than anything he wrote for the church press or included in the book published two years later. Now he explains further that after his published plea for a more friendly attitude toward other believers had brought him into disfavor, his articles in Swensson's paper could have no pecuniary value. Then follows this explanation, showing that Olsson took a more tolerant view of the Waldenstromians, now that they had moderated their position, having cast out the extremisms of the turbulent seventies and set their house in order. He says: "I know very well that with Waldenström and among the Mission Friends there is no broad tolerance, of that you may be sure. But for two parties that have sprung from the same revival in Sweden to be forever quarreling and blackening one another, that grieves me sorely. And because I contributed much toward this scandalous animosity among Christians, I sought to put in a conciliatory word. But it will never do, that I see very clearly. The way I am learning church history ought soon to qualify me for a professorship in that department."

Commenting again on what happened at the Galesburg convention, he wrote these significant lines in self-defense:

"You think I ought to have said nothing at Galesburg. No, dear Brother, anything but half-heartedness; no submission to such theology as Weidner's. If the Synod permits one whose brow never sweated in its service to come in and set up new points of doctrine in order to disturb the conscience of his brother colleague, that is its own affair. But it is my duty to be *honest*, though it bring me into poverty and disgrace. Now, Brother, you have the whole secret. . . . You people think I have turned a wild-eyed visionary. Not at all. I can truly say that I have been in hell in order that I should know hell. My hope consists in crying to God in need and anguish, that very God whom my Lord Christ has revealed to me. If I may live and die within the Synod while still harboring this my hope, I shall be thankful to God for the privilege. [His book, *Christian Hope*, had been involved in the inquisition.] And should you, dear Brother, live after me, as doubtless you will, speak these words at my grave: *He was not a dreamer, but he suffered, body and soul, in sympathy for poor humanity; he still cherished his hope after his church would no longer tolerate it, and the grounds for this hope he found in the Word of God, although he was not permitted to state publicly the reason for the hope that was in him.* Dear Brother, you know me more intimately than does any other person, and to you I have now confided my epitaph.

"The Lord may grant me grace to live yet a few years with my dear ones and at the same time be of some slight service in some little congregation. After that my dust shall take its place beside that of my beloved Anna, if friends will do me this last great service; and my spirit, yes, my spirit shall, with the Lamb on Mount Zion, witness the coming restoration of all creation and hear the harmonies which after an eon of eons shall praise the God who has the power to make *all things new*. Oh, how my frail body and my miserable soul rejoice in the living God in this hope! Just as the Church of Christ formerly conquered the dualism *'from eternity,'* so shall this same church some future day annihilate the dualism that *'to eternity'* implies. During the *middle ages* of this long period of expectation, individual dreamers and heretics, as they are called, will have to suffer, wait, and hope in silence."

While at Kornthal, just before locating in Zürich for the winter, Olsson received a call from the church in Woodhull, Illinois. This call he would gladly accept, he wrote Swensson, but having stated before that he would not serve in Illinois for fear of being suspected of a desire to get back to the institution he had served, he added the condition, "if I could convince the authorities that I intend *never* to return as a teacher, either to the Augustana Seminary or to any other educational institution in the Synod." For greater certainty he wrote further: "Would you have the kindness to assure the leaders that I have sincerely and irrevocably said good-bye to all official positions in the Synod. ... If I come to Woodhull, I will be in the very midst of orthodox and learned men, so it will not be possible for me to do any damage. ... On the one hand, there would be the president of the Synod [S. P. A. Lindahl], on the other, Prof. [C. M.] Esbjörn, the keenest man at Augustana College. Seldom if ever was a heretic so well guarded. And, depend upon it, I would keep absolutely quiet."

Toward the end of the year, the Lindsborg church remembered its former pastor with a gift in money,

Pastor Swensson knowing that his means of livelihood after the resignation from his chair in the theological seminary had been much reduced. This token of love he accepted with joy and gratitude. A general offering in his behalf was given by the churches of the Kansas Conference about the same time. When it came to Olsson's knowledge that this was in lieu of salary due him for his promotion work in behalf of the conference school, he felt humiliated to have been thus presented to the whole conference as an object of charity, and that gift was not so thankfully received. At this juncture the home in Lindsborg, a gift from his friends there, had to be disposed of, partly for pecuniary reasons, but chiefly because the owner was determined never to come back to Lindsborg to live. This decision was made despite his great love of the place and its people. It was prompted by a nice regard for his successor in the parish and a delicate balancing of the chances that, if he did so, the good folk would heap their good will upon him in a measure too great for the maintenance of his self-respect. There were two weighty reasons besides: the one, that he was not yet ready to retire from pastoral work; the other and weightier one, his firm resolve not to accept another position with a synodical institution.

In the last of this series of letters dealing with Olsson's relations with the Synod and the Kansas Conference, dated Zürich, January 31, 1890, he wrote: "And now, dear Brother, let us forget it all. The main thing is to see to it that the debt on your school is paid. Leave me and all that concerns me out of account. Kindly refrain from writing about me in *Framåt* or any other paper. Let me be forgotten especially in the matter of collec-

tions. Put yourselves in my shoes for five minutes and
see how you would feel. . . . Do not say a word about
me at the meeting of the Conference. Brethren, what
you need above all else is harmony and co-operation,
because of that great debt of yours. I should be deeply
grieved to have damaged your cause by any word of
mine. . . . I greatly fear that Lindsborg will never understand the attitude of the rest of the Conference as to the
school, and vice versa. In my humble way, I have sought
to do what I could to remedy this situation, but it seems
my efforts were clumsy as well as fruitless. . . . My heart
is with you in prayer to God, although I can not be with
you in the work. But it is not possible for me to see eye
to eye with the rest of you in the matter of the school.
. . . This letter is, by the grace of God, the last one in
which I give vent to my feelings in my own case."

Olsson's second visit to Europe extended over a period
of thirteen months in the years 1889 and 1890. He put
in that time studying Europe, not only seeing it. His
own observations are embodied in a large volume entitled
Till Rom och hem igen (To Rome and Home Again). This
time, his children, Anna, Mia, Lydia, and Hannes, accompanied him, the three last named remaining in Zürich
while Anna was her father's companion on his visit to
Italy in the spring of 1890.

As might be inferred from the title of the book on
his second European tour, Olsson's main object was to
study at first hand the Roman Catholic Church and its
mode of operation in the Old World. The trip was so
planned as to include the famous cathedrals, the great
art museums, and the places where church history had

been made. Beginning at Antwerp, the route took in
Cologne and many other points in Germany, extended
as far as Constance, and ended for the time being in
Switzerland, where most of the winter was spent at
Zürich. There Olsson settled down to study and put his
children into a private school. The magnificent Alpine
panorama was a constant delight to them all. A climb
to the top of Uetleberg one afternoon in November afforded them a most charming view of the city, the blue
lake, and the surrounding mountains tinted in glorious
colors by the westering sun.

One day in March the two travelers, spellbound by
Alpine winter beauty, were on their way to sunny Italy.
The first point of interest was Milan and its great cathedral. Palm Sunday was spent at worship in St. Mark's
cathedral, followed by a view of the glories of Venice
from its tower. In Florence, viewing Santa Maria del
Fiore, a cathedral built at fabulous cost in honor of the
Virgin of the Flowers, Olsson finds glorious sunshine outside, but medieval darkness within. Here, as elsewhere,
he finds Catholicism a mixture of heathenism and Christianity. Its ceremonial grandeur seems to him to have
been borrowed from India, China, and Tibet. Looking
at the picture of Christ above the high altar, a thin, weak,
pitiable figure, he reflects: "Here is the key to Catholicism. When Christ is portrayed as a repulsive person,
the Virgin and the saints are the more easily presented
as saviors. Read what Luther says about the pope's
Christ. The Reformer knew what popedom stands for."

Arriving in Rome at last, the traveler hastens to St.
Peter's, "a holy place where one will surely find God."
But he is disappointed. Everything points to the pope.

He finds himself in agreement with the comment of Fredrika Bremer, the Swedish authoress, who wrote: "This magnificent temple impresses me as a Christian pantheon rather than a Christian church. The monuments of the popes take too much of the space."

One monument in St. Peter's he looked upon as an eternal shame to the Swedish nation—the magnificent sarcophagus of Queen Christina, daughter of Gustavus Adolphus. What, he thought, would the great defender of Luther's church have said if he could have known of his daughter's embracing the Roman faith? Olsson surmised that the pope must have dedicated this monument with a derisive laugh.

In the ruins of the Colosseum the traveler recalled with horror the blood-curdling scenes when countless human victims were sacrificed before Roman emperors worshiped as gods, just as the pope is now worshiped in St. Peter's as a new Roman god. Yes, and the popes, too, have taken their toll of human sacrifices. Do some travelers think this too harsh a judgment? If so, they must have overlooked the Vatican palace—headquarters of the Inquisition.

On Easter morning, he surveys the Eternal City from Monte Pincio, bathed in the mild sunlight of Italian spring. He sees no signs of resurrection, only a grave. Old Rome lies buried here. All that his eyes behold is the tombstones that remain of the Rome that once was and the monuments to the Rome that now is.

Typical of Olsson's whole attitude to Romanism are his reflections after visiting the Christian catacombs near the Appian Way, here given in summary: "What shall we look for here? Life—eternal life. Up there in the

bright sunshine we found death, only hopeless death.
Down here in the dark underground passages we find
hope of life eternal. All signs, symbols, and mural paint-
ings may be summed up in these two passages: 'For me
to live is Christ, and to die is gain.'—'I am the resurrection and the life; he that believeth in me, though he
were dead, yet shall he live.' "

Finding most of the niches in the catacombs empty,
this close student of church history comments: "Rome
has made enormous sums on the sale of bones of martyrs
and saints. The catacombs became veritable gold mines
for popish propaganda. The Catholics have done their
utmost to prove that the very first Christian congregations were popish and Roman Catholic. Naturally they
also maintain that the heavenly paradise will be Roman
Catholic. Roman law protected the places where the
dead were buried. The pagans were much more humane
than the followers of the pope in the Middle Ages and
after the Reformation. The ashes of heretics were then
thrown into the rivers in order to obliterate every trace
of those whom the church had condemned. No community dared to harbor the remains of a heretic. How anyone
can remain calm and indifferent when thinking of the
dreadful misuse of papal power is hard to understand.
In this underground graveyard popedom is so cleverly
mingled with the early apostolic church that only a sharp,
historically trained eye is able to tell the two apart."

In bidding farewell to "heathen Rome" from the
highest gallery of the Colosseum, Olsson felt like reciting
the sixteenth chapter from the book of the prophet Ezekiel. Like most intelligent travelers, he found Rome an
intensely interesting city. "If I had the means, I should

want to live in Rome for a whole year," he wrote after his return.

Visiting Genoa on the return trip, Olsson looked up the Waldensian church at sunrise and there held morning worship alone. The Waldensian pastor in Rome, a charming Italian who spoke Swedish, was visiting in La Tour, where his countrymen had built a church and a memorial, Casa Valdese. Here the Swedish-American clergyman had the pleasure of listening to a sermon in French by this vivacious Italian pastor on Sunday afternoon. Speaking of the Waldensians, in the story of his trip, Olsson gives us this glimpse of his boyhood: "The Acts of the Apostles and the history of the Waldensian people were my first love in church history. They will no doubt be my last. Perched in a birch tree near a little gray cottage in Värmland, I used to read the New Testament in my early youth. I also read of the 'Land of Martyrs.' Give a lively child a book that interests him, and time can not erase the impressions made on his soul by that book. The struggle of these people for religious freedom threw the little Värmland boy into ecstasy, you may be sure."

On their return from Rome and Italy, the travelers were again thrown into raptures by the Alpine scenery. The majesty of the Alps inspired pages upon pages of sustained poetic description such as is found nowhere else in Olsson's works. With his family, Olsson now continued northward from Zürich through Germany to have a glimpse or two of Sweden before returning to the United States. What Olsson writes of the land and the place of his birth sometimes runs into rhapsody. "Oh, to travel through Sweden and again pick flowers on one's native soil! Who could forget the little homes—the charming

red or gray cottages with white trim? The snow-white
curtains—the lilacs—the calves I played with—the birch-
es, the rocks, the moss—my prayer-stone, the church."
Tears fill his eyes. He weaves beautiful dreams of the
home of his childhood and youth and of his spiritual
home. He visits his teacher Sedström in Fredsberg, Västergötland, a loveable old man whose joy at meeting his
former pupil was indescribable. In Sunnemo, Värmland,
he meets some of the members of his former pastoral
charge, his last before leaving for America. "In Uppsala
I spoke to no one," he says, "only to Dr. Fjellstedt at
his grave and to a few other friends in the cemetery."
Stockholm—the Venice of the North. Ah! A whole book
could be written about Italy and Sweden—Stockholm
and Venice. A visit was paid to Riddarholmskyrkan, to
Johanneskyrkan, to the National Museum, and to the
grave of Rosenius. One of the few living persons in
Stockholm visited by Olsson was Bernhard Wadström,
the noted author and divine.

Olsson's visit with his former teacher deserves to be
pictured in greater detail. The life sketch of Sedström,
elsewhere noted, describes the meeting between teacher
and pupil in these words:

"Olsson's appearance in the Fredsberg church on this
occasion became somewhat of a sensation. He had just
arrived at Töreboda. It was on a Sunday, and he wanted
to grasp the opportunity to worship once again in the
old church at Fredsberg. The services were drawing to
a close when a stranger in travel attire entered and took
his seat on the balcony. It was 'Värmlands-Olle.' After
a cordial but hasty greeting, Sedström yielded his seat
at the organ to a visiting organist. The Holy Communion

was being celebrated. The two old friends soon passed down the center aisle side by side. The stranger stops while Sedström steps inside the railing and whispers in the ear of the officiating clergyman. The congregation is all agog, wondering what the interruption means. At the next distribution, the stranger advances to the rail, kneels, and receives the holy sacrament at the exact spot where he had partaken of the communion for the first time at his confirmation. The solemn episode made the day great and memorable for the two friends. That afternoon they were joined by a third, August Gustafsson of Mårby, a member of Olsson's confirmation class. It was a touching sight to see these three friends walking hand in hand all that Sunday afternoon, talking over old times together and, of that we are sure, exchanging thoughts on the weightiest questions of life. To Sedström, Olsson's first teacher, that day remained one of the most cherished memories of his life."

From Sweden, Olsson and his family returned via Denmark and Germany, visiting Copenhagen and Bremen, and finally at Bremerhafen embarked for America. The tour concluded the interval of two years or more, during which time Olsson's activities were purely private, severed as he was from direct connection with the church body he had hitherto served. The account of his tour completed in the summer of 1890, Olsson again took up work within the Augustana Synod by assuming pastoral charge of the church at Woodhull, Illinois, the same year.

XVIII

THE CHRISTIAN THINKER

An inquiry into the thought life of Dr. Olsson would be incomplete were it to pass by any of his writings, for even the more casual products of his pen, such as letters of travel, official reports, college news letters and announcements, and especially his private letters, are likely to reveal some bit of his philosophy or give one an unexpected glimpse of the man's true inwardness. A man of strong feelings and a tender heart, zealous for the right and impatient with wrong, his sympathies and antipathies were equally strong, and he made no effort to conceal either kind. The diplomatic trick of employing words to cover up one's thoughts he had never learnt. Rather did his sincerity often lay him open to attack from those who were not above taking undue advantage of that trait of his.

In much that is quoted throughout this volume, Olsson reveals himself and his thought on the problems of temporal life. The course of his thinking as a Christian philosopher, while evident in his sermonic and forensic works, we find most clearly marked in three small books from Olsson's pen. The two of these which were published earned for him a reputation for mysticism, and one of them raised doubts in certain quarters as to the correctness of his theology. The third he never published.

The first of these, entitled *Vid korset* (At the Cross),

is a little volume of profound meditations on the redemptive and atoning passion of Christ. From the hot controversy of the seventies over the true significance of the Atonement this came as pure gold out of a melting pot. It was written as a vindication of that doctrine, which is not only Lutheran, but ecumenical. Coming as it did some time after the subsidence of the schismatic struggle in the midst of which Olsson stood, the book is devotional in character and calm in tone, even though it was a summing up of the arguments against the New-evangelicals in general and Waldenström in particular. An excerpt or two from a recent rendering into English will serve to indicate the author's thought and treatment:

Such Is Our God

God is love. Jehovah is righteous in all his ways, and gracious in all his works. 1 John 4. 8, (Psalm 145).

It is at the cross we learn to know God. It is vain to seek this knowledge elsewhere. "This is life eternal, that they should know thee the only true God, and him whom thou didst send, even Jesus Christ." If to know God is eternal life, how needful then to seek this knowledge. It is when we stand at the cross and consider what is accomplished there that we are able to say in truth, "Who is a god like unto thee?" For nowhere else does the fire of God's love and zeal flame as at Golgotha. Here, if anywhere, God is revealed in fullest measure both as the God who is love and as the One who is "righteous in all his ways" and "gracious in all his works." Let us therefore dwell for a moment at the cross in quiet meditation on the love and the righteousness of God.

Here you behold the God who so loves that He spares

not His only Son, but delivers Him up for you and for
all men. You behold the Son of God humbling Himself,
"becoming obedient even unto death, yea, the death of
the cross." You behold Him in whose presence the
cherubim and seraphim cover their faces in holy adora-
tion, giving as a sacrificial offering Himself, His own life
and blood—yea, all. And this for His enemies, for the
redemption of sinners. Who can grasp the unspeakable
greatness and glory of God's love in Christ? Behold the
depth of its earnestness and devotion when He, who might
have had joy, "endured the cross, despising shame";
when He, who "was rich, yet for your sakes became
poor, that ye through his poverty might become rich."
Behold its exalted worth, when He died for us "while
we were sinners"! And finally, behold this love when He
has mercy upon all in like degree—tasting death for all
men. Behold its riches when the Lord out of His hand
gives "doubly for all our sins." Behold it as a love in
truth. For "love is the fulfillment of the law," and this
word must certainly have its fullest application in the
redeeming love of God, God's love in Christ. Surely
God's love in Christ is in completest measure the fulfillment of the law. It is a love that prepared salvation for
sinners, not by setting aside or despising the righteous
law which because of their sin condemned them and held
them in bondage, but by this, that He who was born
under the law, through obedience to the law, redeems
those who are under the law, that they might receive the
adoption of sons (Romans 5. 19; Galatians 4. 4–5). It is
a love that, since He desires not the death of sinners,
saves the sinner from the wrath and from the judgment,
death, and condemnation which are the sentence of the

law upon him, not by overlooking this judgment or declaring it void and meaningless—which would be a blasphemous thought—but by His taking this judgment upon Himself, by becoming a curse for us, by making a sacrifice of infinite worth for our sins, by becoming through His active and suffering obedience an atonement for our sins. This is love indeed, a love just as glorious and great in respect to grace and mercy as in respect to righteousness and holiness.

Olsson's second little volume of meditations, *Det kristna hoppet* (Christian Hope), was published not long after the death of his beloved wife. The loss left him steeped in sorrow. But this bereavement caused him to focus all the powers of his mind on the existence that is to be the consummation of a Christian's life on earth, and to it we owe doubtless the profoundest treatise on the state of the soul after death and the hope of eternal life written by any American Lutheran author. The book is not available in translation, but Dr. Hjalmar Johnson, deeming it of peculiar interest to students of Christian philosophy, has summarized its contents in English, and from that summary we have been given leave to quote:

SUMMARY OF DR. O. OLSSON'S "DET KRISTNA HOPPET"

Suffering and sorrow have come into existence because of sin. But sorrow is also the remedy for the evil of sin. "Affliction is the greatest theological seminary in the world. What does it profit a man that he is often called a doctor in the midst of this world's learned theologians if he has not won his degree in the university of sorrow and suffering? What harsh and dry teachings the theological doctors generally write and speak about God just because they have not been bowed down and crushed by affliction, the cross, and suffering. What does the person who sits among his books in all quietness, ease, and honor know about the temptations and sorrows of human life and about God? The humblest, the most despised and broken human heart must beat within the breast of the one who shall learn to know God."

What we need most of all to know is not the omnipotence of God but the heart of God.

It is in the Holy Scriptures that we find the record of the revelation of God's heart. "I must learn to know the heart of God, or I will sink in helpless despair." Scripture tells me that God is the Father, that He is love, that He loves me but does not love my sins. God's love does not cause Him to forget His holiness nor does His holiness cause Him to forget His love and grace. Both the love and the holiness of God are manifest in the Reconciliation accomplished through Christ. "In vain do I seek for such a God apart from Christ." "Read Paul's wonderful words in Romans 8. 35–39! How could Paul be so indescribably wise and full of assurance of God as love? He studied Christ night and day." "If, then, I become calm in the bosom of Jesus, I shall find the answer to all my anguished questions." Because the Saviour suffered for my sin, all of my suffering and sickness is transformed into blessing.

"Would God be God if death were the final ruler of humanity?" This does not mean that the Christian does not mourn when death takes away his dear ones. "Could I and ought I be more Christian than Christ Himself?" The tears of Jesus beside the grave sanctify my own tears.

Christian sorrow in bereavement is true sorrow. But there is a little Book which was precious to my dear one and which is also precious to me. "It is the New Testament, in which I search out the fourteenth to the seventeenth chapters of John's Gospel." These words, so old and familiar, have now become for me "a letter just now sent from my heavenly Father, a letter of comfort to me in my deep sorrow." I read also the eleventh chapter of John and the fifteenth chapter of First Corinthians. Now I have that which transcends philosophical proofs of immortality. "Now I have the word and the resurrection of Christ as the foundation of my hope."

Christians in their human frailty are prone to assign one mode of death pre-eminence over other modes of departure from this life. "Thus we have conceived the idea that God must take His children home in a very impressive, magnificent, and majestic manner." Then, too, there are Christians who reduce saving faith in Christ to such small partisan proportions that only members of their own party or group can enter heaven. But the Lord Jesus does not seek to make saving faith as intricate as possible, so that He should not need to receive too many into heaven. "He, our blessed Saviour, assuredly goes much farther in saving grace than we can think or pray for." "What a blessing it is that the Word of God is so simple and that faith is there described as a sighing and a longing, a hunger and thirst after grace."

On the authority of 2 Corinthians 5. 10, Dr. Olsson is constrained to write a word of caution to those who suppose that at their death believing souls are instantly cleansed from the sins that beset all. "We are not permitted to regard, as we often do, the taking away of the believers' besetting frailties and sins as such a minor matter. There is reason for us at least to listen to the view that this requires a longer work of grace after death" (p. 48). Nevertheless, "my dear ones who fell asleep in the Lord are indescribably blessed even now. Of that I am certain on the basis of God's own steadfast word."

We know that our dear departed are with the Lord. We know, too, that the Lord is with us always, even unto the end of the world. Where the Lord is, there are the spirits of those made perfect. And we shall again meet and know our dear ones. How could we be completely blessed if this were not true? "He who desires to condemn me for this utterance may do so. I know Jesus, I know my Father in heaven, and that is enough for me." In heaven, love to God does not remove love to man.

All of nature is to undergo an infinite and glorious transformation. The human body is not excluded from glory. Christ possessed a true human body which was raised from death. And in eternity we too shall have incorruptible bodies which will share the soul's supramundane life. The power of Christ will transform our imperfect and corruptible bodies into spiritual bodies of grandeur and glory. They will be like the glorified body of Christ, no less real because spiritual and heavenly. Nothing shameful or impure, nothing diseased or deformed will be found in them. Not the slightest trace of sin will corrupt them. Then there will be an altogether pure and holy soul in a perfect, pure, and holy body.

Not only is the body of the believer to be glorified. Together with the children of God, the whole creation will have a new birth of glory. Such is the teaching of Romans 8. 19–22, James 1. 18, Revelation 21. 1, Matthew 19. 28. All creation shall share in the redemption of God's people. Glimpses of this future glory appear in Psalm 96. 11–12, Isaiah 55. 12–13, 11. 6–9, 35. 1–2. Man born anew will in his future glory be united with nature which has also had the rebirth of glory, accomplished by God's judgment of fire.

"The greatest thing of all is that God gives heaven as a free bestowal and gift of grace." All boasting is excluded. "Nothing else than grace can bestow and foster the mind of heaven." "If we surrender the gospel of grace, it is all over with heaven and salvation." "As it is God's grace alone which receives us into heaven, so it is the same grace of God which must give us the heavenly mind, the heavenly love, and the heavenly spirit of brotherhood. It is this heavenly mind, this heavenly love which the Word of God calls 'eternal life.'" "As Jesus is, so is heaven. If we know Jesus, we are acquainted with heaven. Precisely as Jesus was and is, so is the spirit which rules in heaven." "Nothing other than the love of God, the purity and holiness of God, the beauty and truth of God, the blessedness and peace of God will then be found among the saved. That is heaven."

Now we can understand why the Lord Jesus spoke so often about the coming of the Holy Spirit who was to establish the work of the Spirit and the kingdom of the Spirit in the hearts of His disciples. "First heaven in our hearts and in our life through the Holy Spirit. After that we can go to heaven because heaven is ours."

But will we then in heaven be occupied only with songs of thanks and praise? By no means. Just as on earth the service of God includes all the varied work of love, all the fields of knowledge, together with prayer and songs of thanks and praise, so in heaven the inexhaustible fullness of God will guide us into all that is good in being and doing. We will be developed "into the highest perfection in all that concerns true knowledge, true skill, true culture." "With reference to this, we can not with sufficient fervor and earnestness affirm the Biblical teaching of the transformation of the body and of the entire creation to a heavenly life."

The Scriptures also teach that even though the Spirit is one and the unity of love prevails, there nevertheless are different degrees of glory in heaven. But if we remember that it is of heaven that this is affirmed, this truth contains only a blessed hope. In heaven the greatest delight is found in consecrating human gifts to the service and joy of others rather than to self. There the words of Paul in Philippians, chapter two, are perfectly fulfilled.

Our earthly life is a school preparing us for heaven. It is of no avail, however, to carry on arguments with those who deny the reality of heaven and the glory of the Christian hope. Man must have spiritual discernment of God if he is to have any desire for heaven. "Therefore, when we are nurtured for God, we are being nurtured for heaven, and when we are nurtured for heaven we are being nurtured for God." In His law God requires us to be what He is, namely, Love. "In the gospel He gives us that which He demands in the law and that which He is—Love." The fullness of the Godhead dwelt bodily in Christ. And who shall say that Christ's earthly love was empty and without significance?

Can anyone experience a greater fullness of life and glory after death than did Jesus? "Since the life of Christ came into humanity, a higher life has been revealed to us. The sun shows us that there is a world of light beyond our world. The sun and the stars show us that this world of light must be infinitely greater than the earth. Christ shows us that there is a life of love, a holy and blessed life beyond and above the world." For that life we are now being prepared even in our sufferings. We should consider long and earnestly Paul's words in Colossians 1. 17–18 and 2 Corinthians 4. 10–11, 16–18.

With specific reference to himself, Doctor Olsson writes, "I can truthfully say that I have known painful bodily suffering not only one year but throughout many years. I can testify from experience concerning anguish, sorrows, and torturing anxieties." But it is in the furnace of affliction that we are transformed into the likeness of God. It is through the birth-pains of suffering that the new and heavenly life of man must each day be born. We are being nurtured for heaven even as we have fellowship with Christ in suffering. Such is the triumphant assurance of Paul in 2 Corinthians 1. 3–4, Colossians 1. 24, and Romans 5. 3–5.

As Doctor Olsson was about to conclude his book on "Christian Hope," he chanced upon a little book by Lavater containing letters purporting to have been communicated by a departed and blessed spirit to a friend surviving on earth. Doctor Olsson had the moral courage to do what was regarded as heresy at that time. He included an abridged statement of this alleged spirit communication in his own book. He explained: "The contents seem to me to be so beautiful that I can not

refrain from sharing a summary for the comfort of those
who need the same reassurance as I do. Read and receive
from it whatever you desire and are able to receive."
The spirit communication summarized by Doctor Olsson
states that not infrequently are the spirits of the blessed
drawn into relationship with those who are yet on this
earth. Noble living on the part of the earth-dwellers adds
a sacred joy to the bliss of the departed. But wickedness
on the part of the survivors repels the spirits. The bliss
of the blessed departed consists in holy love. They live
in light and love. Any mortal on earth who lives in the
love of God and man attracts to himself thousands of
the higher intelligences of light and love. "The man Jesus
who was full of light and love was a shining center constantly attracting to Himself legions of angels." But
dark natures, evil characters attract evil supramundane
intelligences and become ethically and spiritually darker
as a result. "There is much about this in the Bible if
we will seek for it." There is a constant communion
between the visible and the invisible worlds. There is
an unbroken communion of saints between those who
dwell on the earth and those who are in heaven. There
is a mutual and blessed influence of the one world upon
the other. "Forget not that there is joy in the kingdom
of loving spirits over your growth in pure self-denying
love. We are as near to you as you suppose that we are
distant from you." Man can enter into an inconceivably
more intimate communion with the blessed departed
than he thinks possible if he will only expose his soul to
their influences through love. "All who love on earth
and in heaven are one through love." The communion of
saints is thus a profounder and richer truth than many

realize. Thus far a summary of the treatise on the communion of the departed with their surviving dear ones, as found in "Letters to Empress Maria Feodorowna of Russia" by J. C. Lavater, written in 1798 and published in 1858.

In the concluding section of the book Doctor Olsson directs a final appeal to any soul who may be perplexed, yet desires to cherish the Christian hope. He says: "Are you able to desire the kind of heaven which the Bible describes? Do you heartily long for and need a life which is like the life in heaven? If you only have that higher need of the heart, you will soon receive a higher faith. And through faith you will soon find both proof and assurance concerning a higher, a better, a heavenly world."—End of summary.

In a letter dated at San Francisco February 29, 1892, Rev. C. M. Esbjörn told Olsson of the appreciation of his book from an unexpected source. Esbjörn wrote: "You may know something about Mr. Ernst Skarstedt. He is a theoretical materialist, phrenologist, fatalist, pessimist, etc. But at the same time he recognizes the nobility of the optimistic world view, although he simply can not hold that belief. The other evening, during a conversation, we happened to mention your book 'Christian Hope.' Then he said, 'That is what I call poetry in prose. I often read that book when by myself in my room of evenings. But I get no further than that.' I thought this a very fine testimonial, and the idea of a materialist reading that book touched me so that I had to tell you about it. I doubt that this work of yours ever received a finer endorsement, and you may be glad that it has

proved the last stay of at least one man who has thrown
overboard all Christian ways of thinking and every other
form of Christian hope."

On the Biblical Meaning of Eternity
(*In manuscript*)

Through the kindness of Dr. Olsson's children, to
whom grateful acknowledgment is made, there is available for the purposes of this study an unpublished manuscript of thirty-four pages of which Dr. Olsson is the
author.   In this manuscript, all of which is in his own
handwriting and all but two pages written in the Swedish language, Dr. Olsson has recorded some profound
thoughts upon a subject which was vital to his warm
heart and keen mind. These thoughts were written down
from time to time, with long intervals, during eight years.
The first dated entry is January 29, 1887. The manuscript is concluded with a note written July 6, 1895. For
the following analysis of this manuscript we are likewise
indebted to Dr. Hjalmar Johnson.

"If, after my death, some one happens upon these
notes—let him pardon their paucity. My deep, fervent
conviction concerning the ultimate and complete victory
of the good and of God is based upon thorough studies
of the Bible, even if I do not find the time and opportunity to prove that such is the case. Some day the
indescribably horrible doctrine, the atrocious delusion of
an endless hell will be blotted out of Christian theology.
That will be a reformation worthy of the name. Then
God will win back His glory of which He has been robbed
by the doctors of theology. . . . If I live, I shall write a
little book on the subject. I do not wish to cause offense,

but I do desire to believe and testify to the truth of the Word of God" (pp. 22–23).

According to Dr. Olsson, the theologians have failed to recognize that the Word of God is a telescope as well as a microscope. Their eyes have been closed to the vast perspective of the Word of God. The entry recorded on January 29, 1887, bears the title, *The Theological Microscope and the Theological Telescope*. It reads: "By means of the microscope the learned study the infinitely great within the infinitely small in God's creation. By means of the telescope other learned men investigate the infinitely large in the infinite stellar spaces of God's creation. Can it be that those who are instructed in the matters pertaining to the kingdom of heaven do not have the right, yea, the duty, to use the Word of God which is both microscope and telescope for the purpose of searching out both the work of God in the individual human heart and the work of God which concerns His entire kingdom of salvation? In a time when natural science is making such great discoveries both in the invisible microscopic and in the invisible macrocosmic, all students of the Bible have both the right and the duty to extend their researches in both of these ways" (Pages 6–7).

How urgently Dr. Olsson felt the need of this enlargement of theological vision appears from his entries recorded on October 31, 1888, under the title: *Also a Subject for a Reformation Meditation!* "During my residence in Moline, especially on Sunday morning, October 14, 1888, my thoughts turned to the Copernican system, that is, the question concerning the geocentric or the heliocentric theory of the world. As is known, the teaching of Copernicus and Galileo to the effect that the sun is the center about which the earth moves precipitated a terrible 'heresy' struggle. Catholics and Protestants, popes and reformers totally condemned the Copernican point of view. Consult history in the matter" (30–31).

"One did not see much of God's creation as long as natural science was only geocentric. But after the heliocentric system had been discovered, an infinite number of new 'solar systems' were unveiled to our view. As long as we confine ourselves exclusively to the small earthly span of human life and leave the remainder as a hard, immovable, and endless eternity, we do not see much of God and His kingdom. If we could begin to interpret God and His kingdom from the point of view of the 'aion,' God would become for us infinitely greater in grace and glory. His kingdom would receive an altogether different meaning for us" (8–9).

"It is the orthodox, generally accepted teaching that the earthly span of life which is usually called the time of grace is the only time about which all the ages move; the time on which the eternal state of the whole human race depends. Only on the last day after man's span of time and life on earth does Christ pronounce judgment, and this judgment can never be changed throughout endless ages. Such is the teaching of the 'church.' The Bible teaches that the earthly span of time is only a very small part of Christ's reign of salvation. The aions of salvation are related to Christ as the fixed stars to the sun. The earthly span of time is only a small fraction of these aions of salvation, just as the earth is only a small planet in the vast solar system. Natural science has already won the victory over the old geocentric system. When will Biblical science, the glory of revelation, triumph over the ecclesiastical imprisonment of Christ? . . . It is impossible to explain the course of the world with the earth as the center of the life and movement of all the heavenly bodies. It is impossible to explain the Bible if earthly time, man's span of life on earth, be regarded as the only time of grace for the poor human race. How the vision of God's creation and the rule of the world has been enlarged since man discovered that the earth moves about the sun! How the vision of God's reign of salvation, God's ways with men, would be enlarged if man would open his understanding and his heart to the teaching of the Bible concerning the aions of salvation, the periods of judgment and of grace in this world and in the world to come!" (31–33.)

Dr. Olsson anticipated an objection to the foregoing argument. "But, someone will say, natural science is still laboring with so many hypotheses. What would happen if one allowed theology to enter upon such uncertain journeyings in infinite space? Moreover, one is afraid to make any change in the prevailing views. People might be misled and destroyed. Yes, yes, in a former day the almanac was the only astronomy which was available to the people. In our day there are books on the subject which may be easily understood. Even those who lack scientific training are enabled to receive some understanding of the indescribably glorious expanse of the heavens, toward which in many an evening hour the reflective person directs his wondering gaze. Are not the theologians under as great obligation to the people as the astronomers?" (9.)

Dr. Olsson was fully aware of the difficulties involved in discharging this obligation, which he so keenly felt.

"Among our number it is permissible to use only the spiritual microscope. If some one should dare to present publicly his findings arrived at by the use of the Biblical telescope, he would immediately be condemned as a terrible heretic. The time is coming and is even now here when we must extend our vision toward the kingdom of God in the large. The telescope is an instrument by means of which one sees far beyond the range of vision of this world. It is indeed an instrument by means of which one searches out other worlds. The Word of God is for us that kind of an instrument by means of which we may view God's dealings with men in another world and in the ages to come. What great insight one would receive concerning the being and heart and mind of God, and concerning man, and the development of God's kingdom, and the final consummation if one were permitted to make use of the rich Biblical concept of 'aion'!" (7–8.)

Referring to 1 Corinthians 10. 11 ("upon whom the *ends* of the ages are come"), Dr. Olsson maintains that "this passage alone ought to be sufficient to convince everyone who regards the Bible as the highest theology that eternity is not always the same as *endlessness*" (16). In the Holy Scriptures, the economy of salvation is divided into two periods or ages. Each of these two periods or ages is subdivided into shorter ages which are spoken of in the plural form *ages*. Ephesians 3. 21 is cited in the Greek (εἰς πάσας τὰς γενεὰς τοῦ αἰῶνος τῶν αἰώνων) as illustrative of the fact that the whole age embraces the shorter ages (4). The first of the two periods or (whole) ages in the economy of salvation is ὁ αἰὼν οὗτος or ὁ νῦν αἰών. This is the whole age, embracing shorter ages, preceding the rule of the Messiah in the Messianic kingdom (16). The

IMPORTANT CORRECTION

In Doctor Olsson's manuscript the Greek phrase quoted on page 253, line 28, was written: ζωὴ αἰώνιος . . . πυρ αἰων–. The last two words were erroneously printed as one, πυραίων. Comparison with Matthew 18. 8; 25. 41 indicates that the correct form of the incomplete phrase would be πῦρ αἰώνιον.

second period or whole age, embracing shorter ages, is ὁ αἰὼν ὁ μέλλων or ὁ αἰὼν ὁ ἐρχόμενος. This second period or age in the economy of salvation begins when Christ takes possession of the (Messianic) kingdom at His coming to judgment (17). Dr. Olsson records his conviction that this second period (the Messianic kingdom) does assuredly belong to God's economy of salvation. "Assuredly, because the Messianic kingdom is the salvation kingdom" (23). The Lord and His apostles always referred to the second coming as ὁ αἰὼν ὁ ἐρχόμενος. "The Book of Revelation describes Christ's possession of the kingdom at His coming. Then, when the great hallelujah is raised (the hallelujah of Revelation 20 and elsewhere) the second period, the age or ages of the rule of the Messiah has begun. The 25th chapter of Matthew tells of this age or period, the judgment which will take place at the second coming of Christ. The word *eternal* which occurs in Matthew 25. 41, 46, thus clearly refers to this second age, the period or age of the kingdom of Christ" (17–18).

In one brief but extremely significant paragraph Dr. Olsson declares that according to the Gospel of John the return of Christ should be interpreted as a spiritual coming. Dr. Olsson does not, however, develop or correlate the implications inherent in such a spiritual coming with the other eschatological views outlined at length in his unpublished manuscript. The following quotation reproduces the paragraph in its entirety: "αἰὼν ὁ ἐρχόμενος begins at the return of Christ. ζωὴ αἰώνιος and πυραίων begin then. But Christ comes *spiritually* according to the whole exposition in John's Gospel. ζωὴ αἰώνιος therefore enters even into the present time span. Αἰὼν ὁ μέλλων is therefore even now contemporary with αἰὼν οὗτος, under-

stood in a spiritual sense. I do not now have the time
to develop this further" (28–29).

But if according to 1 Corinthians 10. 11 the ages con-
stituting the first age or period come to an end, there
must arise the question which Dr. Olsson asks and undertakes to answer: "Do the ages (or age) of the second
period have no end? Is there no end to ὁ αἰὼν ὁ μέλλων?
This aion begins, as we know, with Christ's taking possession of the kingdom at His coming to judgment. This
period or age will also have an end at the close of the
reign of Christ, when Christ delivers over, surrenders up
the kingdom to the Father. Such is the clear teaching of
1 Corinthians 15. 24. The words are indeed very explicit;
can any one be in doubt? Read the many passages which
state that Christ must reign till He hath put all His
enemies under His feet. 1 Corinthians 15. 25–28; Ephesians 1. 20; Psalm 110. 1; Hebrews 10. 12–13; Hebrews
2. 7–8; Matthew 28. 18; Hebrews 1. 2; John 17. 2. There
must be a difference between *possessing* the kingdom and
delivering up the kingdom, between the *beginning* of the
kingdom and the *end*" (18–19). The aions of the second
period, ὁ αἰὼν ὁ μέλλων, begin with Christ's taking possession of the (Messianic) kingdom at His second coming
and end at the consummation of salvation when Christ
shall deliver up the kingdom to the Father. Accordingly
the "eternal" which is indicated in Matthew 25, verses
41 and 46, "must have an end, since the aion of Christ's
rule which is there indicated comes to a close. It is therefore unbiblical to speak of endless punishment. But, some
one will ask, will not, then, eternal life also come to a
close? No. All is included in that state of being which
the apostle describes in 1 Corinthians 15. 28, 'That God

may be all in all.' 'When all things have been subjected unto Christ,' 'then shall the Son also Himself be subjected unto Him that did subject all things unto Him.' But Christ Himself shall never cease to be. . . . Accordingly, all shall be blessed as Christ Himself shall be blessed. All must therefore continue to exist, otherwise it could not be said that God shall be all in all. . . . 'And there shall be no curse any more' " (20).

This Christian faith in the ultimate triumph of God involves sacred mystery as well as promise. "But if, according to the preceding reasoning, 'the ages' come to an end, how will it then be possible for anything to exist? How did any one exist *before* the ages? 1 Corinthians 2. 7 states explicitly that God has foreordained His wisdom unto our glory 'before the worlds' (literally, 'before the ages'); 2 Timothy 1. 9 refers to the grace which is given to us in Christ 'before times eternal.' Likewise in Titus 1. 2: 'before times eternal.' This sounds strange to us with our notion concerning time and eternity. Nevertheless the language of the Bible is definite and all theology must yield to the words of the Bible. Just as God lived a blessed, holy life before the times eternal, *before* the ages when there was no sin, no evil; so also *after the end of the ages* God will live a blessed life and all beings with Him. There shall be no sin *after* the times eternal, just as there was no evil *before* the times eternal" (20–22).

It was Doctor Olsson's belief that this New Testament doctrine of the final salvation of the entire human race is consistent with the Old Testament teachings concerning God's judgments and God's mercy. On October 8, 1886, Doctor Olsson had listed a number of Old Testament references which, he believed, teach clearly that "grace always follows the judgments in the Old Testament" (22). These Old Testament judgments were eternal but not endless.

Jeremiah 23. 40 states that Jehovah will punish with "everlasting reproach." According to Deuteronomy 28. 46 disobedience will bring curses "upon thy seed forever." Isaiah 25. 8, however, declares that "the Lord Jehovah will wipe away tears from off all faces; and the reproach of his people will he take away from off all the earth." In the restoration promise of Ezekiel 39. 25–29 (cf. Jeremiah 17. 4), Jehovah declares: "Now will I bring back the captivity of Jacob and have mercy upon the whole house of Israel . . . and they shall know that I am Jehovah their God, in that I caused them to go into captivity among the nations, and have gathered them unto their own land; and I will leave none of them any more there; neither will I hide my face any more from them . . ."

In Ezekiel 26. 21 Jehovah says to Tyre: "Thou shalt no more have any being; though thou be sought for, yet shalt thou never be found again." Isaiah 23. 15, however, states that "Tyre shall be forgotten seventy years."

Zephaniah 2. 9 (cf. Deuteronomy 23. 3 and Jeremiah 48. 42) states that "Moab shall be as Sodom and the children of Ammon as Gomorrah . . . a perpetual desolation." But compare with this passage from Zephaniah the following from Jeremiah 48. 47, "Yet will I bring back the captivity of Moab in the latter days, saith Jehovah. Thus far is the judgment of Moab." And also Jeremiah 49. 6, "But afterward I will bring back the captivity of the children of Ammon, saith Jehovah." According to the prophecy in Ezekiel 16. 53–55, addressed to Jerusalem, Jehovah will "turn again their captivity, the captivity of Sodom and her daughters and the captivity of Samaria and her daughters and the captivity of thy captives in the midst of them. . . . And thy sisters, Sodom and her daughters, shall return to their former estate; and Samaria and her daughters shall return to their former estate; and thou and thy daughters shall return to your former estate."

Judgment accordingly was not so final that no further restoration was possible. Jeremiah 25. 9–12 does indeed speak of "perpetual desolations" but the context indicates that in duration of time the "perpetual" desolations equal seventy years. II Kings 22. 17 does state that Jehovah's wrath "shall not be quenched." Read also Isaiah 22. 14; 30. 13; 34. 10; Jeremiah 7. 20–34; 9. 11; 34. 22 and Ezekiel 20. 47–48. But then, read the wonderful chapters in Jeremiah, 30 and 31, and learn that punishment is followed by restoration, "for, lo, the days come, saith Jehovah, that I will turn again the captivity of my people Israel and Judah, saith Jehovah" (Jeremiah 30. 3); cf. Jeremiah 16. 15; 24. 6; Ezekiel 37. 11–14; Amos 9. 11–15; Zephaniah 3. 14–20 and Acts 3. 19–21).

Doctor Olsson does not fail to note that "Even Babylon receives a promise. Read Psalm 87" (15). His earnest study of the Old Testament accordingly led him to the conviction that "the Old Testament never refers to an endless judgment, but rather to an eternal judgment. Grace always follows the judgments in the Old Testament. The New Testament never refers to endless torture, but rather to an eternal condemnation. Judgment in the Old Testament and condemnation in the New Testament are identical, as the words in the original indicate" (22). "The Old Testament teaches that just as there shall be no dualism on earth in the time of consummation, but the whole earth shall be full of the knowledge of the Lord, so also there shall be no dualism on the other side, in 'sheol,' but Sodom, Judah, and Israel shall be one in the Lord, Ezekiel 16." Doctor Olsson refers also to the divine promise of ransom from the power and destruction of Sheol as recorded in Hosea 13. 14, "a precious text discovered on the morning of October 8, 1886, after a night of anguish."

But there is yet another objection raised to the doctrine of the final salvation of all men. God, we are told, is perfectly free and is therefore under no obligation whatever to a world which is lost in sin. "There is so much reference to the freedom of God, that He is under no obligation to save all. Alas, that one does not understand *love!* Did not Luther vividly explain how love is free in the act of *serving* all" (26). It is a betrayal of Holy Scripture to interpret the holiness of God exclusively in terms of punishment. "No, its reality is found in the work of sanctifying, making holy, freeing from sin" (27). As Paul declares in Romans 11. 32, God has shut up all unto disobedience, that He might have mercy upon all. "Mercy, accordingly, is the purpose of the punishment. The state of being shut up unto disobedience is clearly a punishment, yea, God's severest punishment, as the context indicates, but this punishment is inflicted *in order that—*" (10). " 'For God so *loved* the *world!*' Oh, what a marvelous word! Such a one is not found in the Westminster Confession. God's love is not found there. There is only the condescension of the highly exalted God and His favorably disposed mercy toward some wretches and favorites,—a high nobleman's whimsical favor to some of his peasants while he is flogging the others to death. There is no more hideous example of the dismemberment of the Word of God, of the total lack of a sense of Biblical perspective, of an atomistic exegesis, than the Westminster confession. O Lord, how long will the kingdom be able to endure such a presentation?" (28.) "Our Saviour has expressed Himself in the sternest manner against the hard, unmerciful legalistic spirit which banished love and mercy from God and man. By so doing the Lord has established the basic principle of the true theology and rejected the principle of all false theology" (12). When love does not exist in a man or an institution, it is impossible to know God. " 'No man hath beheld God at any time: if we love one another, God abideth in us, and his love is perfected in us' (1 John 4. 12). God is revealed and becomes visible through love. When love becomes universal, fervent, and vital in the church, she learns to know God. Where mutual love does not exist, it is impossible to know God. Accordingly, as long as inquisition, persecution, and barbarism were present in the church, it was altogether impossible for the theology of the church to have a true conception of God. Note this with reference to the history of dogma on the subject of eternal punishments" (24–25).

There was a glorious enlargement of the spiritual vision of the early Christians. For Doctor Olsson that enlarging vision was a contemporary experience. "In a class, on December 13, 1887, the prolog of John's Gospel became especially clear and vital to me. The significance of the Lord Jesus for the whole world and for the development of the world is there set forth in the most vital and simple manner. One should first notice carefully the historical development of the very word λόγος in the Greek philosophy, and in Philo!" (25.) "And note Philo's importance for the New Testament language" (29). "Then one should observe the divine fullness which John pours into this word, since λόγος is identical with Messiah. Jesus, the Messiah, is the creator of the *world*, the life of the *world*, the light of the *world*. All life, all light, all the true, beautiful, and good, even within heathendom, all light of reason has come forth from Him, and therefore He is the Saviour of the world. Now one can appreciate the meaning of the words: 'Behold the Lamb of God that taketh away the sin of the world.' Obviously the horizons of the evangelists expanded as did the horizons of the prophets of the Old Testament. . . . Note also how Paul's horizon was extended as we observe in the 11th chapter of the letter to the Romans, and as we especially note in his letters to the Ephesians, Philippians, and Colossians, and also in the 15th chapter of 1 Corinthians. For God so loved the world" (25–26).

Dr. Olsson concludes his unpublished manuscript with a signed paragraph written in "the solitude of a quiet hour" on Saturday, July 6, 1895: "During the course of the years I have found that I am not able to bear the small anxieties. How then should I be able to bear those which are vast? . . . I am not able to have the care of even a few in time. How then could I bear to be concerned about the countless human beings who have entered into eternity? Moreover, I by my concern and speculation can not save even one soul. I have therefore entirely discarded all speculation of the kind indicated in the foregoing notes."—End of summary.

Many good churchmen have differed in their conception of the Biblical term *eternity*. Learned exegetes, with no more than human ideas of time, have thought the six days of creation to be ordinary days, but have forgotten to explain the seventh day, leaving us laymen to puzzle over the question whether after one week's work God rests forever. Scholars have speculated on whether a God of love and righteousness has instituted punishment of long duration only, or endless punishment, for a lifetime of sin. As a Christian thinker, Olof Olsson was among those who hold that God will not tolerate evil forever and who believe in the restoration of all things. He ransacked human thought and searched the inspired Word for a concept of God as a merciful Father, with a sense of justice and a quality of mercy like that of His crucified Son, who admitted a last-minute penitent into His eternal kingdom. In Olsson's view, it does not behoove the finite mind of man to stake out limits for God's love or to stipulate the duration of times and seasons and eons for Him to whom a day is like a thousand years and a thousand years like a day.

In their work entitled *Jubel-Album*, published in 1893, when Dr. Olsson was again on the faculty of Augustana Theological Seminary, besides serving as president of the chief institution of learning in the Synod, Dr. Carl Swensson and Dr. L. G. Abrahamson gave their estimate of him in a short character sketch covering various sides of his personality. Their knowledge of Olsson was intimate, and in the light of their characterization he stands out

clearly as the versatile genius whose dominant position
was not to be denied and whose leadership in the Synod
after Hasselquist no one could contest. This appreciation, probably the most accurate measure of the stature
of the man ever taken, is here reproduced in large part:

"Doctor Olsson's fitness for the position to which he
has been assigned by the Synod's trust in him is beyond
question. He is undoubtedly the most scholarly clergyman of our Synod, being particularly well versed in the
science of theology. The theologians of our time and of
the past, with all their peculiarities, with all the movements and systems they have stood for—none of them
are unknown to him. To this point he has attained, not
only through profound study, but also by personal association with many of the great minds of our time. If we
understand the matter rightly, there is no other way to
lay the foundation for a theoretical knowledge and for
that independent thinking which is a necessary acquirement in a theologian. Such a one is not to jog along in
the ruts of the religious thinkers of past ages; to merit
the high name of theologian, he must feel called to be a
leader in the spiritual development that must go on
within the church, not least in that church to which has
been given the great trust of being, in preference to all
other churches, the promoter of the science of Christianity. . . . The confessional writings must not be minimized, but on the other hand it can not be held that with
their adoption the development of religious knowledge
has come to an end. Men of humble mind and other
requisites will find new depths of knowledge of God and
His revelations, not opposed to the confessions, but in
full accord with them. Such a development must, as we

see it, go on for time and eternity. . . . This has been said to stress the fact that theologians must have the right of independent research in the truth and of telling what they find; but we have the right to demand that they also defend the confessional writings which they are especially set to guard. Now, as to Dr. Olsson, he has clearly shown that, speculative theologian though he is, he submits to the Word of God and bows to the authority of the confessions and traditions of the church. Think of how he led our church to victory over the thinly disguised rationalism of that new doctrine of Atonement which caused so much damage in our fatherland! By the gospel of the cross he broke the power of that teaching in this country so completely that it never rallied, there being now very few among the Mission Friends who dare confess adherence to that form of the doctrine. A more decisive victory than that has never been won among us. Again, ask our younger pastors, if you would know what Doctor Olsson has meant to them as a teacher and a spiritual leader of the youth at our institution of learning. They may find it hard to say what in him they admire most, his sparkling wit, his great gifts as an educator, or his positive Christian character.

"As a preacher, Doctor Olsson is known to our people in all parts of the Synod. How gladly we hear him! And why? Because of the way he puts his whole person into his words; because he speaks at once to our emotions and our intellect; because he yields to the purely human its full rights while proclaiming the fullness of God's mercy; because one senses that as a sinful man who has received the grace of God he speaks to other sinners as to brethren in order to lead them to the mercy-seat of God.

"In the matter of polity in the Synod, many no doubt think Olsson has gone rather far to the left. We have understood this much, however, that in theory he follows the liberal trend in church polity and is an outspoken opponent of the centralization movement in our church body. Our young church, he maintains, has a history of utmost importance to us, in that it points the way our future development ought to go, and we grant that in this he has stated a truth well worth heeding."

XIX

THE LITERARY CAREER

The pen which signed the initials O. O. was a busy and a potent instrument in the service of the Lutheran church of America for almost three decades. Early in 1873, as a pastor in Kansas, Olsson began writing on questions of doctrine and polity as touching the Augustana Synod and published these in a paper of his own. That enterprise the reader will find recorded elsewhere in these pages. After having merged his paper with *Augustana*, he was co-editor of that periodical, the mouthpiece of the Synod, intermittently for a number of years. At first his contributions were scarce, as Hasselquist privately complained, but upon his removal to Rock Island to become Hasselquist's colleague as theological professor in the Augustana Seminary the studies incident to teaching seem to have given fresh impulse to his pen. He had continued a series of articles in rebuttal of Waldenström, begun in *Nytt och Gammalt*, and now became a valiant comrade in arms to Hasselquist all through the theological warfare of the seventies, recorded in another section.

In 1877, while the war was still on, he began to plan writings of a noncontroversial character. He was one of four teachers at the institution who formed a little group called "Ungdomens Vänner" (Friends of Youth), which set up as its aim "to promote the spiritual and temporal welfare of the children and the youth." The other three

were Hasselquist, C. O. Granere, and C. P. Rydholm,
to whom were added members of the senior classes. What
with teaching, administrative duties, and editorial work,
Hasselquist's schedule was already full, and the other
members not being writers, the literary end of this enterprise would naturally have to be carried by Olsson.

The objectives this group had in mind were stated
by C. A. Swensson of the class of '77 in *Jubel-Album*
(1893), where he said: "The year 1877 was a remarkable
one in the history of our Synod. Great spiritual revivals
began, especially in Illinois. Doctor Olsson, then in the
full vigor of his manhood, preached the gospel of the cross
with a fire that kindled thousands of hearts. At our
common institution of learning in Rock Island, strong
spiritual winds were blowing. In that connection we
asked ourselves the question, What can and ought to be
done throughout the Synod to save our young people for
Christ's kingdom and the Evangelical Lutheran church?
The members of the first graduation class at Augustana
College . . . were vitally interested in this youth problem."

Literary activities by the group thus headed by
Olsson were hardly begun until about a year after its
formation. After six small tracts had been issued, its
first book was published in 1878. This was a small devotional work by Olsson, entitled *Vid korset* (At the Cross).
It was the substance of what he had said before in con-
troversial form, now toned down to calm meditations on
the passion of Christ. This book was for a number of
years the best seller of the publishing group later named
the Augustana Tract Society. By 1892, five editions had
been published here and one in Sweden.

The next publication, *Ungdoms-Vännen*, a monthly

periodical for young readers, was started in January, 1879, with Olsson as editor, assisted by John A. Enander of Chicago, editor of the weekly *Hemlandet*. Upon his return from Europe in the fall, Olsson launched his second literary undertaking within the year. Together with Swensson, newly ordained pastor, he edited in time for the Christmas season the first issue of *Korsbaneret*, designed as a historical and devotional yearbook. It proved popular enough to warrant its continuance for several years by the Society. The publication was then taken over by a private corporation known as the Augustana Book Concern, which passed it on to the authorized publishing house of the Synod in 1889. This was one of several enterprises started by Olsson which have survived to the present day. As a synodical publication, *Korsbaneret* has been issued annually, the 1940 edition marking its sixtieth anniversary.

Having whipped into shape his notes and letters relating to his European tour, Olsson followed in 1880 with his fourth publication of note, *Helsningar från fjerran* (Greetings from Afar).

In the year 1883, the Society added another periodical, *The Olive Leaf*, to its list of publications. This, a Sunday school paper, was its first venture in the English language. It, too, has endured through the years, being still published by the Synod as one of three papers for Sunday school pupils. The same year saw the publication of the Society's most pretentious book, an illustrated volume entitled *Luther-Kalender*. It was put out in commemoration of the four-hundredth anniversary of Luther's birth. Olsson was the moving spirit in the synodical celebration at the institution in Rock Island, quite a large-scale event; so it seems only natural that he should have editorial charge of the memorial volume. We find him as the author of three of the ten chief contributions to its contents.

At this point the activity of Olsson in connection with that publishing society ends. When its affairs were surrendered to a concern clearly organized for profit and as general publishers in outright competition with a house authorized by the Synod, he practically withdrew. Back of the publication work sponsored by him lay a benevolent and unselfish motive. At all times, he had an eye single to the welfare of the school. He had sought, though without success, to benefit the institution financially by his modest publications. They had hardly clashed with the interests of the authorized publishers, Engberg and Holmberg, who were his personal friends. When a small stock company started cut-throat competition with them on the specious plea that the school would reap a large profit—after they had first taken theirs, Olsson's experience told him the scheme was suspect. After two years the rivalry had grown so fierce that the head of the private concern openly denied the rights of the authorized one, and that while the Synod was still collecting semi-annual payments for those very publication rights. A documented account of the feud is found in the fiftieth-anniversary publication of the Engberg-Holmberg Publishing Company, entitled *En bokhandelshistoria.*

"If anything is undertaken in opposition to the publishing house in Chicago," wrote Hasselquist as early as December, 1882, "I for one shall withdraw." Pastor S. P. A. Lindahl, who headed the rival concern in August 1883, had given this assurance: "The Society does not intend to start opposition to anyone." (Letter to the Engberg-Holmberg Company, August 13.)

In a kind letter to Mr. Jonas Engberg (January 25, 1886), Olsson explained his attitude, stating that he did not then belong to any publication company. "An enemy of either party," he said, "I can not and will not be . . . I certainly can not appear as an opponent to those with whom I associate daily. Here we are bound to think of our poor school, the economic future of which looks so dark to me. . . . It is not right of us to proclaim against one another and put the worst construction on everything. Oh, how we sin in this respect! Such things gnaw at the very vitals of our church life."

Olsson never submitted any book manuscript to the interloping concern. His next book, *Det kristna hoppet*, was published by the authorized Chicago house in 1887. So was his second book of European travel, his largest work, *Till Rom och hem igen* (To Rome and Home Again), which appeared in 1890. Hasselquist later took the same view as Olsson. More or less under compulsion, he had favored the new firm which was printing the Synod's paper under contract. When Lindahl, as its head, not only sought to dictate *Augustana's* policy, but started a rival paper, *Hemvännen*, the veteran editor's conscience rose in revolt. Early in 1889 Hasselquist resigned his position on *Augustana*, giving as one reason that "He had thought for some time past that two papers with programs as similar as those of *Hemvännen* and *Augustana och Missionären* could not be issued to equal advantage [for the Synod and the private firm] by the same publishers when the one was owned by the firm and the other was practically rented or farmed out to it."

The publication work of the Synod is here viewed merely at the points where it touches Olsson's career as a writer. But even within that narrow scope a number of questions arise. Anyone who examines and correlates the facts finds it only harder to understand such things as these: Why the Synod bought an outside concern which had taken every advantage of it, when the honorable thing was to repurchase its authorized publishing house, which had played fair with it for fifteen years. Why Lindahl's all but bankrupt plant costing the Synod more than $50,000 is spoken of as a gift. And, more oddly still, how Dr. Lindahl can be said to have founded, in 1884, an enterprise the cornerstone of which was laid by Olsson's labors more than six years earlier. A careful study of the records has convinced the present writer that whatever honor lies in having planted the seed out of which grew the Augustana Book Concern, the Synod's third official publishing house, should have gone to Olof Olsson.

SUMMARY

The character of Olsson's authorship appears from surveys of his chief writings made under other heads, where his doctrinal stand, his travels, and his thought life are dealt with. His mind and his pen were not often at rest. If all that he wrote had been issued in book form, it would have run to many more volumes, but as it is, these seven may be listed as his major works:

Vid korset, devotional, 1878. Six or more editions, including one published in Sweden. English version in preparation.

Helsningar från fjerran, book of European travel, 1880. Republished in 1916.

Luther-Kalender, 1883. Published in commemoration of the 400th anniversary of Luther's birth.

Det kristna hoppet, devotional, 1887.

Till Rom och hem igen, book on his second European tour in 1889, published 1890.

Predikningar och föredrag, a posthumous volume of sermons and lectures, published in 1902.

Samlade skrifter, 1916. The collected works of Olof Olsson in a series of volumes not completed.

Minor publications and pamphlets from Olsson's hand are:

Reformationen och Socinianismen, 1878, Moline, Ill. Republished in Stockholm, Sweden, 1880, under the title: *Reformationen, Socinianismen och Waldenströmianismen.*

Echo från reformationsfesten vid Augustana College, 1878.

Grunddragen av en sann medborgares karaktär (Character of a True Citizen), 1883.

Något om känslans bildning och förädling. No date.

Kristi rikes hemligheter och satans djupheter samt de hemliga sällskapen och Kristi kyrka. No date.

A Pilgrim Story from Augustana College, 1896.

Julbetraktelser, 1906. Four Christmas sermons (1866–1895).

The periodicals which Olsson edited or with which he was associated editorially from time to time were:

Nytt och Gammalt. A religious monthly, published and edited by him at Lindsborg, Kansas, in 1873.

Augustana or *Augustana och Missionären,* published monthly or weekly. Contributor from 1874 on and associate editor at intervals.

Ungdomsvännen. A literary and religious monthly, started at Olsson's initiative in 1879 and edited by him in collaboration with John A. Enander.

Korsbaneret. An annual, started by Olsson in 1879; its first issues edited by him with the assistance of C. A. Swensson. Now in its sixty-second year as the Swedish yearbook of the Augustana Synod.

Skolvännen. A paper edited by Olsson in the interest of Augustana College and Theological Seminary and published for irregular periods, first in 1878 and again in 1883 and 1887.

The Olive Leaf. A juvenile paper started in 1883 by the Augustana
    Tract Society and edited by Olsson. Still one of the Sunday
    school papers published by the Augustana Synod.

Framåt. A weekly to which Olsson contributed as solicitor for Beth-
    any College in 1888.

The articles contributed by Olsson to the official organ
of the Synod grew to hundreds in the course of the years.
The signature "O. O." seldom failed to attract the eyes
of its readers, it mattered not whether it was suffixed to
a doctrinal treatise, a letter of travel or pastoral visitation, an official report, the story of a convention, or one
of his many news letters from the Synod's school. His
versatile pen had a large range. Only once, however, was
he known to venture into the field of fiction. The result
was a historic fantasy describing a visit to "Lynnsbury,"
with the scene laid far in the future. The story, which
was used effectively in Olsson's promotion work in behalf
of Bethany College, was published in *Framåt* in 1888 and
reprinted in *Lindsborgs-Posten* forty years afterward. The
title of this story reads: "Julbesöket eller hundraårs-
festen i Lynnsbury 1993."

A literary critic once said of Olsson's language, written
or spoken, "It is poetry in the form of prose." Yet he
himself disclaimed poetic ability. The nearest he ever
came to writing verse was as a member of the first
synodical hymnal committee. Several hymns from the
Swedish Psalmbook were rendered into English by him,
and three of these are found in the present Augustana
Hymnal. It has been shown elsewhere, and it may be
restated here to complete this summary, that the first
English Hymnal of the Synod was in large part the result
of the labors and the directing energy of Olsson as head
of the commission which produced that work.

EARLY AUGUSTANA SEMINARY BUILDING
Where Doctor Olsson lived and taught

XX

IN CATHEDRA AND PULPIT

The Augustana Synod at its annual convention in 1875 instructed the college and seminary board to call Pastor Olsson to a teacher's chair in the Augustana Theological Seminary at Rock Island. In the fall of the year the call was issued. It was declined. President Norelius then urged acceptance of a renewed call but with certain misgivings. In a long letter of December 15 he said of this call: "My idea about your call to Rock Island you already know. I believe the Lord will bless your work as teacher in a theological seminary just as much as, if not more than, that of pastor of a congregation. Yes, I should rejoice if the Lord has ordained a place for you there, for I know it would redound to the good of our entire church body. At the same time I must tell you frankly, as I have told you before: I do not believe that Prof. Hasselquist and you are going to pull well together, even with the best of intentions to do so. You are too sensitive to be able to put up with his peculiar ways and often arbitrary acts. Forgive me for saying so, but I wanted to tell you plainly what I think. Yet I dare hardly say that this would be sufficient reason for you to decline a renewed call if it should come. You would have to examine yourself before the Lord to see whether you would be able to keep calm under such circumstances and pursue your calling cheerfully, not

273

failing in love to and confidence in that beloved man because of his peculiarities."

The call was renewed in January 1876. Again it was seriously considered, many brethren pressing him to accept, while others, especially those of the Kansas Conference, prayed him to stay in Lindsborg. The following month, Olsson went to Rock Island to confer with the authorities, carrying with him letters from his church and from individuals setting forth the hardship it would work on both the congregations and the Conference Olsson was serving should he be persuaded to leave. While recognizing the justice of their plea, the board of directors would not yield. They used every argument at their command to urge his acceptance, maintaining that at the seminary he would be in a position to serve all the congregations and pointing out that the interests of the Synod were now, and had for some time past, been suffering from a shortage of men equipped for training its future pastors. It may be recalled in passing that men of high repute in the Church of Sweden, such as U. L. Ullman and Waldemar Rudin, later bishop and theological professor, respectively, had been called without success to the position now offered to Olsson, thus leaving the bulk of the work in the seminary to Hasselquist, who was president of the school, pastor of a church, and, for good measure, editor-in-chief of the official church paper. Many years before, in sending *Augustana* to Olsson in Sweden, Hasselquist made the admission (January 8, 1869): "My other duties do not permit me to give it the attention I should wish. All I write, and all my other work as well, has to be done in haste."

The outcome of the conference was in favor of the

school. The call was accepted conditionally. Granted leave of absence from his two churches in Kansas for the year (1876), Olsson came to Rock Island, leaving his family in Kansas, and taught temporarily for a year, his leave extended for that purpose. When in 1877 the Synod reissued the call, it was definitely accepted, and Olsson became permanently connected with the Augustana Seminary where he taught for twelve years, until ill health caused him to resign in 1888. After this decision, the family moved to Rock Island, which was to be their permanent home, except for a short interval. It was not without hesitation, regret, and a deep sense of deprivation that Olsson left Lindsborg. The attachment between the pastor and his flock was very strong—almost vital, one would infer from expressions of mutual devotion and love. This parting was no sweet sorrow. From the time the first call was issued, Olsson's mind had been torn between two opposing interests. On the one side pressure was brought to bear on him to stay with the church and community he had founded, on the other, to give his services to the entire Synod, through its educational institution. His attachment to his pioneer parishioners made leaving Lindsborg one of the greatest sacrifices in his life, he often avowed in after years. That in part explains the length of time it took him to make his final choice. Other factors made decision difficult. Pastors in all parts of the Kansas Conference brought their cumulative influence to bear on him. Thus, A. W. Dahlsten of Salemsborg, J. Seleen of Mariadahl, C. V. Vestling of Topeka, S. J. Österberg of Kansas City, J. S. Benzon of Omaha, and L. P. Ahlquist of Swede Home jointly petitioned him to stay. Their plea was based on good grounds such as these: (1) There was then no other pastor in McPherson County, with a mass of settlers who would not let their pastor go. (2) His love of the work among the pioneers and his patience amidst the contingent sacrifices and difficulties. (3) The Conference could ill afford to lose a man of his gifts and knowledge. (4) Few pastors had a heart for the work in the West. (5) "Because very likely we will soon have to think of starting a small school in our own territory, possibly also a newspaper. The growth and development of our population in the West has no doubt only begun." (6) "Now that we are soon to constitute a 'Western Synodical District,' surely you will be needed here more than in any other part of the Synod." The appeals from the other side and in the Synod at large were equally strong. Its educational institution was at this time being practically re-established, and all efforts were now bent toward making the school strong and permanent. "If needed," wrote Erland Carlsson, president of its board of directors, "I will tell you that you have the undivided confidence of the older as well as the younger brethren in the ministry. . . . The board asked me most seriously to put this matter upon your heart and insist that you do not decline the call. Should you not yet be ready to sacrifice [dedicate] your powers and gifts to the good of our institution of learning for the rest of your life, do give it at least one year. No one of the men called from Sweden are able to come this fall, and it is uncertain whether any will come at all. . . . We need you, and we are expecting you. The Lord give you grace to accept this call for His sake and for the sake of our school and our Lutheran Zion . . ." Norelius, president of the Synod, pleaded in a private letter: "Do you know, I think the Lord has actually intended you to be a professor. The situation within our church body is such that nowhere could you be of greater usefulness and blessing than in Rock Island. One must look at the general good in the first place." Other brethren added their voices to those urging Olsson to accept the chair of theology. Thus, Pastor John Telleen of Des Moines, Iowa: "I believe you have been predestined by God for such a position. Pastors and people all unite in this request—so far as I know. . . . Do not dare to say no." And Pastor Håkan Olson of Swedesburg, Iowa, after inspecting with others the new building at Rock Island: "It seemed to us that we ought to advise you to accept the call for the Lord's sake and for the good of the cause. In the unity with which the Synod acted in this matter you surely see and feel a power you ought not to resist." Hasselquist, as head of the institution, was somewhat less importunate, yet the most imperative of all these appeals came directly from the school. "You must accept," was the burden of a message from Prof. Henry Reck, a member of the Augustana faculty. He sketched the situation for Olsson more clearly than any of the others:

"I feel that we can not be too energetic in equipping this college and seminary for the accomplishment of our great work in this land. We must add to the number of our pastors, teachers, and evangelists as rapidly as possible, and these men must be as *thoroughly educated* as possible. . . . This the Synod felt when at its recent convention it authorized the Board of Directors to call certain persons as professors. We can scarcely expect Theol. Lector Ullman to come to America. Pastor Lagerman has withdrawn, and Tutor Wihlborg gives only half

of his time during the coming year. Under these circumstances, therefore, it will be *absolutely and imperatively
necessary* that YOU ACCEPT the call and come at the
opening of the school this fall. . . . I see and feel most
deeply the need of an educated ministry in the West and
of pastors who can also preach in the English language,
[so] that I will abide with Augustana College and contribute my poor mite of ability toward her establishment
and enlargement."

Prevailed upon by so many voices, Olsson gave to
the institution the year of service Carlsson had asked for.
In the spring of 1876, at the end of the school year, he
rejoined his family in Lindsborg. When the Synod, at its
annual convention, instructed the college board to re-
issue the call to Olsson with a view to his permanent
tenure of the professorship, he was again faced with the
necessity of making a momentous decision. Much thought
was given to the matter that summer, while Olsson was
occupied with preparation for the fall-term teaching when
not filling engagements to preach or lecture. It was not
until close upon the opening of the fall term in the seminary that his mind was fully made up, under renewed
bombardment of requests from both sides, but his final
decision was in favor of the school. His service as permanent professor began in January of the following year
(1877).

The Lindsborg people and others in the Kansas Conference were profoundly disappointed at the step taken
by Olsson. Their regret was further aggravated when
Rev. F. Lagerman, who had been tried out as a teacher
at Augustana and relieved, became Olsson's successor in
the Bethany Church and fomented trouble from the

start. On Lagerman's plea that he wanted to go to Kansas to repair his wretched state of health, Olsson had suggested him to one or two churches with pulpits vacant, and Bethany engaged him for the time being. Lindsborg, it would seem, proved no healthy place for him, the hope being expressed from there soon after his coming that he might see fit to accept a call to Salina, a few miles away. Pastor Seleen warned Olsson: "I don't believe we ought to have anything further to do with Lagerman. We have been criticized, both you and I, for having recommended him in a way to Mariadahl." Again he wrote: "It has always been inexpressibly dear to me to receive letters from you, and especially [is it so] now that Satan is attacking me from every side. That I should at the same time be beset by Lagerman—why, oh why? . . . Oh how gladly I would carry out the request in your letters with regard to Br. L[agerman]! But there is no possibility, for the congregation would not agree to it. Furthermore, I believe that wherever he may intrude among us, it will cause further dissensions in our martyred Conference." In his eagerness to be of service to a brother minister who pleaded dire need, Olsson had been prompted by Christian charity to put himself out for him even to the point of assuming responsibility for debts incurred by Lagerman in Kansas. This sponsorship for his pastoral services in Lindsborg, however, seems to have been limited to a promise to see to it that there would be a monthly pastoral visit, a student to serve as supply during the vacancy. His responsibility ended when, in November 1877, Carl Swensson, a student, was called as his successor, to take full charge after his ordination in 1879.

In September 1876 Olsson found himself located in

Rock Island, "a country parson transformed into a professor against his will," as he told his friend Norelius. In his new position, he was met with love and respect, but not all things were to his liking. It seemed that he was shifted around a good deal from the start, being required to teach Christianity in the college classes besides his subjects in the seminary. Before the end of the first term, he wrote, "Now I am in great anxiety over whether to remain at the school." The troubles in Lindsborg, started by Lagerman, seemed to require Olsson's return to his church and his remaining there. "My desire was to keep on tending a little plantation in a hidden corner of the Lord's vineyard," he added.

When Olsson accepted, it was with difficulty he could bring himself to take this step, such was his attachment to the flock shepherded by him since 1869. The decision finally made, he sought to lessen the pain of parting from the Lindsborg church and to reconcile the neighboring brethren who protested his leaving the Kansas Conference. A band of musicians from Augustana College, which included a number of divinity students, was invited by him to make a tour of the group of churches in the Lindsborg area to edify them with music and the preaching of the Word. This would doubtless make it possible for him to leave with better grace, and it could not but serve to endear the school to the Kansans, he pointed out to the president of the institution. With his consent and that of the board of directors, the tour was made. The Augustana Silver Cornet Band entrained October 5, 1876, and reached Lindsborg the 7th after a first appearance in the Salina church. Olsson and his congregation were gathered that morning to cut the crop of broomcorn grown on the church farm, but prevented by rain, they gathered in the church to hear the visitors sing, play, and preach. The next day being Sunday, people flocked in from neighboring churches, and the students took part in two services which took the character of religious mass meetings. This unique harvest festival was continued for the next three days, work begun and ended each day with music and devotions and then closed with divine worship on Thursday. The evening before, Pastor Olsson had conducted the visitors and a small group of parishioners to the top of the nearest bluff of the Smoky Hills, where in conducting a brief prayer service he bade farewell to a prospect he greatly admired and a scene he could not leave without regret.

From Lindsborg the students were personally conducted by Olsson on a tour of the churches at Fremont, New Gottland, Gibson Creek, Salemsborg, Assaria, Falun, Mariadahl, and Walsborg. The visitors made their appearance in Lindsborg at an all-day "thanksgiving and jubilee festival," and at Mariadahl they helped to make the convention of the Kansas Conference impressive. There Pastor Olsson, who had recently served as conference president, made his farewell address, based on the tenth chapter of Hebrews. With the band, returning at the end of October after a tour of twenty-five days, Olsson came to Rock Island to stay. He had every reason to be gratified at the good impression left in Kansas by the group from the synodical school whose tour he had sponsored.

The event marked Olsson's definite step from the pulpit to the cathedra. Not that he ceased to preach from then on, for throughout his life he was constantly asked to fill the pulpits of his brethren on commemorative or other festive occasions, and such requests were far too many for him to meet them all. His chief work for the remainder of his life was, however, that of the teacher of theology. His teaching career covered the years 1876 to 1888 without interruption. After an interval of three years he resumed his chair in theology upon his election to the presidency of the college and seminary in 1891, serving in both capacities until his death nine years later.

Of Olsson as a teacher, both in the seminary and the college department at Augustana, we have the testimony of one who enjoyed his instruction in Christianity from the very first years of his teaching career—from 1876 on. This student was Gustav Andreen, who in later years became Olsson's successor as president of the institution. From personal knowledge Dr. Andreen has thrown light on Olsson as an educator. Shortly before his death he wrote the following appreciation: "Teachers and students rejoiced when the young and learned champion of our faith was called to teach at the Synod's central institution in Rock Island. Old and young hailed him when he arrived in the fall of 1876. Even we of the college had the privilege of sitting as pupils at his feet, for during several years he had charge of the instruction in Christianity in the upper college classes in addition to his regular work in the theological seminary. As a teacher, he impressed us all by his ability to throw a floodlight on gospel truths and to accentuate fundamentals of faith. Our class studied the Epistle to the Romans under Olsson, and his development of the Pauline theme of justification by faith was inspiring. We listened attentively, and to our edification, to his sermons and addresses. Later, as a law student, I often attended the morning devotions at the college, and when I recall some of Olsson's chapel addresses it seems to me that I have never since heard the Word expounded with more spirit and power.

"He took a personal interest in the students, their struggles, their spiritual development. The small enrollment at that time gave him occasion for private conversation with each one of us. Later, when I was the youngest member of the college faculty, he invited me to his study, and when we parted he gave me Tholuck's works in practical theology, *Von der Sünde* and *Von dem Versöhner* (*Of Sin* and *Of the Redeemer*) which have given me food for mind and soul all my life.

"Some of Olsson's addresses seem to me almost epoch-making. Among these were his first Reformation address in Rock Island; his patriotic address on the anniversary of Washington's birth; the festival address he delivered in 1883, when the 400th anniversary of Luther's birth was celebrated at the institution he served. Of his many synodical addresses, I will refer especially to those made at Moline, Galesburg, and St. Peter. His sermon-address in Lindsborg at the time he undertook to help save Bethany College from financial disaster I recall as an appeal of overwhelming power. As I remember Dr. Olsson, he was a most impressive public speaker. Full of earnestness, his voice vibrating with emotion, he evoked response from the heart of every sincere listener. He possessed unsurpassed ability to throw light of electric brilliance on any point he was endeavoring to make clear.

"Olsson was an indefatigable student, endowed with a memory that was remarkably retentive. He acquired languages easily and handled them well. As a newcomer from Sweden, he astonished his colleagues in the Kansas legislature not only by his grip on the English language, but still more so by his understanding of legislative problems; and in the power and elegance of his diction he stood out as one of the foremost speakers of that body. It was the verdict of Bishop von Schéele of the Church of Sweden that Dr. Olsson was the most learned man in our Synod."

"Dr. Olsson was my teacher in Hebrew, Catechetics, and Homiletics, and he was a historical scholar of the first order," said Dr. A. F. Almer when asked to note down some impressions of his teacher. "One day he gave us a lecture on the development of the fundamental Christian doctrines from the days of the apostles down to our own times. Starting with the question of church discipline, he showed that it had its roots in divine love and how it had developed down through the centuries, sometimes in its human administration assuming the character of police discipline rather than the manifestation of the love of Him who died righteous for the unrighteous. In his lectures on history, Olsson always endeavored to trace the workings of God toward the one goal revealed to us in Christ. In the oral examinations, he would keep going deeper and deeper into the subject in hand until he reached a point beyond which the student could not go. There he would stop, thus having found what the student lacked, but without giving him the mortifying feeling that he had fallen short. In discussing the language of the pulpit, he once gave us the wholesome advice to use the pronoun 'I' sparingly in our sermons. 'When I catch myself using it in preaching,' he said, 'I feel ashamed of myself, for it is not my word I am proclaiming, but the Word of God and His Christ.' Dr. Olsson was more than a teacher. He was in all his relationships with us students a fatherly friend," Dr. Almer concludes his testimony.

In a conversation with Dr. Isaac M. Anderson, Rev. Joel Haff, a student of Olsson's back in the eighties, once gave a detailed account of his final oral examination in church history which may be recorded here for the light it throws on Olsson's direct and practical way of probing a student's knowledge. As recalled after many years, the Rev. Mr. Haff's story ran thus:

"After a courteous greeting and a few remarks designed to put me at my ease, the professor looked at me with that kindly smile of his and asked,

" 'Do you happen to remember any idea that Augustine ever had in his head?'

"I was so taken aback by the unexpectedness of the question that I nearly fell off the chair. There was in the back of our textbook a chronological summary of the important events in church history, with date of each event, and for all it was only a summary it covered many pages. This table of dates and events I had studied long and hard; in fact I had fairly mastered it. Accordingly, if he had asked me the date of an ecumenical council or the accession of one of the many popes, I could have answered without hesitation or embarrassment. But this question was quite another matter, and for a little while my mind went blank. Something, however, must be done; and so with a great effort I pulled myself together and said, 'Yes.'

" 'Well, what was that idea?'

" 'Predestination.'

" 'What did Augustine do with this idea?'

" 'He wrote a book about it.'

" 'Well, how was the book received? Did it have any effect upon the doctrinal thought and teaching of the church?'

"From this point I was led on step by step to follow the doctrine of predestination in all its ramifications among the various nations of Europe and America through the centuries down to our own time."

So far Rev. Haff. "And such dealing with history," Dr. Anderson submits, "is *real* history teaching."

As another illustration, the professor of Greek calls to mind an instance in the Catechetics class. Dealing with, say, the thirteenth chapter of First Corinthians, Olsson, after having pointed out how Paul sometimes drops the calm processes of logical reasoning and breaks forth in the language of the heart—poetry and song, would remind his students of similar instances in the classics, Plato in particular.

There were brethren who complained that Olsson spoke out too freely through the Synod's mouthpiece. Of those who counseled "love and tolerance," he said: "They demand that we *whisper* the truth; shout it aloud we must not; if we do, they clench their fists at us." In July 1876, Olsson sent Norelius his resignation from the delegation to the General Council convention to be held that fall. He based his action on the fact that in many parts of the Synod pastors and laymen were tolerating or embracing the totally un-Lutheran tenets of Waldenström while barring fellowship with true Lutherans of other bodies by means of the so-called Galesburg Rule against pulpit and altar fellowship. His protest was in the form of an eight-page letter bristling with arguments against so inconsistent a stand. "It is my positive conviction, based," he said, "not on flimsy suspicion, but on actual conditions, that in practice the Synod is conniving at and thereby countenancing a unionism much more dangerous than that now gaining entrance into the General Council. . . . In my opinion a synodical protest, at this time and under such circumstances, against pulpit fellowship with church bodies which clearly confess and proclaim the Biblical doctrine of the Atonement would be straining gnats and swallowing camels. . . . I must say that to me it was both comical and pitiful to see the whole Synod winking at, instead of combating, an error which undermines the very foundations of Christianity, while at the same time donning gauntlets of steel in order to fight churches which, though failing in certain things, confess with us the basic Christian truths. I say openly that while I turn away in disgust from Waldenström and his school, I hail with joy an F. W. Krummacher, who firmly confesses that Christ died in our stead; a Spurgeon, who clearly proclaims what he calls 'the glorious doctrine of substitution'; a Moody, who exclaims, 'Take the doctrine of substitution out of the Bible, and my hope is lost.' At our recent synod meeting I heard many of our men suggest this rule of action: 'Let us not at all oppose Waldenström, his writings, and his followers, lest the people take still greater interest in his writings!' Thus we would upbraid Paul and Christ Himself for their unwise zeal, their ignorance of our modern way of giving pet names to false teachers in order not to give offense."

In February 1879, Olsson's health was extremely poor. He was too ill to teach for the remainder of the school

year. He went to Lindsborg for rest. Meanwhile he was
planning a tour abroad, intending to embark in March,
if at all possible. "To Sweden I am not going, but to
Germany I have planned to go," he wrote to Norelius,
adding this confession: "For a long time I have been
in great darkness, doubt, and turmoil, but the Lord has
comforted my heart during my stay here. God's promises
are indeed true and trustworthy, but alas for our grievous
faithlessness!" On being granted leave of absence, he
started shortly after on his first tour abroad.

During the stay in Europe, his health was measurably
improved, enabling him to resume his duties on his return
in the fall of the same year. Shortly after the opening
of the second term, however, Olsson's strength again gave
out, and on February 26, 1880, he sent Norelius his formal
resignation, giving ill health as the compelling reason for
that step. To the latter's suggestion that he do mission
work for a time, eventually on the Pacific Coast, Olsson
gave this reply: "It is necessary that I somehow get a
year's rest. I do not think the Lord, who sees that my
mental powers are completely spent, would deny me a
season of rest. It seems to me that rather too much is
asked of me when it is suggested that I, with my frail
wife and my small children, should at once go out into
the wilderness for the summer. It would seem that I
have a right to put that off at least for a few years. Not
that I have done so much for the Lord's cause as to be
entitled to a rest, but it seems that the younger men
ought rather to go out and test their powers."

The resignation did not go into effect. With repaired
health, after a number of months spent in the mountain
region of Colorado, Olsson was able to resume his pro-

SPECIMEN OF OLOF OLSSON'S HANDWRITING

The legend reads: "A silver tongue have I not, neither a golden mouth: I have but a very common human heart. What this heart longs for, whatever makes it rich, hopeful, and glad, that I proclaim to other human hearts."

fessorship, but on his protestation to the Synod he was relieved of teaching in the college, a burden thrust upon him arbitrarily, no such duties having been stipulated in the call to a chair in the theological seminary. No change in his status took place from now until 1888, when Olsson definitely severed his connection with the institution. For him these six years, like the four preceding years of teaching, were filled with a multiplicity of extra duties in no way connected with his theological professorate. Included in such volunteer work was the preparation for the great Luther Quadricentenary in 1883, as elsewhere recounted, and his arduous labors in soliciting funds for the maintenance of the institution. For such work he was called back to Rock Island in 1883 from his summer vacation in Kansas; in fact, a great part of his vacation time was regularly employed by him in promoting the welfare of the school many years before he was chosen its administrative head.

Writing of three outstanding Augustana churchmen (the other two being Hasselquist and Erland Carlsson), Dr. Augustus G. Olsson thus characterized his former teacher:

"Prof. Olsson, using the principle of the Reformation as a starting point, would tell us that our innate ideas or Christian consciousness, as normalized by Holy Scripture, is our true source of doctrine and the starting point of dogmatics; but in his logic he would use Descartes' dictum: clarity is the criterion of truth, and I even heard him use the words of Descartes, "Doubt your way through,' in cases when someone expressed doubts. Olsson was not only a great thinker; he was also a great historian." This student of Olsson's writes of him as "our best informed church historian, theologian, and philosopher at Augustana in the 80's, as he also was the most forceful speaker in pulpit and cathedra." (*Augustana Quarterly*, 1936, p. 49.)

In a short life sketch by Dr. Carl A. Blomgren in the *Valkyrian* magazine (1900, p. 299) the writer, both a student under Olsson and one of his successors on the theological faculty, says of him:

"I have had the opportunity of studying under the direction of very prominent men at three of the foremost American universities, but I found none of them able to inspire a class as Dr. Olsson did in the teaching of his specialty, church history. In that field he was indeed a genius.

"The chief traits in his character were thorough learning, acquired by study and travel, and exceptional gifts; piety gained in the school of the Spirit; an extremely vivid imagination, which often brought him up on Mount Tabor, but as often thrust him down into the slough of despond. He lacked that calm which is peculiar to the greatest spirits of all time."

Of Olsson in the pulpit the most complete portrayal is given by Dr. Sven Johan Sebelius, present dean of the Augustana Theological Seminary, who wrote for this work the following characterization based partly on observation and personal contact:

IMPRESSIONS OF DR. OLSSON AS A PREACHER

I am not attempting to offer a systematic and exhaustive study of the homiletic work of Dr. Olsson. I must confine myself to a few personal observations and impressions of this great preacher's pulpit offerings and achievements. My sources, however, are not only my own memory but also some of the literary products, chiefly sermonic, that flowed from his prolific pen. It was my good fortune and privilege to be a student at Augustana College during the presidency of Dr. Olsson and thus to enjoy with so many others the benefits of his preaching ministry at school and in various congregations. In my own case that ministry was supplemented by a more personal spiritual service which I shall always remember with deep gratitude to God and to His revered and consecrated servant.

Who that ever saw and heard Dr. Olsson when he preached can forget his pulpit personality? At the morning service in college he was always dressed in his Prince Albert suit and the traditional white string tie, but when he preached on Sundays he wore the Swedish ministerial coat buttoned up all the way, and the ministerial tabs of the Uppsala style and size. (For some inscrutable reason the so-called Lund tabs are somewhat larger.) He was well groomed on such occasions, had a fine shock of brown (later grayish) hair on his noble, high-domed head. He looked best, we thought, when his goatee beard was trimmed down to more academic proportions.

But all of these things are external and not the factors that stirred and moved the hearers' minds. They felt the presence and power of an extraordinary personality. Who can forget the play of emotions in his face? It reflected the basic seriousness of Calvary. He had looked earnestly and long upon the Man of Sorrows and went away from His presence with the imprint of His image upon his own soul forever. There was also the paternal smile moving across his countenance like a flock of sunbeams hovering over verdant fields of grain and pasture on a summer's day. That smile was born of the resurrection hope and was eloquent with the note of triumph, "I know that my Redeemer liveth." But let him tell us a little something about himself which will better explain the secret of his personality than the inadequate words of another. In the midst of a critical discussion of the music of Richard Wagner Dr. Olsson makes an interesting self-disclosure:

"My friend, I am a pietist in soul and heart, but a pietist to whom nothing truly human is foreign or indifferent. Everything that is true, pure, beautiful, and good fills my heart with joy. I can fall into ecstasy over a philosophical treatise, beautiful music, a lofty piece of poetry. But there is something else that I treasure more highly than all this, namely, Him who said: "Come unto me, all ye that labor and are heavy laden, and I will give you rest."

When we turn to consider the pulpit message of Dr. Olsson, we discover that it partakes in no small degree of the coloring of his rich and many-sided personality. Yet the kernel of that message is always the pure gold of the gospel of Jesus Christ. I recall a passage in his first meditation in that incomparable collection of Lenten meditations, *At the Cross*, and I recall hearing the substance of that passage in more than one sermon I heard him preach. "A heart-rending cry of woe and lamentation is heard in the writings of every people, and especially in their songs. The Greeks enjoyed life more than any other people, and yet—the greatest poets of this people have sung the most pathetic lamentations in despair over the sufferings in human life. One who has had the opportunity to read, if only in translation, the tragedies of Aeschylus and Sophocles must, if at all capable of human feelings, have felt most deeply shaken. I confess that the reading of these dramas have stirred me in my innermost being. And why? Because these men have expressed the natural groanings and complaints of the human heart over life's sufferings in such a natural and palpable manner that one must feel: they were human beings like myself, and I am a human being like them."

Just as the Capitol Building at Washington, D. C., is the hub of that city, from which great avenues extend in all directions, so the hub of Dr. Olsson's preaching is Calvary, and the major topics of his message are like the avenues or spokes that run out from that center. As an example, a sermon he preached in the First Lutheran Church at Moline, Illinois, on Transfiguration Sunday, 1886, is as good as any. Calvary is glimpsed in the very topic of the sermon, "The Redemption Glory of Christ." Toward the end of the discourse he says: "He [Jesus] came from glory to suffering; He must pass through suffering to glory. From glory man had fallen through sin into suffering. If we were to return to glory, the Lord of glory must suffer and die. The consuming fire of God's wrath and law must needs be vindicated upon the sins of sinners. The guilt of sin must be consumed by the burning fire of God's judgment and wrath. This was achieved in the death of Christ. The Lord of glory was made to be sin and therewith a curse for us. He who was made to be sin for us is the One who is transfigured; He who was made a curse for us is now received up into glory."

The subject of suffering was frequently the burden of

Dr. Olsson's pulpit message. One of the most powerful and beautiful sermons ever delivered by him pictured the real significance and blessing of Christian suffering, something that we do not very often run across in present-day preaching. He used Matthew 16. 24–27 as his text: "If any man would come after me, let him deny himself, and take up his cross, and follow me," etc. The preacher asks: "If we consider the true disciples of Jesus, why do we find a difference as regards the crosses they bear? All must in some degree carry the cross after Jesus, but why must one carry more, as it seems to us, another less? Oh, if only the fire of true brotherly love together with the living faith were found among us, then we should soon find the answer to these questions. We should find that the Lord Jesus chooses some for the purpose of manifesting His grace and glory through suffering and distress. Just imagine, my beloved, if Christ were the life of each and all of us, what mutual congratulations, what universal praises of the Lord's marvelous grace! The healthy person would then stand at the bedside of the sick brother, and one would there hear and feel something which would prompt one to declare: This is a holy place, here indeed God doth dwell. For the two would be comforting and encouraging one another, they would be telling each other of the grace and love of Jesus; the sick man would be teaching the healthy man to thank God for the gift of health; he would point out to him how wonderfully Jesus can manifest His goodness even when one suffers; he would in many instances practically expound the Bible to the healthy brother, for it is most often when in trouble that one penetrates most deeply into its mysteries, so full of life and comfort. . . . And

what would the healthy do to serve their suffering brethren? Assuredly they would come to them with God's
Word in hand and heart to encourage and strengthen the
sick, whose soul powers are often weakened, so that they
forget the Word; they would support the sufferers in the
hours of affliction and darkness which so often multiply
in the experience of a suffering Christian." Then follows
an example of the characteristic Olssonian method of
driving home and personalizing the truth and point of
the message: "No doubt you understand me, you know
what I mean, but perhaps you think that I exaggerate,
that I propose something which can not be applied in
real life. Indeed it can be applied, it has been applied,
wherever a Christian life exists. But what is lacking?
Life in Christ is lacking, the cordial bond of brotherly
love is broken, its fire is gone out."

I should like to present a few more precious nuggets
from the gold mine of Dr. Olsson's preaching, but this
I must forego. I only wish you might have heard him
preach on the authority of the Bible, or on the responsibility of employers to workingmen, or on serving two
masters (in September 1891—a crossroads sermon in the
life of one high school student I know) or on the significance of the resurrection of Jesus (at an Easter sunrise
service in the Augustana chapel 1897), or on the mission
of our Lutheran church in America.

But a few words ought to be said concerning Dr.
Olsson's method and spirit of preaching. That he bowed
to the authority of the Word of God, and not to opinions
of men, however learned they might be, goes without
saying. However, he always proved himself a master in
connecting up with life and of applying the text to the

present occasion. Though he was a great church historian and was able to make the past speak in living word pictures which his students and lecture audiences could understand, yet in his preaching he moved and had his being in the present, speaking for God to the children of men. In a sermon preached by him at the Synod meeting in the First Lutheran Church in St. Paul, Minnesota, the year before he died, we find a good example of the practical side of his preaching. In the introduction he referred to the business sessions of the Synod, saying: "Anyone who listens superficially to our daily proceedings might almost believe that we are a gathering of business men who are discussing the company's profits and losses during the year, or a group of politicians, who are holding a convention to nominate candidates for important offices, and who are greatly excited about the question of peace and war [after the Spanish-American War]. And indeed, we are business men, we are politicians, also statesmen, likewise warriors. But what is it all about? Is it the things of this world only with which we are dealing? No, the discussions are dealing with another world altogether, but at the same time with the present world." Thereupon he plunges right into the matter of discussing practically the subject of counting the cost with respect to the Synod's share in building the kingdom of God in this country (Text, Luke 14. 25–35). He believed in home missions with all his soul, though there was a time when he seemed to think that the Synod's mission was about finished. When the language-fences began to blow down among us, then the larger field came into view more clearly.

Another feature of his preaching method might be

called "wrestling" with his hearers or with an imaginary group of people, exposing in this way the sham and insufficiency of law-righteousness. Listen:

"If any one should ask people in this Christian land if they want to be saved, to be sure most of them would answer, Yes. But if one asks further: Why do you believe that you will be saved?—well, they reply, 'I don't know anything particularly evil that I have done, I don't drink, I don't swear, I haven't murdered or committed perjury, I often go to church, I partake of Holy Communion, I am honest, that's why I believe that God can not condemn me.' But listen to the words of Jesus: 'I am not come to call the righteous, but sinners to repentance.' There are so many, nay, the great majority of men, who base their salvation upon their own righteousness, upon their own piety, upon their imagined keeping of the commandments. . . . It may be true that you are honest in business and conduct, that you have not committed murder, that you have not stolen, that you are charitable and good-hearted toward the suffering; this is all praiseworthy and good before men, but it can not justify you before God. 'But doesn't God take into consideration my faithful church attendance, my coming to the Lord's Supper, the large amount of devotional reading I do? Can God condemn me if I have scrupulously observed all these things?' Yes, verily this He can and will do if as a poor sinner you are not cleansed in the blood of Jesus." The excerpt is from a sermon he preached in Sweden during his ministry in Värmland prior to his coming to America in 1869. We recognize the strong evangelistic note in this and in nearly all of the sermons preached in Sweden. In a conversation with Prof. Hjalmar Holmquist of the University of Lund sixteen years ago concerning Dr. Olsson's ministry in Värmland, which is the home province of Prof. Holmquist, the professor related a number of incidents which throw some interesting light on the character and style of the young pastor's preaching. Professor Holmquist's source of information was his own father, who was *kyrkoherde* in a pastorate adjacent to the one in which young Olof Olsson served as pastor. He gave the following testimony: "Olsson's preaching resulted in a great spiritual awakening in the places where he labored. People came long distances to hear the young preacher speak. They were attracted by his sincerity and enthusiasm and by the urgency of his evangelistic message. Hundreds of people were led to Christ and found peace with God." The young pastor was greatly beloved by the evangelically minded people, and, of course, hated by others, as I could gather from Prof. Holmquist's words.

In Olsson's American preaching the evangelistic note continues to be heard, but the congregational and spiritual culture interest predominates, as might be expected of a man in his position in a church whose membership and traditions are different from those of a state church. At no time, however, do we find in his preaching that Dr. Olsson looks upon his audience as a *massa perditiorum*, as the professional revivalists do, but rather as a field, parts of which are already under spiritual cultivation, while there may also be areas which lie fallow and need to be broken up again and to be brought under the dominion of the Lord unto fruit-bearing and life eternal. Dr. Olsson's work as an educator and teacher exerted a powerful influence upon the style of his preaching, caus-

ing him to stress the pedagogic aspect of the gospel rather
than the one-sidedly evangelistic. Under his disciplined
direction the gospel rang as true in the one field of interest
as in the other.

I have referred to Dr. Olsson's method of "wrestling"
and of direct personal address in his preaching. A Lenten
sermon of his, preached in the chapel of Augustana College on Sunday evening, March 7, 1897, made a very deep
and lasting impression upon the minds of many student
listeners. I am grateful to his daughters, Anna and Lydia,
for placing the sermon manuscript at my disposal, so
that I could refresh my memory on certain points. But
it was especially the personal address and the manner of
it that riveted our attention on the speaker and upon the
great cause he pleaded for. I can still hear the deep tone
of his rich voice, feel the eloquence of his facial expression, and remember the inner reaction to the force of
his message:

"My friends," he was saying as he was bending forward a little, "you are young, and you can not be expected to be much given to contemplation. Have you ever
been standing before a picture of Christ upon the Cross,
and have you then been so attracted in your inmost
heart by the sight before you that you could not help
asking the question, What did the suffering Saviour do
for me on the cross? And did you ask that question with
such an intense desire that you had to have a definite
answer? What, then, was the answer? Can you tell yourself and others what Christ did for you? Or when you
read the passion history and other Scripture passages on
the death of Christ, do you then see what Christ did for
you, and would you be able to give in plain words what

the death of Christ was and is for you? Or, when you sing our passion hymns, do you then realize that your heart is in harmony with the thousands, the millions of hearts who in those hymns have found the expressions and the keynotes to their devotion and their belief?"

Dr. Olsson's sermons were always well prepared. They had the background of a general preparation extending over a lifetime of hard study and experience and of a special preparation from week to week. The exegetical basis of his sermons was solid and reliable; he had the advantage of a thorough knowledge of Hebrew and Greek, but he never brought the tool-box into the pulpit. On occasion he could preach a sermon without special preparation, not the kind that one hears so-called "inspired" or elocutionary preachers deliver, but an expository sermon rich in thought and sound in doctrine. One Sunday morning the pastor of one of our larger congregations found himself in the middle of his sermon facing an exegetical problem that he could not solve. He admitted it publicly in the presence of a congregation of 1,500 people, among them a number of students and professors. Dr. Olsson was present as a worshiper, occupying a pew well to the front. The pastor looked in his direction and said, "I shall call on Professor Olsson to help us out of this difficulty and to continue where I left off." Dr. Olsson calmly rose to the occasion, relieving the pastor of his embarrassment and saving the congregation from a depressed and awkward state of mind.

May I conclude my presentation and my impressions with the question, How may one learn to preach as Dr. Olsson preached, if indeed it be possible to duplicate him? I shall let the great preacher himself answer that question, only he would never permit *himself* to be used as a standard. To him Christ was the supreme standard of preaching and of life. In his travel book, *To Rome and Home Again*, Dr. Olsson relates an incident in connection with his visit at the Santa Maria Delle Grazie in Milan, Italy, where he viewed Leonardo da Vinci's "The Last Supper"; this is instructive and interesting and a self-revelation of this distinguished father in Christ. He writes:

"If now we had a group of evangelical ministerial candidates with us, we should show them how one learns to preach Christ 'unto wisdom from God, and righteousness and sanctification, and redemption.' Do you see the Italian painter seated underneath the large painting, brush in hand, at his small canvas? He turns around and bids us welcome to Jesus with that fine, easy courtesy peculiar to the Italian people. Thereupon he continues his work of painting. Thousands of times he has looked up into the face of Jesus, but for each little stroke of the brush on his picture of Jesus, he looks long and often at Leonardo's Jesus. Now he turns his brush to John, only a little stroke at a time; look, now he puts color on his black Judas, again only a small feature at a time, meanwhile always looking up at the original and then at his own figures. Now he returns to his figure of Christ. There he made a mistake in the coloration of the facial expression. He looks and looks again at the original. Now he corrects the mistake. How slowly the work proceeds, what extraordinary care and precision; the picture must resemble that of the Master, no matter how much time and toil are required. Do you notice, dear preacher, you who are called to paint Christ-pictures according to

the evangelists and the apostles—the image of Jesus
according to Matthew, according to Mark, according to
Luke, according to John, according to Paul and the other
apostles and then the composite portrait of Christ according to all of these original artists? How are you getting
on, dear painter of Christ's portrait? Perhaps we ought
to make a study of how Luther painted the Lord Jesus,
since we are Lutherans. And what of Calvin, Zwingli,
and whatever name they bore, all those whom we call
reformers. You know what a reformer means, don't you?
It is one who paints the Saviour, the Lamb of God, to
poor sinners. Do you know of any faithful and good
Christ-painters in recent times? Do you have any really
good and true pictures of Jesus among your books? Bring
them out, so that we may see. You have painted a Christ
yourself, a picture to be seen in your home, in your social
fellowship, in your private and public life? What do
people say when they look at the Jesus that you are in
the act of painting in your life?''

XXI

THE COLLEGE PRESIDENT

At the death of Hasselquist in the winter of 1891, after his twenty-eight years of service as president of Augustana College and Theological Seminary, the Synod was confronted with the task of finding a worthy successor to that capable educator and patriarchal leader. It was a new problem, and many set themselves to solving it by suggesting men thought suitable, while a few held forth their own claims to the office. Olsson was not among them. After his resignation in 1888, followed by his farewell to synod meetings and to all synodical offices, his only desire was to be let alone. Since his return after a year's stay in Europe, he had been in pastoral charge of a little church at Woodhull, putting in spare time on an account of his visits to Germany, Switzerland, Italy, and Sweden. His secluded place as a village parson was quite to his liking.

But on March 3, one month after Hasselquist's death, Olsson was called by the college board as acting president of the school, pending synodical action at the June convention. The temporary call was accepted, contrary to the expectation of board members who opposed him as well as some of those who gave him their vote, and Olsson was present at the meeting of the board a month later. On May 6 it was "*Resolved*, that Prof. O. Olsson be and is hereby nominated by the Board of Directors to be president of the Institution."

These steps were taken not without a brush with partisan interests which mustered the same old group in opposition to Olsson. That S. P. A. Lindahl, his opponent three years before, should now be a rival candidate for the same office was no mere coincidence. His ambitions were not easily sated. President of the Synod, head of its publication house, and for a succession of years chairman of the board of Augustana College and Seminary, he now aspired also to the presidency of that institution. Before the Synod met, three Conferences, Illinois, Iowa, and Nebraska, besides the college board of which he was a member, had recommended Olsson for the permanent presidency, yet he did not withdraw. He maintained that the board had no authority to appoint an acting president. At the synodical convention he used the weapon of innuendo against the rival candidate, but all without effect. Of Olsson's opponents in the board the assistant editor of *Augustana* wrote privately (to Norelius, March 6): "Being part of the Peter Sjöblom crowd, they naturally wanted one of their own men appointed so as to obtain control of everything—the college, the synodical paper, and the presidency [of the Synod]."

After some preliminary campaigning by this group, during which, as persons present have recalled, a renewed effort was made to call in question the soundness of Olsson's theology, the Synod, by a rising vote, unanimously instructed the secretary to cast all the votes for the recommendation of the board, namely, "That Pro-

fessor O. Olsson be elected president of Augustana College
and Theological Seminary and professor in the seminary."

When the voting for college president was over, the
Synod instructed the board of the institution to issue a
formal call to Olsson, making his election definite. And
when the vote for president of the Synod had been taken,
Rev. Lindahl had been replaced by Rev. P. J. Swärd.

Writing of the choice of Olsson as president of Augustana College and Seminary, the late Dr. S. G. Ohman
said: "When the Synod was to fill the vacancy after
Dr. Hasselquist, that grand old man, there was but one
name on the slate that could be seriously considered
as acceptable to the great majority of informed voters.
Brushing aside certain church-political aspirants and
schemers, the Synod chose the man best qualified for the
position—Olof Olsson. Again he thanked the Synod for
its confidence, but not for the election. He had not sought
the office; he did not want it. However, the Synod had
spoken, and the Synod was dear to his heart. He had to
respond to its call, and in submission to the will of God,
expressed through it, he accepted the heavy responsibility placed upon his shoulders."

What Pastor Lindahl, as president of the Synod, said
of Olsson at the opening of that synodical convention
should be read in the light of what happened later in the
same convention in order to be understood in the sense
in which it was meant. In his annual message we read:
"As painful as it felt three years ago, when Professor
O. Olsson, downcast by deep sorrow and broken in health,
resigned his position in the Synod to seek needed rest, so
joyous it is today to bid him welcome back to take up
the fallen mantle of Doctor Hasselquist. The Lord has

trained Professor Olsson especially for this, and may He now grant him health, strength, and grace to wear it for many years."

When called to the presidency of Augustana, Olsson was at the same time returned to his professorship in the Theological Seminary. That chair he did not occupy until the next school year opened in the fall, but he entered upon his administration as president early in April 1891.

In his first report to the Synod, he paid tribute to his venerable predecessor and gracefully acknowledged the services of Professor Foss as vice president. We read: "But for the grace of God and the love of our Christian people, Augustana College and Theological Seminary would no longer exist, even though many Zion Hills in Rock Island were covered with palatial college buildings surrounded by magnificent parks where flags were flinging the name of the college to the breeze. . . . From this fact, and this alone, we realize what the services of Doctor Hasselquist, who established our educational work, mean to us and to our institution. From this, too, we realize the importance of our calling in continuing the work of this school. . . . During the past year, the presidency of the institution has really been held by Professor C. W. Foss, to whom the Synod is greatly indebted for his calm devotion to duty and his unassuming zeal. I shall never forget the friendly self-denial and the noble courtesy he has shown me during my unforeseen two-months visit at the institution."

From records and reports for the period that Olsson served, practically beginning in the summer of 1891 and closing with his illness in December 1899, items which throw light on his administration are here culled.

In the divinity school, Olsson took the chair of Practical Theology. The very first year, the scholarship requirements in this department were raised. A two-year course was abolished, and three years of theological studies were prescribed for all seminary students, a full college course being fixed as the general entrance requirement. The faculty no longer approved of the short-cuts of the past for entrance into the ministerial calling. Admission by two-thirds vote of a Conference was eliminated, thus narrowing the gate by which men of insufficient education sought to enter the holy ministry in the Synod. In 1892 the degree of D.D. was awarded by the faculty to Olof Olsson, Erland Carlsson, and Eric Norelius. It is to be noted that the recommendation had been made in 1889 and then tabled until now. The adoption of a new and more definite constitution for the school was urged to counteract disintegrating influences and promote unity. Speaking of student protests and dissatisfaction with certain teachers, the president unbosomed himself in these words: "At such times, the life of him who is called headmaster is made so bitter that he could wish to be far away from everything that bears the name of school. It were probably better to have at the head a harsh, ruthless autocrat of brilliant learning and unbending will power. Then school life might again be what it was in the Old World in olden times—a life without love and tenderness, a life without humanity. The heart is a troublesome thing to carry with oneself through this mundane life, especially through school life."

Combined with the commencement exercises of 1893,

the three hundredth anniversary of the establishment of
the Church of Sweden at the historic Uppsala Council
was celebrated at Rock Island by the college and the
Synod. In preparation for the event, the campus was
beautified, and improvements were made on buildings
and grounds. The front was terraced and finished with
a retaining wall financed by the young people's societies
of the churches, and the main building was completed by
adding a portico and a dome. The guest of honor was
Rt. Rev. K. H. Gezelius von Schéele, Bishop of Visby,
official representative of the Church of Sweden, who with
crozier and in the vestments of his office took active part
in the combined festivities. He was invited by the synod
authorities, and it fell to Olsson and his family to entertain Bishop and Lady von Schéele while in Rock Island.
With his dislike for the pomp and circumstance of the
state church, Olsson did not do so with good grace. Dr.
Ohman has furnished the explanation: "Olsson was in
the true sense a bishop in his leadership wherever placed,
yet the title, though Biblical, he could not tolerate. The
jewel of consistency on this point was not his. He was
rather tactless toward the church ambassador from Sweden. I was a guest of Olsson's at the time, and when
he noticed that I did not approve of his conduct toward
the bishop, he said, 'Aha, you too have been blinded by
the episcopal halo!' I do not blame Olsson for his attitude,
after all. Two more radical contrasts than Olsson and
von Schéele one could hardly find. In my opinion,
Bishop von Schéele ought not to have been a bishop but
rather a high official at some royal court a few centuries
ago. Whatever sentiment there might have been in our
Synod in favor of adopting an episcopal form of jurisdic-

tion, that sentiment was all but destroyed by the three visits of that thoroughbred aristocrat, who surely gave us a wrong impression of the Christian episcopate by his high-hatted demeanor. He was the least suitable bishop from Sweden to visit the Augustana Synod. That episcopal type no longer exists over there."

Among those singled out for honors conferred by the university at the celebration of the same event in Uppsala, Olsson was one. The honorary degree conferred on him was that of Doctor of Philosophy. He was invited by Archbishop Sundberg to be present at the Uppsala festivities, and the board granted him leave of absence, but he found no time to go.

On the matter of titles Olsson commented in the church press in 1892: "And now on top of it all, they have played me a trick in my old age by starting to call me 'doctor.' I am thoroughly ashamed, but what am I to do? My old friends frightened me by saying, 'You must yield for the sake of the school.' Well, for the sake of this American childishness I accepted, otherwise I would have shown the 'doctor' the door direct from the platform of the chapel."

On the episcopate he wrote in 1893: "Our stern Spartan church fathers in the Synod complain of course that matters are being handled in slovenly fashion among us because we do not have real bishops (*rite vocati*, to turn suddenly learned), but, dear, good, kind Brethren, please let us oldsters die first and go home to our true Bishop; after that you may run things in a better way. We love you just as much, and you love us, and with such bishops as we have we fellowship in hearty simplicity and child-like confidence."

In 1894 Olsson again came to the Synod praying that the mutual relations of the Synod's higher institutions of learning, which were increasing in number, be properly adjusted. "Our honor as Christians ought to forbid contentions among us, whether openly or in secret," he pleaded. A movement was on foot to separate the seminary from the college and locate it elsewhere. At the synod convention of 1894 it showed such strength as to give great concern to Olsson and others who saw in it a menace to the institution. The Synod's answer to Olsson's plea is found in the new constitution adopted that year and ratified in 1895 by an overwhelming vote. One article stated: "The Synod shall maintain and govern the common educational institution." The movement thus thwarted would not down, but although the idea of splitting the school in two has been entertained in certain quarters, it has lost ground whenever discussed. As the one school controlled by the whole synod, Augustana had its position further strengthened by a decision to raise for its support an endowment fund of $100,000, to be completed by the year 1900. This work got under way after a year. While it was the understanding that Rev. John Jesperson, the treasurer of the school, and a subscription committee was charged with the raising of the fund, the board instructed the committee to make arrangement with Dr. Olsson "so that he can spend his time in the congregations in the interest of the institution." No money, it seems, could be raised for Augustana without him and his power of appeal. Olsson's administration coincided with the hard times of the nineties, and for the school, encumbered with debt as it already was, the outlook was dark indeed. The board of directors asked the teachers to take a cut of fifteen percent in their salaries for the next two years, "owing to the depressed financial condition of the institution." Salaries at this period ranged from $800 to $1,600 a year. Kept busy with appeals for funds, Olsson, to his regret, was often compelled to neglect his work as teacher, but he kept a keen eye on the inner workings of the school and was always on the alert for improving its standing and usefulness. Realizing that "as newcomers in this land we must have two mother tongues," Olsson did more for the advancement of teaching in the English language than any man at the institution before him. Certain subjects were still taught in Swedish, but under him the school became on the whole an American institution. English was introduced in the Christianity classes and was made the exclusive language at daily chapel devotions. Public addresses at commencements and on other occasions were now generally in English. What meant still more, the college courses of study were being uniformly revised upward, while in the school of theology scholarship requirements were made more strict from time to time.

In Olsson's last annual report to the Synod, made in 1899, we read: "Anxiety, fear, and misgivings have filled the unreadable inner side of my annual reports from our common educational institution during the past eight years. At every synodical convention the one who bears the title of president is obliged to sit in the place of the accused and await the verdict of life or death for the institution he represents. . . . The zealous friends of our conference schools seem to think, because it is our specific duty to guard with care our common institution, that we are and must be unfavorably disposed toward those of the Conferences. It is not so. . . .

"The Synod must defend its good name and reputation before the high schools, colleges, and universities of the land. What it means to keep up with the times, in a true and worthy sense, in educational matters the Synod at its present maturity can well understand. The times will not wait for us. If we do not keep step, we will be left behind. . . ."

"The Synod is more dead than alive so long as it allows its educational institution to be buried under a heavy debt. We ought to wear weeds so long as there is a spirit abroad in the Synod which makes it possible at any convention by a majority vote to stop up any of its sources of income or cause it to flow in some other direction."

For his measures looking toward advancement of the school the president did not always have the whole-hearted support of the board. There he had to work with men who had opposed his election and who were not in sympathy with his policies. Rev. Lindahl was an influential man on the board during Olsson's entire administration and held the chairmanship most of that time.

While the president was constantly casting about for ways of inducing the Augustana people themselves to give adequate support to the key institution of the Synod, the board was getting one glittering proposition after another holding out prospects of easy money through devious schemes. In the nineties there broke out an epidemic of speculation in "pay dirt" of all grades from farm, fruit, and truck land to gold-bearing ore of the highest assay. The synod folk, lay and clergy, were smitten by the pest. The first money-making scheme offered to the college was to come from the president of its board of directors. On April 6, 1892, its secretary recorded this action: "*Resolved*, that Prof. O. Olsson, Rev. S. P. A. Lindahl, and Mr. Gustaf Johnson investigate the territory in Texas handled by Rev. Haterius." The trap was carefully concealed and well baited with promises. Olsson fell into it. After the junket of investigation, there appeared in *Augustana* over his signature a highly colored account of things that were to be conjured forth from a wild tract of land near the Gulf Coast— fertile farms, fruitful orchards, beautiful parks, and in the center of it all a flourishing city not far from the "Lavaca seaport." Included in the new Eden was Wolf Point, which had been rechristened "Paradise Point" for better effect. He rejoiced as he saw the prospect of a group of congregations planted there, and added: "We have some older congregations farther up in Texas, where the people no doubt feel at home, but we had no time to visit them." He began with this warning: "I will not lure you to the South. Under no circumstances will I coax you away from a good, beloved home to unknown regions." Then he drew his extravagant word picture, closing the story with these assurances:

" 'But did you not dream about the land down there on the point donated to Augustana College?' Certainly we did. We wished the colony all success in order that we might come into actual possession of that land, and that there we may plant all kinds of fruit trees, so that our school in ten years will have an inexhaustible source of income. Now you laugh again. We shall see. He laughs best who laughs last. . . . If we run away down to the South Sea to secure for our dear school a well-needed permanent income, it will not help unless the blessing of God is with us. . . . We have enough knowledge of human nature to know that those who like to be mean will say that our dear president of the board has promised this land to our school in order to fool people to buy land and that I went down to Texas to play a part in this comedy. No, no, my friends, this is no comedy; yet we repeat: Buy no land on the Point and don't move there unless you like the land and the environment. Do not suppose that pioneer life is child's play. Some are fit to be pioneers, others not at all. That I well know from my pretty rich experience in pioneering."

Rev. C. J. E. Haterius, the promoter, and Rev. S. P. A. Lindahl, editor of the paper which published this fine piece of fiction, may well have been pleased, but it doubtless brought Olsson much regret. The grand project in which he had placed confidence and for the boosting of which he had lent his pen practically came to nothing. When the present writer, as a Chicago journalist, visited the same region two years later, this is what he found: "Paradise" was a low stretch of bare, parched prairie between shallow bayous, the few settlers without the means to get away still inhabiting shacks miles apart. Port Lavaca, the "seaport," was a rambling village rebuilt on the site of a town washed away by a tidal wave and now clinging to the end of a railroad line for support. Of the projected city in the heart of the prosperous colony the only trace was the name Olivia attached to a knot of settlers around a little church worth $200 and called Eden, a name to which it still adheres. Of the gift to the college, on the other hand, no vestige appears in the records. The "donation" spoken of was an empty promise of commissions yet to be earned.

A similar donation recorded in the minutes of the board was one of $13,500 given by Jernberg and Rylander, real estate speculators operating in the suburbs of Chicago. Here also the assumption was that the college authorities should promote the scheme of the firm, but the "gift" was never transferred from the board's records to the treasury of the institution.

Still another gift came late in 1892, when Houghton and Huxton donated 25,000 shares in the Loop Gold Mining Company of Denver, Colorado. This was followed early the next year by another gilt-edged benefaction—10,000 shares of stock in the Magnolia Mining and Milling Company of Colorado. In *Augustana*, Rev. John Jesperson, treasurer of the board and business manager of the institution, announced the donation from the Loop concern, stating that their mine was located a mile from Colorado Springs, where "five different veins cross each other" and gold ore is found in "almost inexhaustible quantities, averaging $40 per ton in gold." He added that shares were selling at 12½ cents. Shortly before, it had been announced that a gold mine had been given to Bethany College.

Seeing no dividends forthcoming, Olsson grew skeptical about the shower of gold so suddenly flooding the schools and gave it as his opinion that the only gold mines Augustana could count on were those in the hearts of the people of the Synod. He had made his mistake and was sadder and wiser for it. This he admitted two years after. On his return from the far Northwest, which had strongly tempted him to exaggerate, he wrote: "I shall try not to overstate the advantages of any place I have visited. I have burnt my fingers before in this respect." He reminded himself now that when he first came to Rock Island, he was sent out as a beggar boy *per civitatem cum sacco*. Recalling where the support of the school was to come from, he suggested the ingathering of a jubilee fund for the college in 1893. He set the amount at a modest $100,000 with this apology: "I beg your pardon for this fantasy, for I know it is an empty dream. At the same time I ask to be pardoned for accepting the call to a chair made for a miracle-worker, not for a weak man."

Of Olsson as educator and administrator we have this sketch from the hand of Dr. E. F. Bartholomew, who worked with him throughout his administration: "Dr. Olsson had a lofty conception of Christian education and of the educational function of our church schools. It pained him that our schools were not measuring up to the standard. He said on one occasion that if Augustana College did not stress the religious element in its educational endeavors, there was no good reason why it should exist; that it was the primary intention of its founders that it should be the instrument in the hands of God to promote the religious life of our people. It was established in the beginning to raise up an educated and godly ministry, and secondarily to produce an intelligent Christian laity, and it is incumbent upon us, to whom a solemn trust has been committed, that we be true to that high ideal and loyal to our commission. On this subject I often heard him speak with great earnestness and even with tears in his eyes.

"He was fully abreast with every movement in the

educational world of his day. He was up with the times, but not in sympathy with everything that was called progress. He had little sympathy with the numerous fads that were even then coming into vogue under the name of the 'new education.' Not everything old should be discarded because it is old, neither should everything new be encouraged because it is new. In education there is really nothing new; the same principles which the leaders of yore strove to promote still persist. Education means now what it has always meant, namely, the development of the soul's mental, moral, and spiritual powers. In the so-called new measures in the educational theory of the day, he saw a tendency to minimize the spiritual elements and to exalt the temporal and worldly. He deeply deplored this trend and fought against it with all his might and on every occasion. He said again and again that the primary object of education must be the formation of a godly character. Our young people must be trained to appreciate and estimate correctly spiritual values. An education which neglects the spiritual side of life is not a blessing, but rather a curse. On occasion he could be a little severe in his denunciation of what he considered the worldly spirit of modern education. At times he was, perhaps, ultraconservative, but under the existing circumstances this was excusable and should not be rated as a defect in his character. He was progressive in the true sense of the word.

"I remember what interest he took in a certain movement for the formation of what was called a Civic Federation of Rock Island. Leading citizens felt that the morals of the city were not what they should be, and the object of the proposed federation was to improve the moral and civic life of the city. Dr. Olsson saw what this movement meant for the welfare of Augustana College, and it was on his suggestion that a personal invitation was given me, September 6, 1894, to attend a citizens' 'law and order' committee meeting in the old Y. M. C. A. building. He wanted the college to be represented in that movement, because a reform of that kind would create a better moral atmosphere for the school. While he avoided making himself conspicuous in civic affairs, he was behind all such movements in good earnest and supported them in every possible way. This showed his fine public spirit.

"At one of our faculty meetings a committee of the students asked permission to participate in competitive ball games. Dr. Olsson was not favorable to the proposition, because he saw in it the beginning of what later came into such prominence in our American college life, when the glory of the athlete eclipsed the glory of the scholar. He was not opposed to athletics as such; he appreciated the value of wholesome games and of supervised athletic activities, but he feared and deplored the extremes to which such things are prone to run.

"In Olsson's day no Greek letter societies were tolerated in Augustana circles. He did not think they had any educational value; they tended only to foster an exclusive, selfish spirit, and that was not in harmony with the example and teachings of Christ. He did not stress the social element to the extent that is common in our day.

"Dr. Olsson valued very highly the daily chapel exercises. He believed that the brief period spent each morning in attendance on the reading of the Scriptures, and prayer, and the singing of sacred hymns, had in it a power for good far greater than we can estimate. He regarded the morning prayers as an essential part of the daily educational program, quite as important as any of the subjects taught in the different classrooms. In those days it was the custom for the clerical members of the faculty to conduct the morning prayers turn about, and they served a month at a time. It frequently fell to my lot to serve in that capacity. I have heard many students of those days say that they received more benefit from the daily morning prayers than from all other things that entered into their experience. Unfortunately that view is not prevalent now in all church schools. In those days it was not an easy matter for any student to get an excuse from chapel service. Dr. Olsson granted such an excuse only for extraordinary reasons, and it rarely occurred. He himself was always in his seat at morning prayers and entered into the service with a devout frame of mind. He would tolerate no sort of frivolity or inattention, but insisted on preserving a devout attitude on the part of each one, and he spared no effort to create a reverential atmosphere in connection with the chapel exercises."

Dr. Bartholomew concludes his sketch with these words: "As an educator, Dr. Olsson had a high conception of the dignity and sacredness of the teacher's office. To give instruction in the various subjects of the curriculum is only a minor and less important part of the teacher's office. There is something far above the mere technicalities of the art that makes the teacher's office only second to that of the pastor. The great aim and purpose of the true teacher is to develop the student's personality, to draw forth into action the sublime powers

that lie dormant in his soul. Dr. Olsson prized a mag-
netic, sympathetic personality above all other qualities.
He did not regard a Ph.D. degree of supreme value in
the teacher's qualification for his office, as has come to
be the custom in our day."

Late in the year 1899, Olsson's strength began to give
way, and on December 5th the board on the advice of
his family physician released him from his duties until
the opening of the next term in the seminary. A linger-
ing illness compelled further extension of his leave. On
April 24, he sent to the board this communication, which
was to be his last:

"DEAR FRIENDS:

"Permit me to try, in a few simple words, to extend
to you my deepest and most sincere gratitude for your
great kindness to me in my sickness and distress. Your
generosity to me has been much larger than I could ever
reasonably expect.

"Thanks, from the bottom of my heart. At the same
time I wish to mention my most heartfelt appreciation
of the kind readiness of Prof. Foss, my colleagues in the
Seminary, and our manager, Rev. Jesperson, to do my
duties. My future is in the hands of God, of you, and
of the Synod. I can promise nothing. I feel better, but
it takes time to regain strength.

"Yours, most thankfully and sincerely,

O. OLSSON."

XXII

RESTING FROM HIS LABORS

At the close of the school year of 1898–99, there was
another period of abatement in Olsson's vital powers,
such as had occurred often before. His most intimate
associates knew that he was spent, that it took all his
will power to keep him at his manifold duties. They
looked to the ensuing summer vacation to bring him
relief and remedy. He attended the synodical convention in St. Paul and made a none too hopeful report on
the state of affairs at the institution for whose pecuniary
support he had had constant worry for the past eight
years and oftentimes before. From there he returned
home with the outlook in no way bettered. After a trip
south to visit the churches in Texas, he was in still poorer
health, due to impure drinking water and the unaccus-
tomed heat, his physician believed. Yet he discharged
his duties as president and as teacher until December,
when his strength gave way. Up to that time, his mind
was in his work and his heart with his fellow workers.
So we learn from Dr. Anders O. Bersell, to whose sickbed
at this time he often came with words of comfort.

In January 1900, Olsson's condition was such that
his temporary sick leave was extended to a leave of
absence for the remainder of the school year. "What is
the board thinking of?" he exclaimed when apprised of

this action, for he was scrupulously observing his doctor's orders, confident that he would soon be well.

In the long, lonely days of sickness, he nevertheless dwelt on the thought that death might cross his threshold sooner than expected. One day he said to his daughters, "I feel so very weak—I could die at any time. But whatever is to be, I am contented." To some visiting friends he said, "If this be an approach to death, it is certainly nothing out of the ordinary." Early in February, when presentiments of his departure began to press upon him, he drew up his last will and set his house in order.

He set his heart on attending the meeting of the Illinois Conference at Moline in March. When that was not possible, he was yet able to meet many of his brethren at a concert given for the delegates in the college chapel. Then and there, in words heavy with meaning and hallowed by the solemnity of the hour, he spoke his farewell to the school and to the church he had served. "A remarkable thing about him," says Dr. Bersell in describing his last days, "was his serenity of mind and the total absence of the nervousness and melancholy which he often showed when in better health. He now took everything with admirable calmness and contentment. While his earthly house was being broken down, his spirit seemed to grow stronger and press on toward clarity and light. As late as the twenty-sixth of April, he conducted the examination of a theological candidate in the subject of esthetics with the same live interest he was wont to show. The nearer he came to the end, the more one sensed the atmosphere of peace that pervaded his sickroom. Up to two days before his death, he conducted the family devotions himself.

"Even when his vitality was so low that one might look for his passing at any moment, that same light beamed from his eyes, that same calm was in his voice when he regained momentary consciousness. Time and again his mind made pilgrimages to the spots cherished in his boyhood memories, guided by a map that hung above his sickbed. Then also the bride of his youth stood so vividly before his mind that one night, thinking he saw her standing at his bedside, he exclaimed with outstretched arms, 'Mother, Mother!' When one of his children asked him if he wanted to die, his answer was, 'Yes, it would be well, yet I should like to live for your sakes.' He loved flowers. When some lilacs and lilies-of-the-valley—his fragrant favorites—were brought to him, he reflected, 'How strange that these flowers should follow one from Italy all the way to northern Sweden!'

"On Saturday morning, it became apparent that his end was near. Yet he rallied now and then and gave clear answers to questions put to him. When he who pens these lines repeated to him the words, 'Yea, though I walk through the valley of the shadow of death, I will fear no evil . . .,' he clasped his hands and a peaceful smile composed his ravaged features. Half after four that afternoon it became hard for him to breathe. When he sought to raise himself, two pastors at his bedside helped him to a sitting posture and supported him so until a half hour later he breathed his last, falling asleep peacefully as a child in mother's arms."

Such was the passing of Olof Olsson on Saturday afternoon, May 12, 1900. What was mortal in him was laid to rest four days after. In the afternoon of Tuesday, May 16, two impressive services solemnized his departure. The first took place in the chapel of Augustana College. In complete contrast to prevailing convention, all was draped in white, the windows, the railings, the platform, the catafalque. Banked against this background, the floral tributes spoke a more beautiful language. The funeral sermons were preached by Eric Norelius, president of the Synod, and by Julius Lincoln, pastor of the First Lutheran church of Jamestown, N. Y., the one on the text, "Lasarus, vår vän, sover," the other on the theme, "I know that my Redeemer liveth." Of the departed it might have been said on that day, Though dead, he speaketh, for his very silence bore eloquent testimony to the realization of that Christian hope which was his all in all. After a second solemnity, held in the First Church of Moline, where Olsson and his family had worshiped for more than twenty years, the burial took place at the Riverside Cemetery. His last resting place is marked by one of those monuments the Augustana Synod has raised up in memory of its best beloved men. If his wish expressed to his friend Carl Swensson years before had been literally carried out, the monument might have borne this inscription:

> "*He was not a dreamer, but he suffered, body and soul, in sympathy for poor humanity; he still cherished his hope after his church would no longer tolerate it, and the ground for this hope he found in the Word of God.*"

XXIII

A COMPOSITE PORTRAIT

In these pages we have taken every opportunity to hear Olsson tell his own story. Excerpts from his own writings, books, articles, and private letters have been reproduced more generously than is the common practice of biographers. Every man can best tell his own life story. Reconstruction or interpretation is required only to fill gaps in the material he himself has furnished, if that is plentiful, as here; if he has left diaries, memoirs, or a complete autobiography, it is presumption in any other man to write his life. Then that task reduces itself to an appreciation, which self-respect deters most authors of memoirs from writing.

Olof Olsson left no autobiographical material, but in his letters he spoke with a candor which makes up for the lack by disclosing many events in his private life and revealing traits of character not otherwise evident. In addition to this self-portrayal, let us see him as others saw him. Forty years after Olsson's death, many persons were still living who knew him personally, studied under him, worked with him, and were impressed by him in one way or another. Their impressions, kindly conveyed in writing or through interview, are here combined with earlier estimates by Olsson's associates to add lifelike touches in this attempt at a composite portrait.

"Produce, if you can, a superior, or equal, to Olof Olsson, as a stabilizer, in a new land, of the distinctive Swedish piety and religiousness of our forefathers, one who could clothe it in scientific form and do it without a single helper. Who would be equal to the task which Olsson, alone and single-handed, accomplished, despite all the opposition in the faculty and the board?" asks Dr. Augustus G. Olsson, adding, "Just think if Olsson had been given the subject of Dogmatics instead of being held back."

This same student of Olsson's recalls this instance in class to show his teacher's attitude as a theological scholar: "Olsson once grew reminiscent because of reference made to a doctrine defined by Dr. Karl Hase of Leipsic and Jena. He said: 'Once a student arose in the class and respectfully asked Professor Hase if the presentation just made by him was genuinely Lutheran. Then Hase held up his own book on dogmatics before the class, saying, "This book does not present the absolute doctrine of Scripture nor does it pretend fully to present the teaching of the Lutheran church. It only presents what Karl Hase *believes* the Lutheran church *thinks* that the Holy Scriptures teach." ' Then Olsson told our class that this is the humble attitude every truly great scholar must take toward the sublime doctrines of the Bible and their interpretation in the Augsburg Confession. When one stands before such men as this, one does not feel satisfied just to memorize a definition and rest the case on that."

From the time Dr. J. A. Holmén sat as a student "at the feet" of Dr. Olsson, he has many recollections. From his notes we quote by permission: "Once in class, speaking of doctrinal errors, he said: 'I came near being drawn into the Waldenstromian error. What saved me was that I was able to search the Scriptures in the original texts of the Old and New Testament.'

"Olsson himself never sought to shine with scholarly luster, and he discouraged the students from adopting any insignia of learning. When the senior class of 1884 was about to adopt the traditional Swedish 'student cap' at graduation, he dissuaded us by saying, 'Brethren, never mind about that white cap. It would only set up a sort of barrier between you and those not entitled to wear it.'

"To the students about to leave for vacation he once gave this advice: 'Brethren, do not be lavish with love. It is like capital; once spent, there is nothing left when you need it the most.'

"There were those who charged Olsson with erroneous belief and teaching, but not once did I hear any unsound, unbiblical doctrine from his lips. Certain persons sometimes sought to betray him into saying what they might so construe, but without success. He would suspect their motive and put them off with a gesture. Only wholesome advice and sound teaching, safe guidance for time and eternity, ever emanated from his lips. Many a time in years past, I have felt profoundly grateful for the privilege of having sat as a disciple at his feet. I appreciated all my teachers, but my deepest and most enduring impressions were those I received from Doctor Olsson. I do not know of any man in our Synod who was so well beloved of its people as he and who has exerted so wide and beneficent an influence among them.

"Certain students from Sweden were inclined to sneer at some of our teachers for their alleged lack of scholarly attainments. It was doubtless one of these who sought to put Olsson to a test by hiding the pulpit Bible just before chapel devotions one morning and putting a copy of the Hebrew Scriptures in its place, knowing that the Old Testament was then being read in rotation and that it was Olsson's turn to conduct the exercises. Without visible embarrassment Olsson opened the book where his predecessor in the pulpit had left off and read the Hebrew text in fluent Swedish. (Without a doubt, he had studied the morning lesson in both languages—a thing the practical joker had not foreseen.) The test was a hard one, but Olsson stood it without flinching, and from that day the newcomers from Sweden were less boastful.

"It is told of Dr. Olsson that on a visit to an eastern university, without making his presence known, he visited the classes of a noted professor of Hebrew. During a lecture, Olsson humbly asked whether a stranger might be permitted to put a question. What the question was I do not recall, but after granting the privilege the professor was not able to answer. When Olsson himself offered a possible solution, he agreed that it might well be the correct one. At the end of the hour, Olsson having left, the professor asked, 'Who was that stranger?' When informed by one who knew Olsson, the noted teacher remarked, 'Oh, that great Hebrew scholar!' When the story reached our ears, we students grew still more proud of our professor of Hebrew."

Other stories told of Olsson may be more or less apocryphal, but these are manifestly well grounded in fact. In partial evidence, Dr. P. A. Mattson makes note of Olsson's statement to him that during one summer vacation, while a student, Olsson committed to memory fifty-three Psalms of David in the original Hebrew tongue. Dr. Mattson says further: "Three years before I came to the United States, Olsson's book, *Helsningar från fjerran* (Greetings from Afar), was published, and I read this gem with great delight. I looked forward eagerly to the time when I would join his class in the seminary. The first time I saw him, our class had been sitting in the seminary room waiting. Suddenly entering the room, he asked, 'Are they evangelists—all these?' This he said in a way to make us all feel put to the test, and after all these years I still recall how forcibly that question struck my ears. We studied Catechetics, Homiletics, Symbolics, and Evangelistics for him, and it was a joy to meet him in the various classes. Dr. Olsson was an excellent teacher, but above all a gospel preacher. He touched the hearts of his hearers as few have been able to do. He used to say he had no golden mouth, no silver tongue, only an ordinary human heart. What that heart felt he would proclaim to other hearts, that they might partake of the selfsame joy."

Rev. A. F. Bergstrom, who was a young member of the church at Woodhull, Illinois, when Olsson served that charge, has words of sincere reverence for his former pastor. "He was my confirmation teacher—a great teacher, whose precepts I can never forget. Later I studied Hebrew under him, and he succeeded in making even that subject interesting. His sermons were short—not more than thirty minutes—but instructive. Though only a child at that time, I remember many of his sermons to this day. Through his preaching, Christ became very precious to us as our Saviour and Lord."

The late Dr. Carl A. Hemborg, tells us that as pastor
of the First Lutheran Church of Moline in the nineties,
he heard old members still speaking of the spiritual refreshing that came to them when Olsson preached his
first sermon in America at their church in 1869. Among
Dr. Hemborg's own recollections of Olsson are these:

"An incident I never forgot occurred at divine services one Sunday morning while Dr. Gustav Stolpe of
Augustana College was our organist. He was playing an
improvised prelude to the Swedish hymn 328, stanza 3:
'O du härlighetens sken.' Dr. Stolpe's heart was engulfed
in the Swedish psalms. At this time his music seemed
to fill the sanctuary with the effulgence of God's glory.
Dr. Olsson came into the sacristy in a transport. 'Did
you hear it?' he asked. 'Did you hear that glorious
prelude? It was overwhelming—it was divine!'

"When we were gathered at the school to bid Olsson
Godspeed on his 'way to Rome,' he spoke, as I recall it,
of human friendship, comparing it to the different kinds
of soil in the parable of the kingdom. [And well he might
after his recent experience at Galesburg.]

"At one of my visits to his last sickbed, Olsson lay
studying a large map of Värmland. Dropping into a
revery, he said, 'Oh, how one is carried away by a longing
for home while retracing the roads and footpaths traveled in the days of youth!'

"Dr. Olof Olsson did not escape the scourge of criticism. There were those who said he did not carry himself,
in the presidential office or at high academic functions,
with a dignity becoming to a theological professor and a
college president. But if there was no artificial solemnity,
no dismal dignity about him, neither was there any

slovenly disregard of propriety. We thank God for what he was to our educational work."

Incidents showing how Olsson's heart went out to those in need or trouble could be multiplied. He took a fatherly interest in the welfare of the students of the institution where he taught. One of the many instances of this is here given as the personal testimony of Rev. C. A. Bergendoff. It should be stated that he was not even one of Olsson's students at the time he was so cordially befriended by him. "About the middle of the first term in my freshman year," Pastor Bergendoff told us, "I was taken sick with typhoid malaria. As I was one of those who had no home to go to, Professor Olsson invited me to come and stay at his home. There I stayed two months or more. Shortly before Christmas, I had gained so much strength that I wanted to do something besides reading. So I went down to Peter Colseth's organ factory in Moline, where I had worked one summer, and got permission to make a piece of furniture. What I had in mind was to make a sofa for a Christmas present to my benefactor and his family. When the work was finished and brought to the home, Professor Olsson wanted to know where I expected to find room for it. When I had explained my object, he permitted me, but not without protestations, to place it in his study. The reason why I make special mention of this is that, not long after, Mrs. Olsson passed away lying on that sofa."

Other instances of Olsson's kindness of heart shown in like situations are cited by Dr. L. G. Abrahamson. Writing his memoirs at the age of eighty-four, the veteran pastor and editor recalls several such instances woven into his own experience while pastor at Altona, Ill., in the early eighties. He says in substance: "Professor Olsson made a request that students without homes might be sent to us for care when taken sick, and my wife and I consented. This promise entailed serious trouble, but it also gave us joy. One day a divinity student named Vixell came to our home with a letter of introduction from Professor Olsson. He remained with us during the better part of a school year. In the measure his health improved, he assisted me in my work, and in 1884 he was so far restored to health that he could be ordained a minister of the Synod. Another student who stayed with us quite a long time while rallying from an illness was A. P. Martin, ordained to the ministry in 1886." (*Augustana*, 1940, p. 165.) Dr. Abrahamson mentions a third student similarly befriended for a year's time at Olsson's request, and it may be fairly assumed that these were not the only students who in like circumstances became the objects of Olsson's benevolent concern. It is worthy of remark that it was not the president of the school, but one of the teachers, who thus looked after students in dire distress. Anyone asking why would have to find his own answer in the heart of compassion that throbbed in Olsson's breast.

One of Olsson's many acts of friendship of which we have been told may well be noted as adding one more character line to the portrait here drawn by many hands. It was an unusual response to an unusual request. A daughter of Pastor John Telleen had died, and the bereaved father came to Olsson saying he had no place where the child could be buried. With his accustomed willingness to help and to serve, Olsson opened his own burial plot to his friend and neighbor, and to this day the maiden sleeps under an unmarked mound in the Olsson family lot in Riverside Cemetery of Moline.

Asked for some impressions of Olsson, Dr. E. F. Bartholomew, who taught English at Augustana College during his presidency, gave the writer for use in these pages an appreciation dealing chiefly with Olsson in that capacity and found under that head. Included in it was this assay of his personality:

"In my association with Dr. Olsson extending over a period of about ten years I learned to value the composite elements of his character. One had to know him intimately in order to form a right estimate of his personality and worth. On casual acquaintance he did not always appear to the best advantage. To strangers he seemed distant and reserved. But those who were privileged to see him in his inner life recognized in him a lovable personality and a congenial friend. The executive side of his office as president was not at all agreeable to him. He did not like to administer discipline to wrongdoers. Those faculty meetings when we sat as a stern court martial, deliberating on the fate of some poor, misguided transgressor, were exceedingly obnoxious to him. They made him nervous and brought on a violent headache. It was hard for him to preserve his composure. He was not even-tempered. There were times when he was joyous, even sportive; and there were times when he was low-spirited and melancholy. I have seen him in despondent moods when all things looked blue, and I have seen him when his countenance beamed with a heavenly radiance. But whatever his state of mind may have been, he was always a cultured gentleman and a warm-hearted friend.

"Dr. Olsson was a broad-minded man. This is justly illustrated by his attitude toward the language question, which was at that time seriously engaging the attention of the leaders in the Augustana Synod. On December 10, 1898, at a meeting of the general faculty held in the old college building, it was decided that thereafter the English language exclusively should be used in the chapel services. This was an event of far-reaching significance. Dr. Olsson took a very earnest part in the discussion. His whole soul was in his speech, and his words and manner thrilled with interest. He loved his native mother tongue, and it was hard for him to see it receding into the background. But he was broad-minded enough to realize that it was for the best interests of the churches and schools of the Augustana Synod to make the language of the land its official language. The issue was inevitable, and it was the part of wisdom to meet it in the best manner possible. The time was at hand when this question must be settled once for all. I remember distinctly with what earnestness and insight he spoke on that occasion. Contrary to my expectation, he was heartily in favor of the proposition under consideration, and the motion was passed without a dissenting vote. His attitude made a profound impression on every mind. I admired the wisdom with which he spoke and particularly the magnanimity and gracefulness with which he yielded to the inevitable. Many in the Synod criticized his attitude toward the language question, but that did not seriously disturb him. He followed the path of wisdom, no matter what the critics might say. What leader was there ever, in any great movement, who was not censured for his actions by men of inferior ability and insight?

"Our Augustana church all too poorly realizes what it owes to the services of Dr. Olsson as pastor, as theologian, as college president, as organizer of our church music, as a writer, as a beautiful personality, and as a devoted servant of the Master," is Dr. Bartholomew's concluding tribute.

"He having been my teacher in the seminary and I having been very close to him in my work for nine years, it would seem that I would have a great deal to relate about Dr. Olsson, but I have not," writes Rev. John Jesperson, who as business manager of Augustana College saw him mostly in his administrative capacity. Yet certain features in the portrait are accentuated in what he does say: "Dr. Olsson was a man with an artist's temperament. Though people in general thought he was an open book to everybody, he was a closed book to most persons. He was a great man, greater than they knew, but he had his faults and peculiarities that one who stood near him discovered gradually. But it was not easy to get so close to him as to be able to analyze him. He had many and great gifts, but not all gifts. He was a great teacher, preacher, and writer, and had he not been a Christian at heart, he might have been one of the greatest agitators, for he could sway the masses."

One whose relations with Olsson were quite intimate was Dr. Sven G. Ohman. Shortly before his recent death, he put down his personal recollections of his old teacher for use in this work. Of Olsson's student days he says: "At the Fjellstedt school in Uppsala he was known as a very devout young man, an earnest and bright student. Dr. Fjellstedt, the noted Bible commentator, founder and rector of the school, declared later that never had the

school graduated a student whose Christian character and
scholarly attainments gave so great promise for the future
as did those of Olof Olsson. He was mentioned occasionally as a model to us students in much later years at the
same school. At Uppsala University he impressed his
teachers to the same degree. They sought to persuade
him to remain at the university, hoping to see him placed
in due season as a regular professor on the theological
faculty.

"On a visit to Rockford once, Olsson, sitting in my
study, reviewed the course of his life, and when I referred
to those tempting prospects, he turned his benign face to
me and said with a smile, 'Yes, I remember. They wanted
me to stay at the university. They held forth many good
inducements and painted my future in rosy colors. But
I don't miss those things. I could not see my calling that
way. No doubt the Lord guided my steps.' Olsson gave
himself to the Augustana Synod as a 'living sacrifice.'
He was a great divine gift to the Synod and an equally
great loss to its mother church in Sweden." Of his teaching and preaching Ohman says: "As professor in our
theological faculty he was probably placed at the height
of his efficiency. To his students he was marvelous, winning at once their love and their veneration. After the
usual rehearsal of our lesson, he would lecture on the
subject, and he knew how to make it most vivid and
interesting, even Old Testament Exegesis! In history he
developed very fascinatingly his views and visions, holding us spellbound the while. He pointed out the connecting links in history showing how one event gave birth
to another. He made history a teacher to us, giving
generously of his own wealth of knowledge and ideas.

"His spiritual influence on the students went deep and far in Christian character building. To some weaker intellects it was so captivating that they wished to adopt in their personal bearing his pious mannerism, perfectly natural to himself, but transparently an amusing caricature when assumed by anyone else. At the morning devotions in the chapel, Professor Olsson's sermons were always rich and impressive, a spiritual breakfast giving strength for serious endeavor. He was equally great as preacher and teacher. His pleasing voice could easily be heard all over the church, and his plain and fluent language in the pulpit had a touch of the poetry and music of his soul as it flowed from the spring of his living faith and conviction.

"I believe that the greatest and happiest period of Dr. Olsson's life embraced the years he so fervently and cheerfully devoted to the theological seminary as a professor. There he was in his true element. There he could make his deep and comprehensive learning most fruitful. I feel very grateful to all my teachers, but none of them left so enduring an impression on my soul-life as he."

Of his college presidency: "The multiplied duties later imposed upon him as president of the whole institution were less congenial and less agreeable to his disposition. It was a forced intrusion, yea, even a loss to his personality which evidently was much more of an idealistic than of an executive nature. If I understood him correctly, he had no desire or inclination for executive office of any kind. I remember once, when he was elected vice president of the Synod, how he rose from his seat and said: 'I thank you for your confidence but not for the election.'

His estimate Dr. Ohman sums up in these words:
"Dr. Olof Olsson was in some respects the greatest man
we ever had in the Augustana Synod. His distinction
could not be compared with that of anybody else because
it was unique, so entirely his own. He was no copy, no
product molded in any dogmatic foundry, no type of any
particular school. There was no 'ism' attached to his
theology or his philosophy. His position was that of a
Lutheran, but his conviction was based independently on
his conception of the Word of God and the sacraments
of the Lord. Intimate with the original language of the
Bible and well versed in ancient as well as modern art
and literature, he was himself truly original. His strong
and lovable personality had its peculiarities, and in certain matters his attitude was debatable, but that detract-
ed nothing from his greatness."

In his book, *Från östervåg*, Pastor Karl A. Martin
touches incidentally on two of Olsson's traits, his self-
denial in money matters and his taste for fine art, both
exemplified on many occasions. Describing a visit to
Portland by Dr. Olsson on a tour of New England in
1892, the writer says: "The church was thronged with
devout hearers. As agreed, the collection was to go to
Dr. Olsson. At that point he protested, 'Dear Brother,
say nothing about that.' 'But the purpose of the offering
must be stated,' I said, 'for there are many strangers
present.' 'Well, then, you may say that much, but please,
do not make any plea,' he conceded. In this we recognize
that devout but modest man, who did not want much
said of him. The next day I hitched up my horse to let
my guest see the city. When we passed the Episcopal
church, he asked, 'What church is this?' At my reply he

said, 'Then let us go in. They usually have such beautiful art windows.' Dr. Olsson had marked taste for fine art, and I still remember with what manifest pleasure he stood viewing those stained-glass windows. From there I took him to Hartford to see the Catholic cathedral recently completed. He wanted to see its style of architecture."

"Perhaps I might give you two pictures," was the response of Dr. Peter Peterson, late president of the Illinois Conference, when asked to record some personal impressions of Dr. Olsson. He first pictures to us the prophetic preacher, then the college president, overburdened by concern for the finances of his institution. Dr. Peterson wrote:

"Dr. Olsson was not only the erudite scholar, the historian, the philosopher, and the theologian, but he had a very definite picture of the future of our church, her opportunities, problems, tasks, and sacrifices. At a convention of the Augustana Synod held in the First Church in St. Paul, Minnesota, Dr. Olsson preached at the Sunday morning service. These words were a part of the text: 'Whosoever loveth father or mother more than me is not worthy of me.' He spoke of the sacrifices of the pioneers, the men and women who organized our congregations and built those modest sanctuaries of pioneer days. He spoke of the sacrifices of the pioneer pastors and of the sacrifices of the men and women who had built and who continued to support our institutions. Then he launched into the future and spoke of new sacrifices that would meet pastors and members of our churches who should live at that time. He said, among other things, there will come a time when it can be said of us Augustana people, 'Whosoever loveth the Swedish language more

than me is not worthy of me.' Dr. Olsson was criticized
in the press for that statement. It was looked upon as
expressive of disloyalty to the traditions and language of
those who founded our Synod. Yet some of us have lived
long enough to have experienced how absolutely true to
future facts and experiences these prophetic words were.
Dr. Olsson was very emotional and very sensitive. Unfair
criticism cut deep into his soul. Augustana College was
in financial distress. Dr. Olsson had the impression that
the Synod and its leaders held him as president respon-
sible for the financial condition. When the Synod decided
that he should go out and raise funds for the institution,
he seemed to take it as a sentence of punishment. I was
serving two churches in southwestern Iowa at the time.
Dr. Olsson came to visit these churches in the interest of
the college. We had services in the larger congregation
in the morning, and Dr. Olsson preached and presented
the need of Augustana College, although he was in very
poor health. When dinner was over and we were to start
for the smaller church, he turned to me and said: 'Brother, I am not able to go. Will you not go alone and present
the cause in connection with your sermon, and I'll rest
until you come back.'

"I could not insist that he should go, so I went alone,
preached, and made the appeal in behalf of the institution. When I came back to the parsonage, Dr. Olsson
was resting in bed. I went up to his room and asked him
how he felt. He looked at me in a way that did not express
physical pain and weakness as much as it expressed deep
sorrow of soul, and said only, 'I believe that I shall be
saved.' These words sank deep into my heart. I still
remember them after more than forty years. It seemed

as if he had emerged from the anxieties and worries of his position and from underneath the heavy burdens connected with his office and that only his own personal relation to his God and Saviour was of importance. The assurance of personal salvation alone had brought calm to his soul," Dr. Peterson concluded.

An unmistakable vein of humor runs through much of Olsson's literary production, though it never crops out broadly at the surface. It flavors his writing like Attic salt, often lending a piquant savor to his discourse on the most profound subjects. His wit was not of the effervescent sort that plays in bubbles on the surface only to spend itself in thin air. Dr. David Nyvall, who has read his books as well as those by his daughter Anna Olsson, bearing the pen name "Aina," offers this explanation in a private letter dealing with his father's friend: "I read Olsson's writings, especially *Till Rom och hem igen*. I also read with delight books written by his daughter, which, I am sure, represent much of his humor, shall I say, repressed more or less in his own writings beneath heavy burdens of responsibility and grim earnest." Nyvall continues his characterization: "My wife, a sister of Skogsbergh from Elgå, often spoke of the young Pastor Olsson, by whom she was confirmed. In fact, most of what I know of Olsson personally came from her rather than from my father, who was a man of extremely few words. It strikes me that Olsson and he were twins in this. Both were really men of aloofness, loaded to the breaking point with interests, let me say universal interests. . . . They were both from Värmland, sprung from the soil of the same parish, and many of the traits indigenous to that province remained with them both to the last."

Looking at the same side of Olsson's personality, the late Dr. Gustav Andreen wrote: "He had a deep sense of responsibility, and all his work was characterized by earnestness. But he could also smile. He associated understandingly with his fellow workers, and on occasion he could even exchange badinage with his colleagues. As an example of his humor, let me recall an incident from one of the early faculty meetings I attended as a young teacher in the spring of 1882. The faculty was to select subjects for themes to be written by the college graduates as a part of their final examinations. President Hasselquist suggested that a few theological subjects ought to be included. Several having been proposed and rejected, Olsson, with a twinkle in his eye, suggested 'Odin's Address to Ansgar upon His Arrival in Sweden.' Hasselquist did not put the motion, but several of us sensed the impetus to literary effort a meeting between the Norse God and the first Christian missionary might give, and a ripple of amusement ran through the faculty room. Subjects related to the group of natural sciences were next in order. When Olsson again made as if to formulate a suitable subject, Hasselquist smiled, stroked his beard characteristically, and protested, 'No, no, we want nothing from you now.' The chairman no doubt had in mind Olsson's opposition to the Darwinian Theory which was then agitating the learned world and influencing some of the men at our own institution, particularly Dr. Josua Lindahl, the science teacher. But he yielded good-humoredly when Olsson insisted, 'I have an excellent topic to propose.' Holding up a copy of a magazine with the features of an ape adorning the front page, he proposed a thesis on the subject, "The Character and

Future Prospects of the Gorilla." The faculty members joined the venerable president in hearty laughter at this sally. As Lindahl and I were on our way home after the meeting, he was still chuckling at the humorous rebuke to ape-ology administered by Olsson."

In notes penned by Miss Anna Olsson, here partly given verbatim, we are privileged to see Doctor Olsson as his children saw him.

His mental recreation consisted mainly of playing his favorite music and—reading the old classics. His favorite study, besides theology, was history, religious and secular. He enjoyed the company of intimate friends, and to all visitors he was an attentive host. His hospitality as well as his benevolences often outran his means. He was never so busy but that he found time for morning and evening devotions, thereby edifying his family and refreshing his own spirit. He never permitted anything to interfere with his devotional reading. One little book was his constant companion—the Greek Testament.

Though never strong, Mrs. Olsson had to do a great deal of entertaining, not only in Rock Island but during the pioneer years in Lindsborg as well. But she was never heard to complain of trouble or fatigue. Pioneering in Kansas meant hardship and sacrifice, but neither the young pastor nor his wife allowed such things to worry them. "Ever since I can remember, we took into our home strangers who were the victims of some misfortune. Several times insane persons happened to come our way. Father and Mother both showed a truly marvelous patience in dealing with these. It was touching to see how these poor unfortunates trusted them. Very seldom did they fail to obey Father. And our Mother

they looked upon as an angel of mercy. Often he would
spend his Sunday afternoons visiting the sick, and Mother
would be helping some one in trouble, perfect strangers
as often as friends. Folks would come to our home seeking
cure for bodily ills, and our parents were always ready
to give them first aid, which also meant continued interest
in their case, whatever it might be.

"Forgive your enemies—this commandment Father
obeyed to the letter. How very willing he was to forgive
those who had wronged him! Of many such instances
we never knew, for he did not even talk about these
things in the home. The word 'malice' was not found in
his lexicon. He was the object of intense jealousy on
the part of men whom we thought were his friends, for
we knew nothing about it until others told us.

"Among his colleagues there were certain men of
narrow outlook who made it very unpleasant for our
Father. Men whose orthodoxy might better have been
termed bigotry sought to brand him as a heretic. But
he was a true Lutheran—more faithful to Luther's teachings than some of his calumniators.

"This is a picture I love to remember: Our Father
sits at his desk absorbed in a book. The doorbell rings.
A visitor—sometimes a farmer, at other times a laborer
from a near-by factory—is shown into the study. Then
Paul or Plato, whoever it be, takes a back seat. The
visitor has Father's full attention. He is asked to give
advice in some delicate matter and more often to render
some service.

"Topelius has a story about the 'perennial student'—
a man who became so enamored of student life that he
never left the university, but studied course after course

for his own pleasure without a thought of being of any use to his fellow men. Our Father, too, was a perpetual student, but with this difference that he studied to be of greater use in life, forgot himself and his own interest whenever anyone stood in need of his aid. To help where help was needed, that was a ruling passion with him."

Pride was hateful to Olsson. He never boasted of anything he had done, but was rather diffident or over-modest. Once, when a couple of his fellow clergymen in Kansas took to using very learned and high-flown language in the presence of the new preacher from Värmland, he began to talk to them in a broad provincial dialect. "When a certain minister who aspired to the college presidency, although he had dodged the college entirely in skipping from the academy to the seminary, told our Father, 'Dear Brother, you were never cut out for college president,' he good-humoredly agreed, 'Well, you may be quite right.'

Olsson's love of home was an inborn trait which remained with him through life, although he was never to have a home really his own. This nostalgia often colored his writings, whether of his native Värmland or his beloved Kansas. "He spoke with feeling of the little red cottage that had been his childhood home. In his dreams he saw another little cottage, on the Kansas prairie, where in quiet seclusion he might spend his last years and, God willing, write the story of his life."

Shortly after Olsson's death, Professor S. G. Youngert, teacher in the Augustana Seminary, published his estimate of him. From the monthly *Ungdomsvännen* it is here reproduced in part as the eulogy of a co-worker and a close friend: "His equal in learning we may see, but hardly his like in depth of soul and nobility of heart, in compassion and understanding for his fellow men, in tireless interest in the fostering of his people of Swedish descent through all-sided education and in solicitude for their temporal and eternal welfare.

"I have met no man who, as I see it, was a better prototype of Swedish national character, who understood his countrymen so fully as he. This applies more particularly to their spiritual characteristics. As is well known, Olsson was a profoundly religious man, but there was, moreover, something very personal and nobly human about his religious life. This trait of true humanity in him became more marked as the years went by. A few weeks before his death, in a long conversation about the mutual relationship between the church and the fine arts, he said in reply to a certain protest against a philosophical trend in our educational work, that we must maintain, defend, and promote human culture in all domains, including those of art and philosophy, even though we thereby expose ourselves to misunderstanding and uncharitable judgments. But this culture, as Olsson saw it, must be thoroughly Christian, for he maintained that all means of true culture, as also the capacity for its acquirement, are a gift of God, which under Christian influence maketh a full man. It was this conception of general culture that made Olsson the great educator that he was and interested him so deeply in all forms of human knowledge. He was withal a lovable disciple of Jesus, in his contemplative hours a St. John, in his fiery and powerful preaching a follower of St. Paul."

INDEX

(Names merely mentioned are not included)

SOURCES

(For conciseness, sources consulted but not directly quoted are omitted from
this list.)

Korsbaneret, Rock Island, Ill., 1901: "Olof Olsson," sketch by Johannes Nyvall.
Anders Fredrik Sedström. By Gust Hultgren. Mariestad, 1930.
Reminiscences by Nils J. Forsberg (unpublished).
Letters among the papers of Olof Olsson, T. N. Hasselquist, and Eric Norelius.
Minutes of the Augustana Synod, 1869–1915.
De svenska lutherska församlingarnas och svenskarnes historia i Amerika. By
Eric Norelius, II.
Min faders testamente. By David Nyvall. Chicago, 1924.
Reseminnen från Amerika. By C. J. N. Kristinehamn, 1876.
Lindsborg. By Alfred Bergin, 1909.
Lindsborg efter femtio år. By Alfred Bergin, 1919.
Emigranterna och kyrkan. By Gunnar Westin. Stockholm, 1932.
Works of Olof Olsson. Listed on pages 270–272.
Augustana and *Augustana och Missionären*. (Briefly designated *Augustana*.)
Numerous articles by Olof Olsson.
Missionsvännerna i Amerika. By C. V. Bowman.
Reminiscences of J. G. Princell. By Josephine Princell.
Jubel-Album. By C. A. Swensson and L. G. Abrahamson. Chicago, 1893.
Till minne af Olof Olsson. Rock Island, 1900. Necrology by C. A. Hemborg.
Religious Aspects of Swedish Immigration. By George M. Stephenson.
Vid hemmets härd. By C. A. Swensson.
Ungdomsvännen, 1900.
Valkyrian, 1900.

ACKNOWLEDGMENTS

Cordial thanks are due a number of persons who have aided the author by writing down their personal recollections of Olof Olsson for use in this volume. Since then, some have gone where no words of gratitude can reach them, among these Dr. Gustav Andreen, Dr. S. G. Ohman, Dr. Peter Peterson, Dr. Peter Henry Pearson, and Dr. S. G. Youngert. Those now living who rendered highly valuable service to the writer by contributing extensive recollections, characterizations, and book summaries are Dr. E. F. Bartholomew, professor emeritus of Augustana College, Dr. Hjalmar Johnson, professor of Christianity and Philosophy in the same institution, Dr. S. J. Sebelius, dean of the Augustana Theological Seminary, and Dr. Julius Lincoln, pastor of the Trinity Lutheran Church of Chicago. In placing her father's papers and letters at the writer's disposal, Miss Anna Olsson has earned his most profound gratitude.

For encouragement in the work and sponsorship of this volume, the author is particularly indebted to the *Augustana Historical Society*.

E. W. O.